THE BEST TEEN

WRITING

OF 2007

SELECTIONS FROM
THE SCHOLASTIC ART & WRITING AWARDS of 2007
Foreword by Billy Collins

Edited by Justin Beltz

a Program of the Alliance for Young Artists & Writers, Inc.

For information or permission contact:
Alliance for Young Artists & Writers, Inc.
557 Broadway
New York, NY 10012
212.343.6493
www.artandwriting.org

Anthology printing, September 2007
ISBN-13: 978-0-545-05931
ISBN-10: 0-545-05931-3

With appreciation to

Hugh Roome
for his vision of an annual anthology of
student writing

Mimi Esguerra
and her staff for finding extraordinary ways to make this
publication possible

Justin Beltz
for his hard work, keen eye, and dedication to authentic
teen voices

Kent Williamson, **Billy Collins**, the **Jurors** and
the **Regional Affiliates** of **the Alliance for Young Artists &
Writers** for their contributions to this effort

And to the **Young Writers** and their **Teachers** whose work is
featured in this anthology

ABOUT THE BEST TEEN WRITING OF 2007

The Alliance for Young Artists & Writers commends the tens of thousands of students who accepted the challenge and submitted their best writing to The Scholastic Writing Awards of 2007. These young writers have joined the ranks of authors such as Truman Capote, Jean Stafford, Bernard Malamud, Carolyn Forché, Sylvia Plath, Joyce Carol Oates, Joyce Maynard, Robert Redford, and countless others who—over the 85-year history of The Scholastic Art & Writing Awards—regarded their work seriously enough to submit it for review by professionals. By doing so, they have taken the first step down a long literary path.

Congratulations to the students and their teachers, who earned recognition through the fourteen regional affiliate programs and region-at-large preliminary to the national adjudication this year. This year 373 young writers were honored nationally through The Awards. For *The Best Teen Writing of 2007*, only 51 works were able to be included due to space limitations. The works selected were chosen both as exemplars of good writing and to represent the great diversity of the national award recipients, including age and grade, gender, genre, geography and subject matter. While every national award recipient manuscript is deserving of inclusion in the publication, the selected works accurately and richly represent the authentic voices of our nation's teenagers, their thoughts and opinions.

A complete listing of national award recipients and a broader selection of works from The Scholastic Art & Writing Awards can be found on our Web site by clicking "Virtual Galleries" at www.artandwriting.org.

The Scholastic Art and Writing Awards endorses student freedom of expression as outlined in the resolutions and guidelines of the National Council of Teachers of English, which may be found at http://www.ncte.org/about/over/positions/category/cens.

table of contents

9. **editor's introduction**
   justin beltz

11. **a message from the national council of teachers of english**
   kent williamson

12. **the possibility of greatness**
   foreword: billy collins

---

14. **fire,** *short short story*
   laura ball, 13. wauwatosa, wisconsin

17. **one last day,** *personal essay*
   zara kessler, 16. new york, new york

22. **spring training,** *poetry*
   amanda picardi, 16. natick, massachusetts

23. **swimming pool,** *poetry*
   grant hailer, 15. milton, massachusetts

24. **the problem with jump-off trees,** *short story*
   erin weeks, 17. greenville, south carolina

31. **on being informed,** *journalism*
   anna isaacs, 16. bethesda, maryland

34. **white woman**
   a prayer for my friend...
   idi amin had a blue windbreaker
   phoebe rusch, 18. interlochen, michigan

47. **of rawls, refutation, and ratiocination,** *humor*
   andrew halterman, 17. norman, oklahoma

51. **far-off yellow,** *science fiction*
   jasmine hu, 16. san jose, california

58. **ma'arat ha'machpela,** *personal essay*
   leila dashevsky, 18. kfar pines, israel

62. **boy,** *short short story*
   suzannah isgett, 16. north charleston, south carolina

65. **of the dangers of lunch lines,** *poetry*
   michael lambert, 16. birmingham, alabama

67. **a traveler's journey,** *personal essay*
   maya de vitry, 16. lancaster, pennsylvania

74. **confessions of a teenage mascot: my life as a bee,** *humor*
   michael yashinsky, 17. west bloomfield, michigan

77. **across the universe**
   eighty percent water
   for sarah
   denise rickman, 18. raleigh, north carolina

85. **she thinks she loves him,** *short short story*
   margaret hayertz, 17. west linn, oregon

88. **it's just too soon,** *journalism*
monica klein, 17. new york, new york

91. **woodnote,** *poetry*
david pederson, 16. edina, minnesota

93. **mapping the streets of chinatown,** *personal essay*
kathryn llewellyn, 16. westport, connecticut

98. **final grade,** *science fiction*
erin guty, 15. camp hill, pennsylvania

106. **the cotton club,** *personal essay*
eugene stockton-juarez, 14. carlisle, pennsylvania

109. **family reunion: china, 2005,** *poetry*
lisa pang, 15. alexandria, virginia

112. **church people,** *humor*
katharine eisenberg, 15. greenwich, connecticut

119. **so old school,** *personal essay*
elizabeth motich, 17. dillsburg, pennsylvania

125. **bouncing back,** *journalism*
kaitlin sanders, 17. newton centre, massachusetts

130. **the witness**
menu planning
sharpening
anne reece, 18. interlochen, michigan

140. **obituary for an *a*,** *poetry*
jack anderson, 13. provo, utah

141. **underground,** *short short story*
alyssa fowers, 15. miami, florida

144. **the last revolution,** *journalism*
naomi funabashi, 16. exeter, new hampshire

151. **the road home,** *short story*
margot miller, 16. wilmington, delaware

156. **slashed skies,** *poetry*
eric roper, 13. greenville, south carolina

158. **rise up,** *personal essay*
jillian kinsey, 14. middletown, pennsylvania

165. **defining you,** *science fiction*
katharine sedivy-haley, 16. riverside, rhode island

172. **brace yourself,** *humor*
thomas renjilian, 16. clarks summit, pennsylvania

176. **aquarium**
quick money
bird watching
cory wallace, 17. greenville, south carolina

190. english breakfast, *poetry*
kayla krut, 15. la jolla, california

191. the funeral, *poetry*
cora johnson-grau, 13. los angeles, california

192. song ever changing, *short short story*
jenna devine, 16. martinsville, new jersey

196. a twisted stomach, *journalism*
joshua p. mcmillen, 17. elliottsburg, pennsylvania

200. on being experienced, *personal essay*
rosetta young, 16. providence, rhode island

203. tantamount, *science fiction*
sindha agha, 13. urbana, illinois

207. the sweet forgotten life, *poetry*
antoinette forstall, 13. birmingham, alabama

208. a small adjustment, *short story*
shalini ramachandran, 18. lilburn, georgia

214. fallujah, *dramatic script*
rebecca mccarthy, 17. greens farms, connecticut

221. the lump of inspiration, *personal essay*
nicole levy, 16. new york, new york

226. nature at our doorstep: four seasons on an ohio farm, *journalism*
john savage, 13. loudonville, ohio

232. finding hope, *short story*
clare grieve, 14. fairport, new york

240. gratefulness runs in the family, *personal essay*
brenna o'tierney, 18. anchorage, alaska

243. tip tap, *short short story*
ryan beiermeister, 16. houston, texas

245. writer's statement
brown or bust
everything i need to know in life i learned from genghis khan
temnete sebhatu, 18. greenville, south carolina

257. my father says he hates poetry, *poetry*
ryan brown, 17. denver, colorado

259. about the authors

266. 2007 writing jurors

267. sponsors of regional programs

269. about the alliance for young artists & writers

271. call for submissions

EDITOR'S INTRODUCTION

Underneath my bed at home in Bluffton, South Carolina, there is a box with the words "Do Not Open" scrawled across the front in red Sharpie. Inside of the box, I have compiled everything I have ever written since the age of ten. Among these items—a short story with talking unicorns, a hokey rhyming poem in the shape of a broken heart and countless journal entries with unnecessary expletives used incorrectly.

As I edited *The Best Teen Writing of 2007* this year, sporadic visions of this box kept popping up in my head. It was difficult for me to conjure up some sort of meaning or connection—how could my "box of shame" possibly compare to writing deemed "the best of 2007"?

I recalled my own bizarre history as a writer. I created my box nine years ago when I sat down at my dining room table one summer and decided I was going to write my first novel. I could imagine the headline in the newspaper— TEN-YEAR-OLD WRITING GENIUS PENS BESTSELLER. I only wrote one paragraph before I decided to play with my cat outside, but it was on that day that I first felt a desire to save what I wrote. Some strange ethereal force in the pit of my stomach told me to hang on, when I knew in the back of my head that my "masterpiece" would amount to nothing of immediate acclaim.

The warning on the front of my box was added when I hit thirteen and suddenly felt embarrassed by everything in my past. I became taller and my box became heavier. Soon, the hard drive on my laptop transformed into the unfortunate new home of my own personal "worst teen writing," and I tossed in everything from repulsive sonnets detailing the beauty of dead squirrels to three-page "abstract" screenplays.

When I arrived home from my first year at college two months ago, I ignored my warning and opened the box under my bed. There was a reason I hadn't set fire to the thing many years ago and I was determined to get to the bottom of it. To my surprise, evil spirits did not lurch from the pages condemning me as a writer; I did not curl up in a fit of shame after skimming through a short story with themes of whimpering angst and rebellion. Instead, I found a wealth of new material. I called friends over, and together we performed theatrical interpretations of my seventh grade journal entries. I even popped in one of my father's Philip Glass CDs for dramatic effect.

And it was then, as the malevolent violins blared in the background, that I realized I was reading the work of someone else. The old me was someone to tease; he was a character whom I would write about for years to come. Essentially what I found in my box was a timeline, solid evidence to chart my progress through the years.

In many ways, I view this collection of writing as the first notch in the timelines of the fifty-one authors represented here. Many have graduated from the confines of "teen writing" and will soon move on to the world of "adult writing"—a frightening place where recognition programs are replaced with picky publishing companies who hand out acceptance letters as generously as Gold Keys. Soon, they must brace themselves for an endless string of obstacles: revisions, rewriting, distractions, failure, the dreaded writer's block, even success. But they are more than ready. And when those transitions are finally made, this anthology will forever remain as that box under their beds—not because one day they will feel embarrassed by their old writing, but because it's the jumping block that pushed them to keep creating their own individual histories. It is a testament to their exact thoughts and feelings as teenagers; it is proof that they had to get started somewhere.

Editing this book was one of the most entertaining things I have ever done. I would like to thank everyone at the Alliance for Young Artists & Writers for giving me this opportunity—particularly Bryan Doerries, Lisa Feder-Feitel, and Alex Tapnio, for their guidance and for patiently listening to my extravagant and unrealistic ideas. I would also like to thank my family for their support, my roommate last semester for putting up with the countless stacks of manuscripts piled around the room, and the writers of the *Chicago Manual of Style* for teaching me the difference between an *em* and an *en* dash. Last but not least, I would like to thank George and Scott at South Carolina Governor's School for the Arts and Humanities for basically everything.

—Justin Beltz

JUSTIN BELTZ earned the Nonfiction Portfolio Gold Award as well as a $10,000 college scholarship from the 2006 Scholastic Writing Awards program. He selected and proofread everything in this book. Justin is a sophomore at the University of Southern California where he is studying screenwriting and comparative literature.

A MESSAGE FROM THE NATIONAL COUNCIL
OF TEACHERS OF ENGLISH

The National Council of Teachers of English acknowledges the dedication and passion of every student who submitted an entry to The Scholastic Art & Writing Awards and salutes the students whose work was ultimately published here in *The Best Teen Writing of 2007*. By learning to look closely at the world around them, sifting through their perceptions, and inviting us to see what they have constructed, these students have enriched thousands of readers and observers. At the same time, they have honed valuable skills that can bring them personal satisfaction for a lifetime.

In its position paper, "Beliefs About the Teaching of Writing," the NCTE asserts that writing is a tool for thinking and that writing grows out of many different purposes. The works in this anthology provide eloquent testimony to support these beliefs. Nothing gratifies a language arts teacher more than knowing that a student has cultivated a passion for artistic communication. So, on behalf of these young writers, their teachers, and everyone who values the difference that powerful communicators can make in our society, NCTE thanks the Alliance for Young Artists & Writers, Scholastic Inc., and the other sponsors of the program for their ongoing support.

Young writers in 40 states, the U.S. Virgin Islands, and international schools in Europe and Israel participated in the Scholastic Writing Awards in 2007. Through its distribution of 15,000 free copies of *The Best Teen Writing of 2007*, the Alliance is making a powerful statement of support for the written word. The skill and subtlety of these young authors allows them to express not only what they know, but to reveal and share personal insights. The result is an anthology that authentically captures the life experiences of young adults at the beginning of the 21st century.

For more than 80 years, classroom teachers have embraced The Scholastic Art & Writing Awards as a way to motivate students, to encourage their creativity and personal exploration, and to reward those who achieve on the highest level. I believe that the work included in *The Best Teen Writing of 2007* is proof of the powerful impact educators are having even as the modalities of writing and reading are changing in fundamental ways. We at the NCTE are grateful to The Scholastic Art & Writing Awards for providing the opportunity to recognize the very best writing by our nation's teenagers this year, and to acknowledge the debt we all owe to their teachers for their commitment to students and the craft of writing. Onward to 2008!

—Kent Williamson

KENT WILLIAMSON is the executive director of the National Council of Teachers of English.

THE POSSIBILITY OF GREATNESS

When Allen Ginsberg's canon-shattering poem "Howl" was published in 1957, I was sixteen years old and installed in a Catholic high school in the suburbs of New York City. Jack Kerouac's *On the Road*, which continues to sell over a hundred thousand copies a year, was also published in 1957. The following year saw the appearance of Lawrence Ferlinghetti's collection of poems *Coney Island of the Mind* and *Gasoline*, and the first book of poems by Gregory Corso. Up until that time, I was a fairly normal, well-behaved child: an altar boy, a choirboy, and a Boy Scout. But the appearance of those books that formed the core literature of the Beat Generation changed everything. In their writing I found a wildness and an outrageousness I did not know could exist. I finally understood the phrase "freedom of expression." The only poetry I had heard, beyond the rhymes of Mother Goose, was the poetry taught in the classroom. The authors were all male, dead, bearded, and each of them had three names: William Cullen Bryant, Henry Wadsworth Longfellow, Ralph Waldo Emerson. The poetry was formal, elegant, sonorous—and it seemed as if it was issuing forth from the grave. The beat poets were spontaneous, angry, ecstatic, and their poems sounded as if they were being shouted from the rooftops of a city. They were "alive" in every sense of the word. Suddenly, "poetry" had a new meaning. It was exciting, rebellious, cool. I was hooked, a teenager in love with this new way to declare yourself in language.

Luckily, no poems survive from the many I wrote trying to imitate these new poets. I wrote as if I were a fellow beatnik, a free spirit, liberated, fearless, half-crazy. The truth was I was still diligently working on my perfect attendance record and making sure my homework was turned in on time. Even though the results of my imitation were ridiculous, I was learning something. I was writing. I had found a way to externalize myself, an outlet, something to do with the inner turbulence known as adolescence. Though I would never tell anyone, in my heart I knew I was a poet.

If anything can be taken from my experience as a teenage writer, it is that writing begins by imitating other writers. A paradox of the writing life is that the only way to be original is to follow the path of imitation. What truly inspires writers is the writing of others. What's more, in order to advance in your writing you need to find writers who make you jealous. Then you must react to that literary envy by writing in imitation of those writers. An "original" writer has really just learned how to absorb a variety of influences, combining them in a new way. Strange as it is to hear, some young writers say they don't read very much because they are afraid it will compromise their originality. Nothing could be further from the truth. Writers learning by reading just as musicians learn by listening and painters learn by looking closely at the paintings of others.

Gathered here in *The Best Teen Writing of 2007* are poems, stories, and plays by writers who have clearly opened themselves up to the influence of other writers. In their work, I can hear the echoes of writers I know, but I can also hear an edge, a tone that is their own. These young writers are standing on the shoulders of others, but they are also reaching to find their own way of sounding. As different as they are, one from another, what strikes me the most is the way each piece dares to declare itself. There is an audacity here that emboldens the writer to speak out regardless of the consequences.

And this is the balance found in the best literature, a combination of indebtedness and curiosity which involves a looking backward and forward at the same time. Finally, the freshest voices speak from a platform nailed together by the writers who have come before them. After he had read *Leaves of Grass*, Emerson—he of the three names—wrote to Walt Whitman: "I greet you at the beginning of a great career, which must yet have a long foreground somewhere, for such a start." Who knows which ones of these teenage writers we will hear from in the future, but let us greet them too and recognize the possibility of greatness, which is impossible without such remarkable beginnings.

—Billy Collins

BILLY COLLINS is the author of seven collections of poetry. His latest is *The Trouble with Poetry and Other Poems* (Random House, 2005). He served as United States Poet Laureate (2001–2003) and poet laureate of New York State (2004–2006). He also served as a National Writing Juror for the 2007 Scholastic Art & Writing Awards.

FIRE

A gentle mew stirred the early morning silence. It was repeated, more anxiously. A third mew followed, shriller, and definitely disgruntled now. But it was the fourth cry that finally penetrated the stupor of the woman curled up on the bed. Her eyes flickered open, and she distinguished a blurry contour of the source of the noise—a scrawny cat, now pacing in front of the bed impatiently. The woman, Angela, groaned and heaved herself to a sitting position, extending two fingers to nuzzle the cat gently under the chin, and glanced at the clock beside her bed.

"Five fifty-seven?" she murmured incredulously. Then her gaze shifted to the cat, who was now sitting erect, his tail swishing rhythmically, his head cocked, his luminous eyes fixed on her. She met his eyes and narrowed her own, folding her arms in a defensive pose. "I don't suppose there's any reason you're dragging me out of bed at six o'clock on a Sunday morning," she grunted aggressively. The cat leapt nimbly to its agile feet and swept out of the room without a backward glance. Angela sighed and clambered out of bed. Knowing perfectly well what the cat wanted, she set off toward the kitchen and began to fix him breakfast.

"Fire, for someone who sleeps twelve hours a day, you sure aren't very sympathetic," she pointed out as she selected a bowl from the dishwasher. The cat rubbed briefly against her legs and leapt lightly onto the counter to watch her. "Really," she continued, pulling open a drawer and reaching inside for a can of cat food, "you act as though you haven't eaten in a week." But her look softened as she looked at Fire's scrawny frame. Angela might get irritated by some of her cat's antics, but he was as good a friend to her as any human she knew. Prying open the can, she pondered aloud, "I must be the only person in the world who would get out of bed at six o'clock on a Sunday morning just to feed her cat." She flipped the can over, and the mush inside it fell into the bowl with a nasty squelching noise. "Well, I guess this means I'll have time to get a few things done before heading to the grocery store," she admitted, and she ran her fingers affectionately across the top of Fire's head as she turned to leave.

Fire nibbled at his breakfast, as was his custom, stopping every so often to preen or stretch or peer through the window at a squirrel in the bushes. Angela was much more efficient, bustling around the house, doing the laundry and the ironing and such assorted chores. By the time Fire had gotten bored with his leisurely breakfast and meandered into the living room, Angela was kneeling beside the vacuum cleaner, plugging it into the electrical socket. She gave him a nonchalant little pat and flicked the switch, turning the vacuum on. As its low drone filled the room, Fire's whole body went rigid. His fur stood on end. His claws ejected, and his mouth slid open in a panicked cry no one heard over the vacuum. The next second, he raced down the hall as fast as his lean little legs would go. Angela tore after him, abandoning the vacuum cleaner, which hummed dully on in the background. Angela groped for the terrified cat but missed and slid into the screen door, knocking it ajar—wide enough for the slim little Fire to slip through. He was gone.

"Fire!" she shrieked, throwing herself after him, allowing the screen door to slam behind her. "Fire! Fire!" she called, tearing down the driveway. She froze for a moment, gasping for breath. "Fire!" she bellowed, loud enough for the whole street to hear. She sprinted into a neighboring yard, crouching haphazardly to glance under their bushes, hurriedly treading on a patch of begonias, completely ignoring the middle-aged woman watering them, who turned to stare in appalled shock as Angela dashed diagonally across the street toward another yard. An oncoming car swerved to avoid her, smashing into the curb, honking furiously.

"What do you think you're doing?" the driver shouted after her.

Angela heard nothing and cared not. She was three blocks away from her house now. Swiveling her head to take in every inch, she raced past house after house and turned into the parking lot of a modest wooden church. Acting on instinct, she threw open the large double doors and shouted in a voice so piercing, so agonized, that it filled the entire room in an instant. "Fire!"

Only then did Angela look into the room and realize, with a jolt of her heart, that church was in session. Rows of pews were packed with the multitudes of Sunday morning worshippers, who all turned to stare directly at her. There was a second of dead, tense silence. Then the entire congregation hastily leapt to their feet and swarmed in every direction, screaming hysterically, fighting their way toward the exits which instantly clogged, but not before Angela had ducked inside. In a surprisingly short amount of time, the church was still and silent, empty of everyone except for Angela, who sank to her knees, peering under the pews. She then dashed up, her footsteps clacking and reverberating eerily, to check behind the altar. Nothing. Her chest heaved as she revolved on the spot to face the cavernous, abandoned church. But was it empty? Out of the stiff, poised silence came the tiniest, gentlest mew.

Angela's breath caught in her chest as her heart leapt hopefully. She scurried down the aisle to the very last pew. There, the streaming, colorful light descending from the stained glass windows overhead fell upon the scrawny figure of a cat, who was reclining on the pew as if it were a throne, basking in the sun, casually twitching its tail this way and that, and displaying on its face a look of complete indifference as though the events of the day were hardly even worth his notice. Angela unceremoniously scooped him into her arms and held him there for a long moment, relishing what she had almost lost forever. If she had had eyes for anything other than the cat squirming in her arms, she would have heard the muffled whirring of sirens heralding the approaching fire trucks in the parking lot.

Laura Ball, Age 13
St. Jude School
Wauwatosa, WI
Teacher: Paula Bond

ONE LAST DAY

I heatedly throw my dance bag into the corner, allowing a pair of *pointe* shoes to spill out, and plop down on the hard gray floor to watch the five-hour-long *Sleeping Beauty* rehearsal. One question resounds in my head, pounding like a never-ending hammer: Why am I here? The SAT book perched halfway between my bag and the floor refuses to let me forget the painful practice test that I took this morning, the X after X after X that filled my answer sheet as I checked for the correct responses. I have vocabulary to learn, formulas to memorize, and grammar rules to review. And that is not to mention my schoolwork—essays, math problems, outlines that I want to finish weeks in advance—that awaits me at home.

So, why am I here? The ballet mistress forced me to come. She snatched my part away from me because I tried to be a normal person, attempted to spend a week in a world where *temps de flèche*, *entrechat six*, and *rond de jambe* are meaningless phrases. I went away to Portugal for the holidays with my family and returned to find the glittering costume, the heavy jewelry and the character shoes replaced with one clunky word: understudy. As much as I struggle to restrain the thoughts from entering my head, ruminations that I never could have imagined having two or three years ago, I cannot help feeling that this may not be the right place for me, that perhaps I am not meant to be a dancer. It's something that my actions have been telling me for months but that I have never let enter my head for fear that they might be correct. I arrive at ballet class with no time to warm up because I am finishing a math assignment that isn't due for a week. I edit and re-edit and re-edit even the smallest English paper rather than sew the *pointe* shoes that I desperately need to wear the next day. The other girls, the students who will wear the gowns and the jewels along with the company members, they're not like me. They don't care about school or family; they don't want to go on vacation, to see the world. They are perfectly content with lives that are one-hundred-percent saturated with ballet.

Yet I stay because I can see the ballet mistress gazing at me out of the corner of her eye and because no matter how much my allegiance to school and to my family draw me outside the studio's mirrored walls, there is still one last glimmer of enjoyment that I may be able to get from watching a Manhattan Ballet Company rehearsal.

The director of the company, David Thomson, enters, and a chill goes down my spine as his sharp, blue Russian eyes, resting under a handsome mane of curly blonde-gray hair, scour over the row of sitting ballerinas. He harshly claps his hands together and without a word, the dancers take their places around the studio. Judging from their attire—ripped tights, bright blue bike shorts, leotards with massive holes gracing the sides, hair not controlled in buns but flying everywhere—one would never believe that they are professionals, but as they begin to leap and twirl around the studio, their sharp leg movements, precise footwork, and delicate arms make the fact incontrovertible.

Henry West, playing the king, enters the scene and performs a small pantomime. David immediately smacks his hands together, signaling someone to halt the music. He exclaims in his refined accent, "You are the king. You cannot look like some man running to catch the bus. You are getting the world's attention; you are the king!" He rushes to the center of the studio and hilariously mimics what Henry did and then proceeds to perform what he desires: grand majestic movements and stately facial expressions. Henry repeats the opening scene, imitating each of David's corrections, and the effect is spectacular, regal, enough to make me feel that I am one of his subjects. Within the next thirty minutes, David transforms into a young maiden, a nervous messenger, a fairy, and a page, each of his impressions funnier than the next, each of his changes immensely improving the scene. As I sit, laughing in enjoyment, I realize that David is not the menacing, villainous, omnipotent director as I have always pictured him. Behind the sharp gaze, he is an affable, approachable boss with a keen sense for detail, an impeccable understanding of what will please an audience, and an innate ability to articulate his expertise.

Jennifer Winger, playing the lead role of Aurora, begins the Rose Adagio, famed throughout the dance world as one of the most strenuous sections of a ballet ever choreographed. Yet, you would never be able to tell that from Jenny's movements. The room becomes silent, everyone left breathless, gazing at Jenny's supple legs and fluid arms. I feel the urge to jump into her shiny pink *pointe* shoes, to have my time to shine amidst a world of observers, to move with the poise that Jenny moves with. She perches in attitude, and one-by-one, four suitors dexterously partner her. I hold my breath as she reaches her final balance, the most challenging component of the arduous section. She removes her hand from the man's shoulder and balances...and balances...and balances; faces around the room light up as Jenny remains poised in position. When she finally gently rolls down through her *pointe* shoe, the studio bursts into thunderous applause. No longer concerned with recalling the definitions of cantankerous and erudite, I beat my hands together, the tears welling up in my eyes.

Everyone is astounded; words praising Jenny dart like arrows through the large studio. But the action is far from over; four men, playing bugs, pull Melly Baron, a friend of mine, a company member, and today, the nefarious Carabosse, into the studio on a glittering black cart. Melly's new to the part, and I observe the nerves swarming around her willowy body as the cart flies past David's gaze. Yet, as soon as she dismounts and begins her wicked pantomime, any apprehension vanishes. Melly plunges into the dramatic role, suspending all chatter with her twisting and contorting her hands, a depiction of the spell that she will place on Aurora, and her silent yet deceitful laugh, engrossing her whole body and causing goosebumps to spring up on my arms. Before I know it, Melly is back on her cart and quickly exiting the scene, leaving behind a smiling David, obviously pleased by her striking portrayal of the role.

After a few more minutes of dancing fairies and maidens, the ballet mistress perceives a the growing restlessness in the room and loudly announces, "Everybody take ten." I sigh, overjoyed finally to be given the opportunity to move about the studio, even if only walking. I stroll around, gossip with a few of my classmates, and then return to my humble abode, my spot on the floor, and settle down again to observe the groups of beautiful blonde girls with big blue eyes and handsome brown-haired young men standing around chatting and erupting in laughter. Sophie and Tess, company members crouched a few feet away, discuss the intricacies of their New Year's Eve plans: "I'll come over to your place tonight at seven, and we can get ready and then we can go to his house at like nine thirty or ten. Did I tell you that I got that dress, you know the green one that we saw in the window at Interscoop? It was on a huge sale. I definitely have to wear it tonight. But what shoes? Hmm…"

Joey and Masa, two short men with bandanas tied around their long locks, have more practical concerns: "Did you see my jumps and turns? Were they good?…Yeah, they looked good…That's a relief. I hope David liked them…" The camaraderie, the normalcy of these focused, gifted artists surprises me, and I burn to jump up and tell Sophie that I saw the green dress in the window, and it would look stunning with her complexion, to inform Joey that I noticed David smiling as he pirouetted across the studio. But I am not part of their world, not a member of the company, not a distinguished dancer.

The curtain closes on the break, and the next dance to be practiced is a huge waltz containing a flock of small children in addition to virtually all of the members of the *corps de ballet*. As I watch tiny girls, their long blonde curls twisted into French braids, waltz around the studio clutching strings of flowers, nostalgia courses through my body, memories of those former days when I too clung to a garland and danced in the spotlight as a miniscule villager. Yet more than the children, more than the handsome men, the dancers that stand out to me the most are the fresh crop of apprentices nervously twirling about the studio. A few months ago, they were students just like me, and now they are there, dancing amidst the *corps de ballet*, the printer warming to produce their contracts. Erin was in my class last year; we stood next to each other at the barre. I secretly shunned her because she did not go to school; she got to ballet hours before our classes began so that she could stretch, warm up, and prepare for the lesson, while I was left to dash in from school with thirty seconds to spare, barely enough time to tie my *pointe* shoe ribbons. Yet I prided myself with the knowledge that Erin wouldn't know the difference between a linear or exponential function, between an element and a mixture. At 17, lectures, notecards, and college applications were the furthest things from her mind. But the truth is that no one in this studio cares that I know the definition of "garrulous," and she does not; that if someone ran into the room with a complex equation, I could solve it in about half the time that Erin could. And I yearn to be like Erin, to forget the stress of Virgil and the quadratic formula, to twirl and leap across a stage. Because look at her now, she is waltzing along with the professionals, she is part of the magic, and I am shunned in the corner, the student understudy.

For the next half an hour, I sit in a trance, gazing at one long-legged beauty after another gracefully float across the studio or soar up to almost graze the double-height ceilings. It's as though I am in a dream; the hard, grueling work, the sweat, the elegance, and the grace combine before my eyes like the colors in a kaleidoscope shifting into place. "You may leave now. The court couples are finished," the ballet mistress nudges, galvanizing me from my reverie. I stand up and slowly tiptoe out of the studio, looking back over my shoulder, still gazing at the scene, never wanting to return to reality. We're done an hour early. This morning that news would have brought a huge grin to my face; I can go home and edit my papers or pour over the SAT website. But now all I want to do is run back into the studio, stay there until the magic is over, sleep there, wake up tomorrow and watch again. I don't want to learn how to graph a sine curve; I want to study each step of the Rose Adagio.

But I must leave, go out into the December air, the bitter cold trying its hardest to ship me back to reality. Yet my absorption in the galaxy of ballet has not left me completely; the drug still circulates in my veins. I return home and again fling my bag off my shoulder. This time the SAT book falls out completely, but I don't pick it up. I read the Manhattan Ballet Newsletter instead. I browse around the Manhattan Ballet Company web site, reading Jenny and Sophie and Melly's bios. I discover that there is a movie on television tonight about the Company's trip to Russia and sit wide-eyed, watching the dancers pirouette across the Maryinsky stage, gazing at them laughing while sightseeing. When the film finishes, I want more; I am addicted. I find the documentary about the Manhattan Ballet Company's *Nutcracker* that my parents had bought me but that I had left to grow dusty under a stack of vocabulary flashcards and slip it into my computer. I sit enthralled, exhilarated by the endless footage of rehearsals and performances. Ten minutes before midnight, I remember from amidst my fervor that it is New Year's Eve. I watch the ball drop, see the fireworks exploding outside my window, yet quickly return to the movie, yearning to hear the end of an interview with a famous ballerina, seeking to discover all of the secrets of a trade that this morning I was on the road out of.

But it's a new year, and new thoughts are entering my head, new ruminations telling me that I am not ready to give up all of this yet.

Zara Kessler, Age 16
The Trinity School
New York, NY
Teacher: Saul Isaacson

SPRING TRAINING

For J.P.

We crouch beneath ballpark sun
six feet west of home plate,
which is bride-white and pregnant
with famous footprints: mine and yours.

I label you, aloud:
Eyelids pulled by puppet strings.
The desert sparkling on your scalp.
A face unshaven and hinting sweat
(though it's only Massachusetts' April).

You kiss my head and offer me the diamond.
I'd prefer Fenway's grass perimeter
(Dirt shivers; wind infiltrates my sweater)
but this field sweats historical devotion,
and you are proud.

I'm too young for baseball's implications—
monetary, patriotic, superstitious.
Your barbed chin scrawls, on my forehead,
some age-old father-daughter secret
regarding love and time and equilibrium.

Like a scar beneath sixteen years of freckles,
I will find it one day in the mirror:
Even past slow songs and soul mates,
past stale gown and ring clutching finger,
I will never love a man so much as you.

Amanda Picardi, Age 16
Walnut Hill School
Natick, MA
Teacher: Daniel Bosch

SWIMMING POOL

We once went swimming
in the town pool.
Our trunks hung down to our knees,
girls lingered by the pool
in chairs
with new breasts.
Their mothers watched.
We flexed invisible muscles
desperate to impress
a tan Aphrodite
veiled in dark sunglasses.
Kids waded by the steps
holding the hands of
fathers, who yearned
to give the wisdom
they were still searching for.

We used to play a game
where we would hold
our breaths for as long as we could,
once I even opened my eyes
felt the burn of chlorine
like the time we got drunk
off your sister's wine coolers.
A hand began to push me down.
I gulped for air, and then
complete darkness.
You said it was all in
fun, just a game
for a little laugh
trying to impress the guys.
Yet here I sit
alone by the pool
still gasping for air.

Grant Hailer, Age 15
Milton Academy
Milton, MA
Teacher: Elisabeth Baker

THE PROBLEM WITH JUMP-OFF TREES

The night Ben and I went swimming was the first time I'd been to the river since Elizabeth Marsh drowned a year and a half before. That spring, a huge storm threw power lines around Rubyridge County like matchsticks. After thirteen inches of rain, the Beauna River was strong enough to strip fences from the ground and livestock from low-lying fields. A week after the water went down, Elizabeth and I went to the river to see the flood marks on the trees. We hadn't planned to swim but it was the first warm day all year and she was always looking to prove herself.

"Bet we'll be the first to swim since the storm," she said, pulling off her shoes. I lost an earring in the dirt and while she ran to jump in, I was hands and knees on the ground. "The water's moving pretty fast," she yelled over her shoulder, and I heard her splash. I never found the earring but after five minutes I went to the riverbank and called her name. In the branches above my head, a tangled plastic bag trembled in the wind. Dried lines of mud stared eye-level at me from the trunks of every tree. Debris whirled in the current and the sound of cold water shook me like a pair of hands. It took three days for scouts from all over the county to find Elizabeth's body.

Ben Henrikson got off work at 8 P.M., and by the time he walked to my house, the sky was royal blue and fireflies pinpricked the night. We were sixteen that summer and at its most complicated, love meant sneaking out to pear orchards at 3 A.M. in the back of a maroon Oldsmobile.

On the front porch, as I waited for Ben, I put my headphones on and lit two citronella candles. I pulled a scrap of paper from the back pocket of my jeans—on it, I'd scribbled my work schedule for the week. I was off the next day. Unlike most of my friends, I'd held my job at Creative Kiln, a pottery-glazing store, for two years. My mother knew the owner well, and she'd given Elizabeth Marsh and me jobs when we were fourteen. On off-hours Elizabeth and I used to sit in the back room practicing French and throwing clay on the pottery wheels.

People expected me to quit after Elizabeth died. I understand, my boss told me, if you don't feel comfortable working with constant reminders. I knew I faced those reminders regardless, so I stuck around for the summer, which turned into another school year, and then another summer. Besides Ben, pottery was the only thing I invested energy in anymore. I kept the finished stoneware in the trunk of my mother's car, on shelves in my room, in boxes in the basement— but I never used them. Since the accident, I'd made sixty-two vases, mugs, pitchers and bowls. Sixty-two attempts to reclaim a sense of normalcy. I tried everything: tall, delicate vases with handles like crescent moons; squat, dark mugs the size and shape of cupped hands; mottled-green bowls with edges like pie crust, faces open to the sky.

When Ben came up the sidewalk, my eyes were closed.

"Margaret," he said from the front yard. I lowered the volume. "Mr. Hodgins died last night." Ben worked at Brodeur, the only old folk's home in town, and got paid six bucks an hour to prepare food and wash dishes for people who couldn't. Mostly that meant he puréed carrots and apples and once, a fish sandwich, but he got to talk to the residents, too.

"The ex-mayor? I'm sorry." Mr. Hodgins used to be mayor of Rubyridge. Just a few years earlier, he'd caught the biggest flathead catfish in county history—a whopping sixty-six pounds—at Douthat State Park.

"It's affecting me more than I thought it would," Ben said.

"My parents won't be back 'til midnight," I said. "We can take the car out. That'll make you feel better." I didn't have my license but I'd learned to drive several summers before at my uncle's farm. "There are a couple good movies playing," I said. "Or we can drive up to Sweetwater. Frank says the pears are ripe enough to pick."

Ben tilted his head. The crickets seemed to lower their voices while he thought and the sycamores rattled their leaves like dry paper in the wind. I got up and set the fallen terra cotta pot—it was empty—back on the steps. A crack branched out from its base and I knew my mother would be annoyed. I sat back down on the porch steps and offered Ben something to drink.

"Let's go to Beauna Point," he finally said.

I'd been tracing the wood grain and at his words I let a finger slip. Think fast. "Ouch," I said. I faked a grimace and pinched my index finger until it was sore. "Splinter." Before he had a chance to speak again, I shoved the hand in my pocket.

"We could just stay here," I said. "We have the house to ourselves."

"Yeah," Ben said. "But I want to go swimming."

"We have an empty house, and you want to go swimming?" I laughed, realizing I'd overstepped a boundary. "You can go," I said. "But I hope you don't think I'm coming."

"Why? I'm not asking you to get in the water."

"We're not even supposed to be there after dark," I said, but even as the words left my mouth I knew it was a weak excuse. Beauna Point was the most popular place in town for teenagers to hang out. I hadn't been back since Elizabeth's death.

"Just drive me there?" he asked.

"I'd really rather stay here," I said. I climbed onto his lap and grabbed his hands. Please look at me, I thought. When he finally did, I wished he hadn't.

"Listen, Margaret," he said. "It's been a year and a half. You won't go near water, but you'll spend five hours a day trying to make the same pots Elizabeth used to make. When people try to talk about her you leave the room, but you saved every stupid newspaper clipping about the accident. I know you did. Your mother showed me the book."

"Are you kidding me?" I threw up my hands.

"She's concerned about you," Ben said. "We just want you back. She thought I could help you."

"She wants you to help *her*," I said, and I stood up. I kicked off my shoes and walked across the grass. A streetlamp buzzed and I wondered if it was really so loud or if I was imagining it. "Get the keys," I said. "I've changed my mind." Ben rose without question. The screen door clanked behind him and I heard the hardwood floors creak as he walked to the back of the house.

Ben emerged a few minutes later with an old bag of my mother's and the car keys. I could see the blue and green stripes of a beach towel peeking out from the canvas bag. He put his hands on my shoulders and kissed my forehead. I grabbed the keys and towels so that Ben could sling his book bag over his back. "Thank you," he said. I stopped myself from asking if he'd spoken too soon.

Every time we passed a streetlight I saw the reflection of Ben's face slide up the inside of the windshield. We drove the first block in silence. At the corner of Woodfield and Jackson, a dog darted into the street and I kicked the brakes so violently the bag flew from Ben's lap onto the dashboard. Drivers in the mountains are bound to hit animals—squirrels, deer, foxes, dogs—but it was partially that ridiculous fear that kept me from getting my license. Don't worry about it, my father told me—when it comes down to his life or yours, you won't think twice. I thought in a split second I would make the wrong decision and end up in a ditch.

"Damn dog," Ben said. "The Hastings need to get a fence." My heart was caught somewhere between my stomach and my lungs. I just nodded. Ben turned the radio on. I resumed driving.

"My mom loves the mug, by the way," he said. "She uses it every morning. I had to remind her not to put it in the dishwasher. She thinks you could sell them for a lot of money."

"They're not that good," I said. I'd considered selling my ceramics before. There was a good market for arts in Rubyridge, but I found it difficult to part with my creations. Selling the work would mean giving the ownership I held so dear to a stranger.

"Your stuff wins awards," Ben said.

"Elizabeth was better." I pulled onto the dirt road that led to the river. Ben rolled down the window and stuck his arm into the summer air. Somewhere in the distance a dog bayed at the moon.

We parked on the gravel at Beauna Point and before I turned off the car, the headlights illuminated a sign that read No Trespassing After Dark. I wasn't sure if the sign was new or if it had been there before and I just hadn't noticed it. The sign post was splattered with mud from a recent rain. Overhead, the sky was cloudless and, except for its mournful expression, the moon was perfect. We were far enough from the lights of town to see every star. They flooded the sky like a school of fish, glinting and shuddering.

Ben cuffed my shoulder. "I want to show you something," he said. He took my hand and we started walking in the direction of the river. The Point didn't look much different from the last time I'd been there. The air was warm on my skin, the gravel was uneven under my flip-flops, the trees on the bank of the river were dark and hunched. We might have been the only people for two miles round. *Void* was the word that came to mind. The stillness struck me at surface-level—I felt it on my skin—but in my gut I knew something quivered beyond the quiet.

The sand on the path got caught between my shoe and my foot. With each step the friction grew worse until I realized I'd stopped moving. I couldn't hear anything over my heartbeat and put my hands over my chest to still the heavy thumping. Why was I so nervous? I'd had seventeen months to mourn. The rest of Rubyridge recovered and by June of the year Elizabeth died, most people were swimming at Beauna Point again. The river wasn't dangerous. Buoys were installed along the bank in seven places. She was foolish to swim after a storm. It wasn't my fault.

How many times had I told myself that? On the riverbank my soft calls for Elizabeth had turned into screams. She was playing a sick joke on me and I was ready to go home. When I realized she wasn't hiding in the underbrush along the bank or behind the fallen tree in the river, I stormed to the dam half a mile downstream. I cursed her—even as I arrived breathless to the nearest house to ask for help; and in the flurry of the next few days as everyone in town grew distraught; and on the week of her funeral when I was forced to dine with her family and tell them the underwhelming details of her final moments. Even then, I didn't blame myself. I was raw and angry with Elizabeth for turning things upside-down. Only after the newspaper articles and the hugs of consolation and pity did I find that while Rubyridge had moved on with its life, I could not.

How does a fourteen-year-old carry on living and bear witness to life's transience? I didn't know how to manage both. Girls I grew up with clutched pink binders, laughing and flirting in the school hallways. Neighbors whose kids I'd babysat walked their dogs past my house and whistled. Cashiers at the grocery store smiled at me and asked about my mother. I wanted to shake them out of their boring, pathetic lives. I wanted to grab their wrists and ask them: "How have you forgotten? Remember me? I don't deserve this."

In the movies, people are haunted by voices—shrieks and whispers fill their quiet moments. I found myself haunted by the sound of the voice that never came. My angry words floated across the river and there was no answer. That absolute, dead quiet filled the space between every breath I took for a year and a half.

A car door slammed. I'd hardly been aware that Ben tore away to grab the bag of towels. Now he walked toward me and I realized that I was being swallowed up from the inside.

"Let's go home," I said. "I shouldn't be here." I had my back to the river and Ben took me by the shoulders and turned me around. I smelled mountains and river water and then I realized what I was looking at.

Down a slight incline, an enormous wooden cross was staked in front of us. It was looped with fake flowers and a couple disintegrating envelopes and dirty teddy bears sat around its base. Dozens of red handkerchiefs were tied on the arms of the cross. Elizabeth used to wear them, so after her death, people began wearing thin strips of that bandana fabric on their arms as a gesture of remembrance. The cross was in a clearing under a few oak trees, which is why I hadn't noticed it before. As we walked closer, the reflection of the moon on the water made it more visible. I stopped a few yards in front of it, frightened to move any closer.

"Some friends put it up a while ago," Ben said. "It's kind of weird to see that when you want to go swimming, but I guess we can't forget altogether. Her parents want to replace it with a stone marker." The cross wasn't by the main jump-off tree but I could see how it would discourage swimmers. Seeing the cross was like seeing a ghost.

I didn't speak. I didn't know what to say. "Sorry" was redundant. A warm breeze came out of nowhere and blew my hair into my face. I reached up and grabbed my earlobes, a nervous habit. I wasn't wearing any earrings. That first warm day of spring had felt amazing and Elizabeth and I were happy to be out of school. We couldn't see beneath the surface of the water. There was no way of knowing right then the strength of the undertow.

I approached the cross and knelt, rubbing one of the handkerchiefs between my fingers. The ground was cool and its contact on my skin made me feel less shaky but I backed away after half a minute. "In the trunk," I said to Ben, and he nodded before I'd finished my sentence. I watched his back as he ran back to the car, keys jingling in his hand. On my other side, the river flowed sluggishly beyond dark, leafy branches. Chunks of moss floated on the surface of the water.

Ben returned with a frayed cardboard box in his arms. Its contents clinked as he stopped in front of me and I reached in to remove a deep blue pitcher. I didn't remember making it but my initials were on the bottom. At the base of the cross, I cleared a spot with my foot. I cradled the round weight of the pitcher for a moment and then set it on the ground.

We left the cross and I felt it watching our backs as we began walking toward the jump-off tree. In the dirt above the steep incline leading to the river,

Ben took off his shirt. Grabbing a branch, he slid down the incline and climbed onto the fallen tree perched over the river. He sidled to its middle and stood up, watching his shadowy reflection dance on the surface of the water. Looking at his back, a chill went down my spine. Just as I yelled "Wait!" he jumped, and the force of his body hitting the water seemed loud enough to shake the trees. I wanted to reach out and stop every ripple in the river. My heart pounded loose inside my ribcage.

Ben surfaced. He shook water from his hair. "What'd you say?" he asked. I looked at him and before I spoke there was a flash in which I thought, silence is not so bad. The feeling that time isn't passing when you're underwater—that you're suspended in agelessness—reached up from the shore and grabbed me for a half-second. I forgot everything. Then it was gone, and I was a teenage girl standing on the dirt banks of the Beauna River, where a friend once died.

"Wait," I said. "Wait for me." And I situated the cardboard box on my hip. I slid down the slope and clambered onto the tree. Ben smiled up at me. The tree bark had been worn away by so many feet that it was smooth under my heels. I took a deep breath and heaved a clattering mess of red, green, blue, and brown into the river. The sound the clay made as it hit the water was like a gunshot at the beginning of a race.

Erin Weeks, Age 17
South Carolina Governor's School for the Arts and Humanities
Greenville, South Carolina
Teacher: George Singleton

ON BEING INFORMED

While reading the *Newsweek* magazine to which my dad subscribed in a quest to create in me an informed, cosmopolitan young woman, I came across an article entitled "How To Stop a Genocide." I'll preface all of this with a confession: I knew only the peripheries of the Darfur crisis before delving into Fareed Zakaria's article. I'd heard of the government-sanctioned rape and murder by means of the Janjaweed, I'd heard of the millions displaced; and I knew, simply and necessarily, where Darfur was plotted on the map.

Several hundred words more knowledgeable, a thought occurred to me. What would happen if I asked a high school student that essential question: Where *is* Darfur, anyway?

I asked several. The answers, sad to say, did not surprise me.

"In synagogues?"

"Isn't that near..."

"No idea."

"I'm not that good with geography..."

"The Middle East?"

And the creativity award goes to: "I don't know, but it sounds like the name of the bad guy in *Shrek*." (I'm thinking of Jay Leno's "Jaywalking" gimmick, in which the journalistic man-on-the-street technique is taken to a satirical level, pedestrians living up to their names and answering that our vice president is

Kennedy. Their voices slide up at the end in question.)

In her *New York Times* column "Public and Private", Anna Quindlen pointed out in the context of the simultaneous Bosnia and Somalia crises of the early 90s that Bosnia, a European country, gained more media spotlight and discussion than Somalia, an African one. Her final line pleaded, "Surely our empathy can transcend race."

And this could be part of it. Africa, in the American mentality, conscious or not, is an AIDS-ravaged, anemic jungle of starvation and suffering, too convoluted to begin to unravel—a lost cause. Perhaps an oversimplified argument would finger-point at racism, and I have no doubt that this bolsters the apathy as with Somalia, particularly juxtaposed with a predominantly white nation.

But what of those who didn't even know Darfur is in Sudan to begin with?

I am getting at a conclusion that might move some, upset others, and still yet cause people to shake their heads sadly and with familiarity: High school kids are not informed.

It's a generalized statement to make—certainly more than a little risky. The part and parcel stress of these four years is infamous; the peer pressure, emotional fallout, and that c-word college are icing on the sour-tasting cake. And there are exceptions to anything, as still others pick up the *Post* once in a while or flip to CNN.

Here, though, is an unofficial compendium of the things even the most intelligent students seem to have plenty of time for: We have time for the Internet. We have time for cell phones and instant messaging and shopping and deciding what color Uggs to wear. We have time for *The O.C.* We have time for tabloids over frappuccinos at Barnes & Noble and we have time for that ever popular Facebook.

So how about that genocide? (I can assure you a copy of *Newsweek* weighs similarly in your hands to one of, say, *Us Weekly*.)

Calculate the price of one Lacoste polo divided by the number of single *Washington Post*s purchasable. I'm cripplingly right-brained, and I can still tell you that that number is significantly large. Don't give up your shopping just yet, but think about it in the scheme of where our priorities lie.

No one is asking anyone at this juncture to become an activist, bite off more than plausibly chewable with a full-time education and various extracurricular activities that constitute a tight, stressful schedule. But chew on this (stick it in your pipe, sit on it, something): The literacy level in our cookie-cutter suburb is fantastic, really. You don't need a data collection to tell you that Walt Whitman

High School kids can read quite well. We tick off Fitzgerald and Hemingway, Austen and Salinger on summer reading lists and then write five-paragraph essays on them. We get As.

A statistic recently publicized states that the average American knows more *Simpsons* characters than Supreme Court justices—if you were looking for one more thing for which we students have time. It also shows that there is no right age to be informed, striking off one more excuse: "I'm too young; it doesn't affect me." True, the peace accords in some far-off country may not ignite a fire in your heart. But it doesn't take much to realize how localized the news can be, from the *New York Times* to our very own *Black & White*; how, yes, you are a part of this world, unless you are living under a rock. If not aware now, then when? Look what happens: you grow old getting your information from a cartoon.

It's a lesson in grounding. It's easy to become ensconced in the bubble of your own life, traipse happily through, unscathed and naive. It's also a simple way to become selfish in your ignorance of six billion others besides you.

After informing one student that Darfur is, indeed, a region in Sudan, I received a not-mean-spirited reply of "Smart kid."

Well, not particularly. I just read the paper.

Anna Isaacs, Age 16
Walt Whitman High School
Bethesda, MD
Teacher: Louise Reynolds

WHITE WOMAN
(EXCERPT)

Characters

CHRISTIAN NGUGI, mid to late 30's, Ugandan, associate director of Liberate The Children, Kampala office. A reserved man; a pressure cooker.

ELLE FORD, early 30's, director of the Kampala office. A traditional American beauty. More pragmatic than she seems at first.

Setting

The screened-in front porch of Elle's house just outside Kampala, Uganda. The screen door is stage left, the whitewashed front door and broken doorbell stage right, so that the audience is facing the porch's side, looking in. The steps leading up to the screen door are whitewashed as well. The downstage center wall and wall adjacent to the screen door are made of material similar to mosquito netting. The wall adjacent to the front door and the upstage wall are whitewashed wood. There is a window next to the front door through which the dim glow of lamplight can be seen. African masks hang on the back wall. There is a sofa, a table with a teapot, a thick stack of papers and a coffee table book entitled *Beautiful Africa: 365 Days.* It is night.

(CHRISTIAN enters stage left. HE is breathing heavily. He checks his watch, squeezes his briefcase handle as if to make sure it is still there, squeezes it again. He steps onto

the front porch, opens the screen door. He squeezes his briefcase handle some more, looking down at it compulsively. Christian spots the thick, disorganized pile of papers underneath Beautiful Africa: 365 Days. *Hands shaking, he moves the book and begins to rifle through the papers, mumbling to himself.)*

CHRISTIAN: Literacy initiative...Toys 'R' Us Children's Fund would like to... Liberate the Children global action campaign...Johnson & Johnson clean water program...Proctor and Gamble extends its warmest regards to Liberate The Children in their effort to...2006 not-for-profit fiscal accountability index...NGO Liberate The Children ranks tenth in...

(There is a flash of movement behind the window. Christian drops his briefcase. He hastily puts the papers back, with the book on top of them, except at a slightly different angle than before. He moves to the door to ring the doorbell but Elle's voice stops him.)

ELLE: *(from behind the door, HER voice quavering)* Whoever is out there, I'm warning you. I have a gun.

(Christian's mouth twists bitterly.)

ELLE: *(unconvincingly)* Hello? Did you hear me? I said I have a gun. A gun, yes, a gun. And I will shoot you if you don't leave right now. I will. What, you don't believe me?

(Christian closes his eyes, almost laughs.)

ELLE: *(babbling)* What do you want? There's nothing out there for you. Except the teapot. Take my teapot. You can have it, I don't care. It's worth a lot of money. I understand if you need the money. Please, take my teapot, feed yourself, feed your family, please, please, please God just take it and leave—

(Christian jabs at the doorbell.)

ELLE: Hello?

CHRISTIAN: It's quite all right, Miss Ford...my family...doesn't need your teapot, although they thank you.

ELLE: Christian?

(Elle opens the front door. She is wearing a brightly colored robe with an African print. Her hair is wet as if she just showered. She stares at him a minute, biting her lip.)

ELLE: *(helplessly)* I...I'm sorry, Christian, I...just get spooked sometimes.

(Christian looks at the floor, his jaw tight. His posture is stiff.)

ELLE: I didn't think you'd come.

CHRISTIAN: I have something to discuss with you, Miss Ford. Concerning the Child Soldier Initiative.

ELLE: *(overlapping)* I-I was afraid. Afraid you wouldn't come.

(She reaches out to touch his arm. He bristles. She looks down, clasps her hands, looks up again. An 'Ah well, if that's how you're gonna be about it' gesture.)

ELLE: Flight's at ten tomorrow. I should arrive in Nairobi around eleven-thirty or so. Christian?

CHRISTIAN: Yes, Miss Ford?

ELLE: For chrissakes, Christian, don't call me that. *(beat)* Office is all cleared out. It's yours now. Congratulations. You'll be director. Director of all Liberate The Children programs in Uganda. Has it sunk in yet?

CHRISTIAN: I am not...director yet, Miss Ford. I am still associate director.

ELLE: But with me off to Kenya, of course you'll be—

CHRISTIAN: *(He gives her a hard look, a 'Come on, now' look.)* I don't want to uh... what is it? Count my chickens. I don't want to count my chickens before they hatch. Congratulations on your new position, Miss Ford.

ELLE: Please look at me. Christian.

CHRISTIAN: I stopped by your house to...discuss some...details regarding the Child Soldier Initiative. I wanted to straighten some things out before you leave.

ELLE: Christian. Please. It's nearly one in the morning.

CHRISTIAN: *(overlapping)* I really cannot be staying long. My children have school tomorrow.

ELLE: Fine. We'll stay out here then. I'll make some tea.

(She crosses to the teapot and removes the kettle, causing her robe to slip a little off of her shoulder. She doesn't bother to pull it back up. Christian glances at her exposed shoulder, swallows painfully, then looks away from her to the stack of papers. He straightens the book back to its original position on the table while her back is still turned. She exits stage right through the front door, carrying the kettle. Christian leans over the table, flipping through the papers without moving them. He hears her footsteps approaching and lets go of the papers. He picks up Beautiful Africa: 365 Days *and pretends to read. Elle enters again, carrying the kettle and a tea tray with two mugs, one box of Earl Grey and one of Kenyan tea. She puts the kettle back in and turns on the teapot, then sets the tray down on the table. She sits down next to Christian, crossing her legs and resting her feet against the right corner of the table, making her calves more prominent. Christian glances at her legs then looks away, back at the book.)*

ELLE: I used to love that book. When I was little. I'd sneak into the living room—my mom never let me in there, she was afraid I'd track dirt onto her furniture—and flip through it for hours. That's when I fell in love. The...tenacity in the pictures. The joy and hope, despite such suffering. Especially the children. It moved me so deeply.

CHRISTIAN: *(His hand is clenching and unclenching around the handle of his briefcase)* I attended a forgiveness ceremony today. Very powerful event. All those former rebels, all those old children being welcomed back into their communities. The arms are...less than open to the rebels but...I have faith that they will open. And when each child came forward to step on the egg, to look at their faces, you would think they really were...reborn. Not only symbolically, but truly. Not...terrorists, but children. One man broke down and actually embraced the boy who macheted his son. *(beat)* There's another one taking place around Gulu in a week.

ELLE: As soon as I'm done with this caseload.

CHRISTIAN: *(stony)* I see.

ELLE: What? *(Christian doesn't answer.)* WHAT?

(Long pause. He sits there, just clenching and unclenching his hands.)

ELLE: *(To end the awkward silence)* How is Josephine?

CHRISTIAN: My wife is...very well, thank you.

ELLE: Did you ever tell your wife about us?

(He stares at her, unkindly.)

ELLE: Well, I think it's a fair question: Don't you?

CHRISTIAN: *(ugly)* Like a horse with blinders.

(Elle reacts.)

ELLE: O...K...Listen, Christian, go home, get some sleep, you've been working yourself too hard, we both have. We'll keep in touch—I mean, I hope we will. Or, have a nice life, I guess. *(beat)* Please just tell me what I did wrong. Do you know how hard it's been for me, going into the office this past month, putting up with your...mean obsequiousness, your silence? Just like that. No explanation. I haven't known what to think, whether you were trying to cope with my leaving by distancing yourself, or what the hell. I'm going to be in Nairobi tomorrow. You at least owe me an—

CHRISTIAN: Closure? Closure, is it that? Ok. I love my wife. I love my children. And I have a job to do.

ELLE: If you want to save face, fine, but not at my expense. Not like this, not on our last night. I thought you had more dignity than to act like a petulant kid for an entire week.

CHRISTIAN: Tell something to me, Elle: are you behind on your work because your mind has been elsewhere? Because this week, this week for me has been about... reprioritizing.

(Beat.)

ELLE: That tea should be ready soon. Earl Grey?

CHRISTIAN: Yes, thank you.

ELLE: Don't thank me. You know, I've never understood why you like such bland tea, I much prefer—

CHRISTIAN: African teas. They are more flavorful. *(He shakes his head slightly.)* You have said this many times, Miss Ford.

ELLE: I repeat myself a lot. Sorry.

(There is an awkward silence. Elle stands up and pours them two cups of tea, one Kenyan, one Earl Grey. She sits down, begins to sip her tea. Christian doesn't touch his.)

ELLE: What was I to you? Just some stupid white woman? Some rich *muzungu* you were with because you wanted to spit in people's faces and couldn't? Did you just do it for a private laugh?

CHRISTIAN: *(Through his teeth)* I would like to discuss the matter of forgiveness ceremonies further, Miss Ford.

ELLE: I'm tired of you. Of your poker face. Of your 'Yes, Miss Ford' and your 'No, Miss Ford' and your Earl Grey and your silence. For caring what people think. For being a lackey.

(Christian abruptly stands up, knocking a sheaf of papers off the table.)

CHRISTIAN: No, you did not care what people thought. You ate it up. You relished it. Miss Elle Ford, Harvard graduate, disowned second daughter of Charles Ford, Miss Elle Ford the renegade aristocrat in her Mexican serape and Moroccan hat, arm around her black lover. *(beat)* My...presence here tonight is...concerning the initiative. Are you honestly so self absorbed that all you can think about is your failed hunt for exotic game?

(Elle looks like he slapped her. She sits there a moment, trying to speak but choking on her self-defenses and apologies before they come out of her lips. After a moment, she looks down. Her hair covers her face. Christian's hands, which were balled into fists at his sides, unclench. His jaw un-tightens. He sits back down next to her. They sit in silence for a moment. Christian gulps his tea. It burns his throat but he stops himself from making a noise.)

ELLE: You thought that I would *brag*? That I would romanticize you like that?

CHRISTIAN: *(speaking to the screen)* I know you wanted to think of me as...long suffering. But my father was lucky enough to speak English, and smart enough to keep his head down. I have not suffered, not really, and suffering is only a part of life. I suppose I am a lackey. But it keeps food in my children's bellies. I do not care if your spirit is stirred by that.

ELLE: I just don't understand. Why you had to end it like you did.

CHRISTIAN: Don't you have any sense of consequences? Or is that a foreign concept? I *love* my family.

ELLE: Okay, so I was reckless. I was attracted to you, Christian. Human beings are attracted to one another, and it makes them stupid. Don't turn this into a Chinua Achebe novel. We're people, not nation states, and yes, I do find black men attractive, and so yes, I was attracted to you. Some men prefer brunettes. You happen to like blondes, and—

CHRISTIAN: Don't.

ELLE: Okay. Okay, I get it. I'm the imperial villain, and you're the noble protagonist led astray. All right. *(beat)* How can you be so cavalier? You said you loved me. You said I had a heart the size of the sun. That I was so intelligent, that my passion was so sexy, that together we could do great things. We were unstoppable. Or was that just lip service?

CHRISTIAN: Just what?

ELLE: Lip service. It means... Look, I haven't been like a giddy schoolgirl or anything, don't...don't flatter yourself, all right? *(beat)* I've just been busy. Been too busy coordinating sponsorships. *(Christian is gripping his teacup so tightly that it looks like he might crush it.)* Christian... *(her face crumples slightly)* We did this together, Christian. We built this together. Just think of what we could have done with five more years, or even two. I don't have to take the offer. I could stay at the Kampala office. And whatever it is that I did, I can make it up to you. I promise. *(beat)* Hey, did I tell you that the *Christian Science Monitor* is dedicating a five-page spread to the Child Soldier Initiative? Pretty soon we'll have more sponsors sending in money than we have children. Phenomenal turnover, highest in years.

(Christian sets the teacup down on the edge of the table, abruptly and a little too hard, and it slips off the corner, falling on the floor and spilling on his foot. He kneels and takes a tissue out of his briefcase, tries to wipe the tea off of his shoes, his good shoes, but gives up, sitting down in the pool of liquid and putting his face in his hands.)

ELLE: Christian? Want some paper towels? *(beat)* Christian?

CHRISTIAN: I think you should attend a forgiveness ceremony, Miss Ford. I think you should see these children face to face for more than a photo opportunity. For more than just kitsch.

(Beat.)

ELLE: Photo ops are necessary for promotional purposes. And I do more good with the time I spend in my office and the decisions I make there than I could any other way.

(Christian gets to his feet and opens his briefcase. He pulls out a picture of a ten-year-old boy and a letter.)

CHRISTIAN: Do you know this child?

ELLE: No.

CHRISTIAN: Yet you found a sponsor to pay for all his schooling and basic needs.

ELLE: I help coordinate sponsorships for hundreds of children everyday. Do you remember every single file that comes into your hands?

CHRISTIAN: His name is Joseph. He is being sponsored by one Maeve Benson of Chula, Georgia. Maeve Benson is sixty years old. Never married. No children.

(Something clicks behind Elle's eyes. She stands up suddenly.)

ELLE: More tea?

CHRISTIAN: Let me read you a letter from Joseph to Maeve. *(He clears his throat.)* "Dear Sponsor, Thank you so much for supporting me in my studies. I am enjoying my classes very much and earning good grades."

(Elle does not look at him.)

ELLE: Would you like more tea, Christian?

CHRISTIAN: 'The situation here is very bad. But since escaping from the rebels, some of the bad things inside me are fading. I now know that I am not a monster. Please send help for all my brothers and sisters who are still fighting in this war. Please write to me or else I think you have forgotten about me. Sincerely, Joseph.'

(Elle takes his cup and pours him some more Earl Grey. She sits back down and takes Beautiful Africa: 365 Days. *She hugs it to her chest, not looking at Christian.)*

CHRISTIAN: A touching letter, is it not?

(Elle says nothing.)

CHRISTIAN: Well written.

ELLE: Stop it.

(Christian pulls another letter out of his briefcase.)

CHRISTIAN: And this is from Maeve Benson. 'Dear Joseph, I will never forget about you. May God bless you, child. You are always in my thoughts and prayers, and in my heart.'

ELLE: Stop it.

CHRISTIAN: 'I have no children of my own. It is a blessing to be able to help you. I look forward to your letters and am so proud of your accomplishments.'

ELLE: *Stop it.*

CHRISTIAN: 'I love you like you were my—'

ELLE: For chrissakes, stop it. Stop it!

CHRISTIAN: 'I love you like you were my own child.'

(Elle stands up abruptly.)

ELLE: *(hysterically)* STOP IT! STOP IT, STOP IT, STOP IT!

(Christian takes several more photos out of his briefcase. He pauses over each one.)

CHRISTIAN: Joseph has been dead for a year. James has been dead for three years. Simon, two years. Christine, four years. And there are other cases, other cases I discovered. My silence the past week? I grew more and more silent the deeper and deeper I saw into your heart, Miss Ford. I wasn't sure if you knew about it at first. I wasn't even completely positive until I saw your face a moment ago. I wanted to assume that it was a mistake. A glitch. And if it was not, I wanted to assume that it did not go very high up. I wanted to give you the benefit of the doubt. Because, for all your faults, I knew you meant well.

ELLE: I'm glad to know you thought of me as a well-meaning fool. I'm glad to know I wasn't any different to you than any other white woman. What do you care about it anyway? The money still went to child soldiers. It's not a case of graft. We could turn a larger profit this way. A larger profit for kids who need it. What do you care about a slip in quality control?

(Christian nearly chokes.)

CHRISTIAN: A slip in quality control? You send sponsors pictures of kids who have been dead for years. You write fake letters to these poor people who think they are doing a good thing because you do not have a large enough supply of pictures of actual *live* children—and you call that a slip in quality control?

ELLE: I am trying *so* hard to keep this office running, Christian. And I will do whatever it takes. The money went to a greater good. That's the way things work in Uganda.

CHRISTIAN: No, that is *not* the way things work in my country.

ELLE: You hate your country. You hate the open gutters, the red dirt roads, the stores with their stupid names like Jesus Died Solely For Your Sins Hardware or God Cares For Tailless Animals Fashion Home! If a toothless beggar tried to touch your hand, you wouldn't even *meet his eyes*. You cheated on your wife with me just like you cheat on Uganda with that ridiculous double breasted suit you ordered from Harrod's, with your furniture, your china, your house with its security system. All your awkward, *awkward* imports. You actually *do* own a gun.

CHRISTIAN: And is it so bad, that an African man should have nice things? That he should have a beautiful, well-educated woman on his arm? I treasure that suit because it is one of only two. My wife presses it every night. And you come here to live out some sort of rich person's rustic fantasy. I think you would go around wearing a burlap sack and holding a sign that said 'peasant' if you could. Or perhaps it would read 'martyr.'

ELLE: So I was an accessory? Is that it? Like a Rolex, to wear around and show off how much of a British windup clock you are? Here, want some more Earl Grey? Take it. Take it!

(She thrusts tea bags at him.)

A PRAYER FOR MY FRIEND, AS BOMBS FALL ON BEIRUT

For Roy Hage

Your phone lines are down.
All I can do from here
is pray. Pray that the noise outside
doesn't shake the kitchen
where your mother pours milk
and smiles for your little brother.
She is a veteran, she knows better
than to look up from the table
unless the flames lick her house.
This is bravery: a straightened cushion,
a watered plant, a thirsty child.

I pray that you will be like her
even as the smell of burnt fuel stings
your nose and warships dot the horizon.
Don't fear for the loved ones you can't reach.
Trust suspends gravity. Squeeze your eyes,
hold your breath as tightly
as your brother's small hand.
Every minute marches;
we must kiss minutes,
run our fingers over them like rosary beads.

I pray for your family and all families
who have never known true peace,
whose every glass of milk is delicious,
for all people suspended
between night and morning. I pray
that as you breathe and I breathe,
our breaths will coincide
and yours will slow so you may sleep.
I pray that you will take tiny risks:
step out on the balcony, feel the breeze
on your face. Go back inside quickly,
knowing there are angels
at your heels.

IDI AMIN HAD A BLUE WINDBREAKER

Idi Amin had a blue windbreaker, European, that he wore against the river breeze when he went fishing with his favorite wife before he killed her. She was his favorite because of her long hair, which was like a white woman's, which he could run his fingers through and forget about matters of state. She liked the squishiness of his cheeks, like a cherub's, but didn't dare tell him so.

Idi Amin enjoyed a good rugby match. He had an accordion that he played often, though with more virtuosity when drunk. He laughed at the rumors from the West: he was a cannibal, he had tea parties with severed heads. A Koran safeguarded his pillow, the cover crumbling, favorite passages earmarked. The ink ran where he had fallen asleep and drooled. His shirts smelled like cigars and French cologne.

He went fishing when he could in those days, when strange fish began appearing farther up the Nile, clogging dams like oversized alewives. He wore his blue windbreaker. His favorite wife asked if she could have a go, and he pressed the rod into her soft hand, guiding it, reeling in a catch over her shoulders, something sliding into place behind his eyes.

Phoebe Rusch, Age 18
Interlochen Arts Academy
Interlochen, Michigan
Teacher: Anne Marie Oomen

OF RAWLS, REFUTATION, AND RATIOCINATION

Since the first day I climbed the torturous stairs to the debate room, my teammates had woven fantastic tales of how exhilarating debate tournaments were. My upperclassman mentor had told me of the intense friendliness and camaraderie that existed among fellow debaters, and also that everyone would be especially nice to me because I was a novice. Despite these reassurances, from the very minute I walked in the door of Benton West High School for my first tournament experience, I was thoroughly intimidated.

Slouching in one of the cheap plastic chairs in the corner of Benton West High School's cafeteria, I waited for something to happen. Our debate team had arrived almost an hour ago, after an excruciatingly long bus ride from Norman High, and we were now confined to the cafeteria until classes let out. I sighed and observed from my vantage point the hubbub that was just beginning. Another bus had arrived, and a stream of people in various states of (un)dress were in the process of staking out their territory in the Commons. The plastic-coated cases, the precious papers with the arguments and evidence that I had spent the previous two weeks honing and polishing, were trembling ever so slightly in my hands. I imputed it to the grande mocha Frappuccino, extra ice, that I had smuggled onto the bus; a thick layer of solidified cream was still adhered to the roof of my mouth and I could feel it by running my tongue over it. To my left, over by the food counter, a group of Cross-Examination debaters had set up their boxes in a circle and were practicing reading their cases out loud. To most of the Lincoln-Douglas debaters like me, the ways of the CXers constituted a persistent mystery. It was reminiscent of some sort of cult prayer circle, with everyone bowing up and down, eyes fixed on their papers, and reading as fast as they possibly could and occasionally shouting out words like "genocide," "infantilized Other," and "global thermonuclear omnicide." Even though I knew I would never be debating them, I was intimidated by their dense jargon and impressive façade of knowledge, as well as the otherworldly vibes I was now quite certain were radiating from the circle.

A corpulent boy with long, unwashed hair, leaving the ritual recitation of evidence, waddled past me, throwing off an aura of uncleanness and dishevelment. It looked as though his suit had lain wadded up in the bottom of his closet all summer, and that his torn and shredded tie had been commandeered by his cat for claw sharpening and pouncing practice. I knew immediately that he was not on our team, because he would have already met an abrupt and painful end from our coach for trying to wear such shabby attire to a tournament.

A few tables away, a very different figure was languidly sitting. He was very tall and well dressed, and handsome by any standards. Several others were crowded around him, listening to him pontificate. "Well *of course* I'm running Kant. Anyone who's not is a complete idiot. Can you believe that someone actually tried to run Rawls against me in class? Against *me?*" I looked down at my affirmative case in my now quite sweaty hands. Rawls' "Veil of Ignorance." I could feel my cheeks getting prickly and hot. The anxiety that formerly had been simmering quietly in the background now leapt fully to the forefront of my consciousness. Whoever this "Kant" character was, I needed to get some of his arguments, and fast. The quick rhythm and strained vocals of Led Zeppelin's "Kashmir" emanating from the tinny speakers of someone's laptop drummed in my ears, further adding to the oppressive feeling of anticipation and expectance that hung in the air.

A balding man wearing a Benton West shirt featuring some witty saying about debate that I was in no mood to appreciate, walked imperiously through the throngs of expectant debaters toward the wall directly behind my booth, and deftly stuck a fluttering piece of paper eye-height on the white cinderblock wall. Immediately, the suit- and skirt-clad horde surged forward, forcing the coach to fight his way back against the tide. A girl clambered onto a table and yelled "postings!" at the top of her lungs, as if there was anyone in that room who was not fully aware of the fact. I found myself caught up in the herd that swarmed around the postings. Engulfed by others also fighting toward the front, I was assaulted by an interesting and invasive medley of smells. Nervous sweat, perfume, and the unique smell issuing from a boy who had just shoved the remainders of his cheese stick and graham crackers into his mouth all wafted through the air, combining in my nose to create a complexly nuanced, yet vile smell. The boy's snacks were now being mashed into an umber pulp that leaked out of the left corner of his mouth as he excitedly gestured to his friend who, judging by the horrified look on her face, was just as repulsed as I was.

Elbowing to the front of the group, trying to avoid having my suit besmirched by the cheese and graham mix, I began searching for my number on the list. I quickly located it on the first column on the left about halfway down, meaning that I was arguing affirmative. My opponent's number indicated that he or she was from Concord High School, our archrivals, but very respected archrivals. My room number was 218, but in this school, that told me very little about where it was located. Looking back at the postings just to double-check my room number, I noticed for the first time a tiny note at the top left corner of the paper saying that the start time for Flight A rounds was 4:00 P.M. I spun wildly around to check the time on the ancient IBM wall clock that seemed at odds with the rest of the perfectly clean and modern building. The big hand clunked solidly one minute forward, now saying that my round had started four minutes ago. A jolt of adrenaline coursed through my veins; I turned and ran.

Trying to remember my way through the tortuous hallways, I began grumbling under my breath about the sick and sadistic architect who would build a school with a seemingly random numbering system and large rectangular depressions in the middle of the hallways. As I dashed past row upon row of closed classroom doors with cadmium yellow signs explaining the standard horrible punishments that would be inflicted on debaters entering rooms without a judge present, palpable fear and excitement exuded from under the closed doors. My shoes squeaked wildly as I whipped past the small black numbers on every door, getting closer and closer to 218. Finally, I saw my door. I zeroed in on the doorknob, lunged forward, grabbed the tarnished metal knob, turned it, whipped the door open, and sprang in. The door flung around all the way open and hit the wall, tearing a jagged gash in some kid's art project. I looked around the classroom that I had invaded, blood pounding in my ears, and the first thing I noticed was that every single square inch was covered in garishly colored works of art. The second thing I noticed was that I was completely alone. Furtively looking around, I crept out of the classroom, hoping that no one would report my infraction of entering a room unaccompanied.

Trying to close the door silently, which proved very difficult because of the jangling metal mobiles attached to it, I heard the sharp clicking of high heels on linoleum, and turned around to see a short girl in a pink blouse and a swishing black skirt sauntering towards me. She had a half-incredulous, half-disparaging expression on her face. "Our judge isn't here yet. He and my mom are having a conversation in the judges' lounge." It suddenly occurred to me that I might be the only one here who did not personally know any of my judges. The half-digested burrito and the Starbucks drink that I had consumed for lunch suddenly condensed into a cold little pellet in the bottom of my stomach. She continued, "So is anyone from your school running Rawls? I heard that some people actually thought it would be a good argument. It amazes me how stupid some people can be." She stared thoughtfully at a pink and green glitter covered paper plate on the wall, and then turned to me. "But I did prepare some answers to it, anyway," she continued. "So what's your name?" she asked disdainfully, inspecting a chocolate smudge on my light blue shirt. Wishing a medium-sized meteor would fall through the room and incinerate me where I stood, I answered hesitantly, "Justin Garfield," extending my hand. She shook my hand briefly, the icy coolness of her fingers matching the expression on her face. "Freshman?" she asked curtly. "Yes," I replied quickly. A small smirk tugged at the corners of her lips before she regained her impassive demeanor.

She carefully sat down cross-legged on the floor, her pleated black skirt folding up with a starchy crinkling noise, and began to flip through a huge black binder ruffled with pages and pages of yellow Post-It notes covered in miniscule pink handwriting. She glanced up, and I realized that my mouth was hanging open like a beached salmon's. "It's evidence," she told me imperiously, as though I was a mentally deficient second grader. "You know, facts? That I can use when I'm arguing? Do you know what evidence is?" Before I could retort, she quickly glanced behind my shoulder and got to her feet to watch a scruffy college boy approaching. My opponent ran the last few yards out to greet him, cheerfully saying "Hi, Matt," who responded "Hi, Claire, how's it going?" completely ignoring me.

Claire began walking next to him before pausing to throw over her shoulder, almost as an afterthought, "Oh yeah, and my name's Claire." We both followed Matt into the room, but I stopped as I walked through the art-bedecked door. I took one last whiff of the hallway air uncontaminated by the metallic odor of poster paints, fearing it would be my last. Tracing my finger over the pitted surface of a crude clay pot, I silently questioned the sanity of spending a weekend verbally demolishing other people for the derivation of some sort of enjoyment. Resigned to my fate, I reluctantly closed the solid wooden door and turned to face my doom.

Andrew Halterman, Age 17
Norman High School
Norman, OK
Teacher: Betsy Ballard

FAR-OFF YELLOW

My first memory is of the window. Steel frames behind muslin curtains, as if floating fabric could subdue harsh metal bars. Glass slightly tinted to allow me to look out, but never to let anyone look in. I recall sunflowers.

The window had been a gift from Mother. In the first six years of my life I had known no other world than the four walls of my room. Mother never explained to me why I was to remain inside. It wasn't until I was three that I realized I didn't look as a child ought to—it was the storybooks, full of pictures of Dick and Jane with their smooth faces and fair hair. There were no mirrors in my room but I was a precocious child and the shadows on the walls and hazy reflections in the wood of my desk told me that my face looked different from the rosy-cheeked storybook faces. I begged Mother to tell me the truth. And that was how I knew I was grotesquely, hopelessly deformed.

I hadn't wept. I hadn't wondered about the source of my deformities, hadn't felt horrified. What difference did it make when only Mother could see me? She thought I was beautiful and so I was beautiful, beautiful until that day.

That day. I was a boy of perhaps eight. It might have been winter—the seasons were never terribly perceptible through a window—because the glass was lightly misted with condensation and she was wearing a yellow sweater. She was a girl my age and she sat on the obsidian sidewalk and sketched a tree. I watched in fascination as branches and dead leaves blossomed from the tip of her pencil. After a while she collected her drawing and left. Dusk settled and the glassy streets were silent, but I could not forget the crude image of a tree. I saw her often from then on—in the late afternoon she would sit on the sidewalk, watching the world with bright eyes.

Before I continue I should mention that my days were not divided into months and seasons but books. In my lonely childhood I had nothing to entertain me except Mother's books, and since I couldn't experience the buzzing of bees or the crunch of leaves, books were how I kept track of time. One January became *Treasure Island*; half of June, *Jane Eyre*; all of October dedicated to *The Count of Monte Cristo*. The first time I saw her, it was during *Love in the Time of Cholera*. Two things happened during *Love in the Time of Cholera*: one, Mother told me what cholera was and two, my feelings for the girl outside my window plunged deeply into love.

It's hard to think that a boy of perhaps eight could fall into the dizzying sort of love that I fell—not fell, *leapt*—into. I don't know what drew me to her. But in my head I was Florentino Ariza, watching Fermina Daza every day from the safe distance that a park bench provided, and I loved her beyond all measure of men or stars. I longed to feel the softness of her yellow sweater and I wept disconsolately when I realized that this was unrequited love at its most pathetic—when one did not even know the other existed and would never have any hope of knowing.

Mother thought I was sick because my appetite waned. When I slept it seemed to be in a feverish half-dream. While awake I hid my love well from Mother, who loved me so completely that it felt like a disloyalty to love anyone else. But while Mother was not present, I wrote and painted for the girl. And I continued to watch for her daily, despairing if she did not come and rejoicing if she stayed for longer than usual.

It remained this way through *Moby Dick*, *Great Expectations*, *Pride and Prejudice*, *One Thousand and One Nights*. With each book I read, she acquired a new facet and identity in my mind. Eventually she became a beautiful conglomeration of Estella and Scheherazade, Elizabeth Bennet's fire and Antigone's fierce courage, the spirit of Fermina Daza hovering like a watermark in the background. I knew very little truth of her, but what I did know I repeated to myself until her nature and my own were intertwined. She liked to read and draw trees. She liked the color yellow. She liked to run. She was my childhood.

I knew I would never speak to her—she would run from my misshapen flesh. But I yearned for a way to communicate, to know she wasn't a wispy figment of my imagination. So when I was twelve and reading *To Kill a Mockingbird* and *The Merchant of Venice*, I came up with the idea to play Boo Radley and leave my Portia gifts in the knot of her tree. The idea enthralled me. A gift was selected— my own crude watercolor of the tree, all gnarled branches and splotched brown leaves with a dab of yellow near the base. To leave my gift, I had to step outside for the first time.

I had stayed in my house for twelve years, and the outside world was something to be wary of. But the need to show the girl—however subtly—that I loved her became so extreme that I knew I had to open the door. I did it at night when Mother went to bed. I placed a scarf over my face, frightened that the halogen streetlights would reveal me to anyone who was watching. Quietly I turned the knob of the front door and took my first step onto the sidewalk. I stood still, senses buzzing from cool touch of obsidian, feverish breath of the wind, too-big velvet skyway above. Aching thump of my heart when I saw her house. I wondered if she was awake.

I never made such a connection with stars before, but now some words in the books I read made sense. *Constant. True—fix'd and resting.* Under the stars' gaze I walked to the tree (senses like static) and slipped my painting in. I made sure it was stuck in a certain way that no eyes but hers and the stars' would notice it. And then I crept back to my room. I dreamt of what her face would look like when she saw my painting—simile after simile flooded my mind, but I settled on yellow daffodils blooming, despite my never having seen daffodils before.

When she came the next day, my head felt light. She did not notice it when she sat down onto the sidewalk and took out her sketch. But just as her pencil traced the knothole, she stood up. I watched with lips like paper. Slowly she took out the watercolor, white paper illuminating her face and her smile—not a daffodil, a star.

I saw fix'd stars long after she tucked my painting away and left. This was the first of many paintings, of trees and sky and birds. The artwork grew more and more skilled with each passing book (*The Iliad, Crime and Punishment*) and by my thirteenth year my birds seemed to flutter. In all the paintings, I included misty yellow. She always tucked them away and I always saw stars.

Once, while reading a T.S. Eliot poem, I went to leave her a painting of my vision of a Parisian street. And as my hand reached into the knothole, I found a folded sheet of paper. Three words were scrawled onto it:

Who are you?

I choked down a half-laugh, half-sob underneath my scarf as I tucked the paper into my pocket and returned home. But not before I crushed Paris with a pencil tip and wrote two words of my own.

A ghost.

For a while I stopped leaving my paintings. I couldn't paint anymore— my hands shook at the thought of being so impossibly near her. But I could not stand her lusterless face after seeing that there was no new painting in the knothole, so I slipped an old portrait of a ballerina into the tree. The next day, a note—*Thank you, my ghost.*

While I was reading O. Henry's short stories, I decided to give her an elaborate painting of a peacock with diaphanous feathers spread wide. I put on my scarf and slipped out, but just as I was about to place the painting, footsteps startled me.

It was her, standing in the yellow sweater.

I dropped the painting and was about to run before she grabbed my arm. "Wait," she said. "I'm not here to hurt you."

Oh! But that's the only thing you can do. The sight of her so close made me feverish. She glowed softly before the night sky, a star superimposed against stars. She told me that she was sorry if she had startled me. She asked where I lived. I pointed to my house. She asked me how old I was. I thought *two hundred and seven books* but I said thirteen. My voice was like paper. "I'll be thirteen next Tuesday," she said. I wondered what today was. I felt for the scarf, making sure that its blackness still shrouded my face. I wondered if she would ask me why I wore it. She didn't.

From that day on we met often. It made me the happiest I had ever been— but I was not used to interacting. She sensed this and made up for my gaps in conversation, but there were many things I never told her. I never told her that I loved her, that she had been my yellow light through the window. How could she love a faceless boy?

She was not the mosaic of heroines that I had imagined. She was too hasty, too young, too imperfect. This was disappointing yet fascinating—I had long ago been convinced that I knew her and now had to reacquaint myself with a whole new person. But gradually I felt that I loved her more than any preconceived notions—she was more a rough draft for a heroine than the real thing, but I loved her, for there is something touching about a first draft in all its jagged entirety.

Slowly I told her why I wore the scarf, why she could never see my face. She told me she didn't *think* it would matter to her, but if it was important to me that she should never see my face, she didn't mind. I was glad, for I lived in perpetual fear of losing her if a chance wind caused the scarf to flutter off my face.

I lent her books. When I first handed her *Love in the Time of Cholera*, her eyes had grown wide. "Where did you get this?" she asked. "The Federation banned…" I told her to read it and she did. The next time we met her eyes glowed and she eagerly took the Eliot poems. With every book I lent her she seemed to acquire a steadier glow, until one day during my nineteenth year (Plato's *Republic*) she told me that she didn't care, that love was blind, that she loved me, that she might have to go away soon, but could we get married?

For one moment I saw fix'd stars, my far-off yellow up close. Then I realized that she was bright and beautiful and she could not have a veil for a husband, a half-formed shadow for a life. I told her no.

She left me during *Lolita* and the tree died afterwards. Mother passed away circa *To the Lighthouse*. I grieved madly for a while, throwing my books and paints at the dead tree at night. And then one night after another bout of feverish tossing, I opened up *Love in the Time of Cholera*. At dawn I sat down and wrote a steady, perfectly composed letter telling her I loved her and we could be married after I sought treatment. There had to be a cure, I told her with lines of hope. I left the letter in the knothole, took my books, and left. I was not sure where I was going, but eventually my sore feet reached a city of glossy roads and people with their heads perpetually down. A far cry from Paris, but I spent the next three years in this city, searching.

I resorted to stealing food at night to survive—no one would hire a veiled man. The scarf drew attention so I kept to small alleys and dark corners, only wandering at night. Once I walked past a man in a blue suit and the *Odyssey* tumbled out of my bag.

"Wait a second," he said. He picked up my book and before he had the chance to say anything more I dashed off.

Gradually I gained information from other outcasts. They were often full of dead ends, and this labyrinthine path to my cure continued for three years. There was no cure in sight until I got my first lead in months from a hooded man. He told me to see Dr. 1244 and to say that I had a yellow mask.

I arrived at the doctor's office the next day and did as I was told, and the receptionist led me to a hidden door in the wall. She told me to sit. A few minutes later a man with a white coat and glasses that obscured his eyes came in—he said he was Dr. 1244.

I took off my scarf and a small convulsion escaped him. He asked me if my father had been a soldier. I told him I didn't know.

He handed me a page of dense words and told me to skim it. *A Great War sixty years ago...Catastrophic consequences...Our Federation—leading biotechnology—won with Mutagen Yellow...Transformed genetics of soldiers—created invincible warriors...Soldiers mostly sterile, but a few managed to have children. Children were—*

"Deformed," Dr. 1244 said when I looked up, "grotesquely deformed in such a manner that no cosmetic surgery could have repaired them." He looked at me—another convulsion. "Forgive me. I haven't seen one of your faces in a while."

He looked down. "The soldiers died off very soon—Mutagen Yellow was a sure carcinogen. The children lived. The Federation was approaching bankruptcy. They did not have the resources for to solve a human rights crisis, so they mandated hospitals to kill these children. As a result 3,000 infants were silently, secretly murdered. But some, as you can imagine, slipped through the cracks. Your mother must have been very brave." He smiled weakly.

"I was one of the scientists responsible for inventing Mutagen Yellow." His face turned skeletal as he spoke. "There hasn't been a day that has gone by when I haven't contemplated putting a bullet into my skull. My sad sort of atonement lies in your cure. It took me almost your entire lifetime to perfect the cure, and if the Federation found out, they would execute me—no one is to speak of the Yellow crisis. I should warn you that the cure will be beyond any pain real or imagined. Many stop after the first treatment."

I said I didn't care about pain. He didn't look like he believed me until I told him I was in love.

I began my treatment with Dr. 1244 during a rereading of *Hamlet*. It was pain at its most base and electric, and I might have screamed but was too delirious to notice. Mother. Window. Flashes of yellow. Sunflowers. Her. During my forty-fifth session (eightieth rereading), the alignment of my features had shifted. According to Dr. 1244 we were halfway done. He asked to borrow *Hamlet*.

It took ninety rereadings of all books before the treatment was complete. Dr. 1244 showed me my face. It was smooth and chiseled, strange and human. I gave Dr. 1244 almost all my books in thanks and left, feverish with anticipation.

I knew she would be waiting for me—first drafts have something obstinate about them.

I saw her from a distance—she was standing in front of sunflowers, in her yellow sweater. I ran to her, laughing as the yellow became closer and closer. She smiled at me, tears running down her face. "I knew it was you," she said.

I pressed her close to me and told her I loved her. She said she knew, that we would live out an eternity together and we laughed and cried. But then I realized that she was not surprised, that she did not even look into my face.

"Don't you see how I've changed?" I asked her. And then I noticed the thin film of white over her eyes, how she seemed to stare at fixed nothings and I felt horribly sick.

"I don't see much anymore, my ghost. Love," she said, "is blind."

I trembled in horror. "No—"

"Yes," she said with a smile. "It took me a while but I found something—It's permanent and now you don't have to worry about hiding your face—Oh, I'm so glad—I got the idea from that book you lent me—*Oedipus*—"

I began to weep. And as her hands fumbled for my tears, she felt the smooth regularity of my features. Her eyes—her beautiful blind eyes—widened in shock. "Oh," she said. "Oh." She hadn't received my letter. She couldn't have read it anyway. She couldn't read anything now—not Eliot, not Shakespeare, not *Love in the Time of Cholera*.

"It's all right," I said as I held her fiercely. "It's all right. I'll read to you every night until we die." And as I held her my tears mingled with sunflower and sweater, a far-off yellow I knew she could not see.

Jasmine Hu, Age 16
Lynbrook High School
San Jose, CA
Teacher: Connie Willson

MA'ARAT HA'MACHPELA

The moment I entered the revered site, I was bombarded by the deafening buzz of hundreds of murmured prayers, rumbling through the large chamber and into the little room I had stepped into. I clasped my hands together, the clammy hands of an anxious defendant awaiting the judge's verdict. A certain lightheadedness rose to my cheeks, leaving me to reach out for the worshippers standing around me for balance.

Oxygen stopped entering my body; all breathing halted as if I believed in the childhood superstition that one mustn't inhale when passing a cemetery, so as not to disturb the souls of the dead. Despite visiting such an important shrine, such significant graves, I was holding my breath for a very different reason. Quite simply, there was no air to breathe. I was slowly suffocating, getting pulled under. Choked by the women elbowing around me, trying to get closer to the crypts. Smothered by the mob of ultra-religious men barricaded behind the wall they had created in their hearts and minds, shutting the rest of the world out; their side locks swaying to the beat of their whispered prayers. I felt my blood pounding wildly behind my temples, and with a sudden rush of anxiety I realized that if I didn't leave I would faint. Frantically, I spun around; tripping over my laces, I lunged forward into the sweating crowd. I was sure that I would never make it out of the heart of the beast—everywhere I turned, hordes of people poured out supplications, their faces contorted, hopeful, ecstatic.

I was disappointed in myself. Where was the rush of excitement, the flash of inspiration one might expect visiting the graves of the forefathers who populate my daily prayers? I was standing in the structure built over *Ma'arat ha'Machpela*, the cave in the largely Arab city of Hebron, where the revered founders of the Jewish people are buried: Abraham and Sarah, Isaac and Rebecca, Jacob and Leah.

For as long as I can remember, every Friday night around the Sabbath table, my father has smiled into my eyes, his hands resting gently on my shoulders, blessing me, beginning with, "May G-d bless you as Sarah, Rebecca, Rachel and Leah..." Now, for the first time, I was at the tombs of these remote, mystical ancestors, standing only meters above their burial chambers. Why, in such a place, could I only think about my claustrophobia, letting my physical needs take over when spirituality is, or should be, the driving force?

I received no help escaping the ocean of people, no miraculous parting of the Red Sea. But finally, I forced myself into a little alcove where not so many people were standing. I turned to find myself staring through iron bars into a little room. The bars obscured my view—spaced just wide enough for my hands to wrap around, but not wide enough to fit my head through. I forced myself to look past the bars into the memorial site for Abraham, the father of monotheism. Before I had the opportunity to study the room before me, I caught sight of three sets of wide eyes staring at me from behind an identical set of bars on the opposite side of the room. There, three Muslim girls were standing in the hall outside the memorial site for Isaac, a place that is forbidden to Jews except for 10 days of the year, during which the Muslim religious authorities are compelled to grant us entrance. A woman beside me followed my eyes and whispered, "Isaac isn't even their ancestor! It's a disgrace that they have the power to keep us out." She glared across at the girls.

The girls' hair coverings were swept over their foreheads with the elegance of a light kiss on the hand of a queen; the traditional headwear bore the familiarity of a mother's touch, snuggling up close to their chins. But I could see their faces, and in their expressions, a mix of interest and mistrust. The tallest of the girls looked straight into my eyes while the other two made a show of pretending to pray, taking turns sneaking glances at me. I stared back at the tall one, intrigued by the person behind those cold brown eyes, those pinched lips perched above a sharp jaw line, the kind I had always envied. Her dark skin was flawless, perfect as a stretch of desert sand. A smile broke across my face before I could stop myself as I tried to imagine her removing the head covering within the confines of her home, rinsing her face with the "Clean and Clear" that Jennifer Love Hewitt represents, parading around the television screen wrapped in a towel. The girl's eyes narrowed in response to my grin, the nostrils on her prominent, ironically "Jewish", nose flaring slightly, her anger somehow only adding to her striking beauty, making her painfully human as her glare pierced into me from across the room, through the two sets of bars. Her narrow shoulders stooped forward as she whispered something into the ear of one of the little girls, never taking her eyes off me, like a guard dog that growls until the stranger reaches the next house. The little one glanced at me and I stared back at her, wondering how often she came here, how many other people like me she has studied at memorial site of her beloved forefather, of my beloved forefather. Of the man whose two sons made their way down such different paths that their descendants have lost all sense of familial connection: Isaac, ancestor of the Jews; Ishmael, ancestor of the Arabs. In a moment of bravery, the little girl stuck out her tongue, then turned and scampered away.

My heart jumped into my throat, the image of her pudgy cheeks and button nose lingering before my eyes. As the cold metal pressed into my forehead, I felt grateful for the prison bars separating us, protecting me. As that gratefulness entered my consciousness, shame washed over me. Were the bars actually necessary, what exactly did I think they would do to me if there was nothing between us? I needed protection from *them*? It was absurd; the oldest must have been thirteen or fourteen. *Look at them*, I told myself, *they're just little kids.*

After a moment the pudgy cheeks returned, flanked by two women dressed in the uniform of black robes with white cloths hiding their hair and necks. Without even glancing at the memorial before them, they pushed their noses right up between the bars on their side and glowered. Their glares accosted me like a freezing shower on a cold, winter night. Tears rushed to my eyes, and I looked down upon at the prayer book I had been grasping, unopened, the whole time. Their hatred shot across the room, aimed and fired straight into me. My teardrops escaped one by one, joining those of the people around me, who were pleading breathlessly to our ancestors to intercede on our behalf. But my crying was different, empty of prayer and awe, filled only with pain and sorrow.

In a steady stream, the tears tip-toed down my cheeks, pausing at my chin, then took the plunge drop by drop, glad to escape the quivering surface of my face. Quite suddenly, my friend Tzipporah's freckles and wide smile flashed before my eyes. I could picture her praying, eyes clenched shut as her slim frame rocked back and forth in the room from which I had escaped just a while ago.

I wondered if there was anger in her prayers, blame for the loss of her brother, kidnapped and murdered by Arabs a week before the start of last summer's war in Lebanon. I wondered how she would react to my tears, tears that she would consider blasphemy in the face of the undying hatred that killed her brother.

The next time I looked up, the women and their daughters were gone. That beautiful teenaged face retreated back into her world, and of course, I knew that I would never see her again. Our separate lives hardly provided opportunity for our paths to cross, but then, why would I even want such a thing? The memory of her glare burned into me, smothering the hope that someday, somehow, there will be peace. More than anything, I wanted to find her and shake her, to feel her bony arms between my fingers, to make her look at me, really see me. But what would she see? The angry frown of her stern mouth had been aimed solely at me, a Jew. I was defenseless and exposed; her entirely human eyes pierced right through me, leaving a small scar on my heart.

Leila Dashevsky, Age 18
Kfar Pines High School
Kfar Pines, Israel
Teacher: Greg Trimmer

BOY

The straw bristles on the broom scraped dust out from under the single bed, dragging airy clouds of particles and specks of white into the black dustpan. The repetitive sweeping of Lilly's broom soothed Boy; its tickling sound meant that she was home so his howling could subside. As always, the yellowed curtains of thin cotton with summery, eyeleted hemming only let a warm light escape from her windows. Lilly enjoyed her privacy and seldom let anyone into the musky rooms of her small shack. Her bed looked shy and exhausted, slumped in the corner as if trying to hide its conspicuous body. Lilly, too, felt cumbersome here, as if she were Alice in the White Rabbit's house; her wide hips, accentuated by patchwork skirts, always bumped into doorways and kitchen tables.

She picked up the dustpan and carried it to the trash, dirt escaping in a frantic dance, falling into the doomed bag below. Boy scratched his paws by the front door, chewing at fleas that hopped onto the faded rug under his brown and black body. The old German shepherd groaned deeply and tiredly at his master as he slowly stood, moving mammoth, creaking bones. His brown eyes peered into hers, asking. *You hungry, Boy?* He stepped closer to her and flicked out his tongue to show his unconditional appreciation. He watched the pink bunny slippers shuffle to the door and he whined when her brown leathery hands turned the brass knob. And as if surprising the son who would never cling to her skirts, never grow up to be a poor loser who mowed white men's lawns for his mother—as if for this son, embodied in a dog, she pulled a ham bone out of the embroidered pocket of her apron with a wild expression in her round cheeks. She tossed it out the door, and Boy scrambled into the night after it.

The only sound now was the continuous ticking of the cat clock hung on a nail in the kitchen. Its eyes looked from her to the door, from her to the door. Its tail was almost too long and barely missed the radio antenna as it swayed back and forth. Lilly studied the aqua plastic on the radio, how the speakers looked mechanical and ugly next to its stylish frame. She and her house were the speakers. She served a purpose, but not her own. She was not beautiful; her black hair had long turned into silver wire. And her home—its purpose was to house the colored maid. *For Heaven's sake*, her pitying employers would think, *where else can she go?* Her house: dilapidated at best. It was left over from a time when the town was rural, when whites owned blacks, before the small town had hidden her shack behind retail shops and Southern homes, before anyone had ever heard of the Cold War or TV dinners or "civil rights." The aged house sighed as her matronly body moved around within it. Its shingles fell and scattered on the ground after a storm. Its wood was splintered, but even so, it was her home. She knew it was the best she could get for a black woman making three dollars a day, so her shack was immaculate.

Boy would probably start scratching at the door soon, but she hated the silence until then. With an ivory fingernail, Lilly turned on the radio. Static filled the room. She moved the antenna to the right and something about a draft, something about free love, reached her ears and satisfied her hunger for sound.

It was just after Thanksgiving, and she still had the leftovers from the dinners she cooked for her employers. Turkey with her own cranberry sauce (of course), collards (her recipe), mashed potatoes with gravy (both white and brown), and pumpkin pie. Very typical, but she liked it and was grateful when Miss Barbara invited her to sit at the table with the rest of the family. Maybe she was more to them than hired help.

But that was not how the Sprouses felt. They lived next door, in their big shuttered-window house with their hair salon; Lilly's shack slumped proudly beside it. She would pull the curtains taut and leave Boy inside to whine when he saw her empty bed, its cotton blanket made with sharp edges tucked under the mattress, taming the sea of blankets, almost militarily, almost beautifully. Tim Sprouse would tell Boy to shut up, shut up, shut up. *One day I'm going to kill that colored woman's dog.* Lilly ignored his bony, alcoholic ankles, his shotgun breath, his unshaven words. She kept Boy inside anyway, sometimes wandering over midday to give him a biscuit to calm his nerves. She got up early and came home late, and the dog stayed in her shabby cottage alone.

She heard a gunshot. *Probably some ol' man shootin' a squirrel.* She opened the door a bit to see where Boy was. *Probably run home wit' his tail between his legs; damn thing got no bravery 'bout hisself.* Instead, she only heard rain, dripping in big teary drops off the roof over her front porch. The rain was thick and cold that night, like honey kept in the fridge too long. Lilly called his name, but he didn't come. Removing her slippers, she stepped her aching feet, now bare like a child's, into the cold rainwater that had collected on her doormat. *Boy!* She slowly plunked down each step, damp wood creaking under her weight. She waited to hear him, but she only heard indifferent cars and molasses rain. She lifted up her skirt and showed her legs, dark brown and speckled with grass and leaves and scars and hair and everything just like little black girls, running behind hollering shacks, through deep-fried kitchens, through brown, green, black, gold woods.

Her breath became labored and panicked as she kept calling Boy's name, over and over. His whining somewhere had stopped, and her voice took over the lonesome howling. Worry struck the soles of her feet as they slapped on the wet pavement around street corners and under telephone poles.

Boy lay bloody in the road. His strong rib cage did not undulate with breathing. His teeth were bared, but not in anger, and his tail did not wag as she approached. *Help!* Lilly called but knew no one would come out of the safety of their white, clapboard houses. The rain stung her eyes and hands and back, but she scooped her hands under Boy's body, cradling him like a dead child—her only child. Her arms, strong from years of sweeping, folding, toiling, picked up his massive body tenderly and solemnly. There was no use for anger. She carried him back home.

Suzannah Isgett, Age 16
Charleston County School of the Arts
North Charleston, SC
Teacher: Rene Miles

OF THE DANGERS OF LUNCH LINES

We were the only two women in
the cafeteria, my boss in her heels
and me, a small tower of faded gray.
We were stuck together, moving
inch by inch past the salad bar, and
I felt inside me this swelling opportunity
to know how far I could push that fake smile
which she always used to acknowledge me.
I let the gloom of my too large
slacks spread its way, like storm clouds,
across her skirt's sky blue horizon.

I asked her what the point was
in ordering her tray—the sweet tea
always behind the red delicious apple,
the carrots lined in groups of threes.
She replied she hadn't thought of it
before, and couldn't imagine
the type of person who did.

Outdone by her buffet tactics,
I said I didn't see the point
of all my breaks, told her
I needed no reminders of
the perks I got under her wing.
She shrugged, adjusted her bread crumbs,
and said most women could die
from stress at thirty, that I should be
careful, knowing that I was older than that.
And left with that, I took the noblest
approach and closed my mouth so
quickly that I felt for
magnets in my lips.

But still I wondered—maybe behind
her hubris lurked something as common
as my outdated bifocals (guarding my eyes

like sentries). What if the ranch
was runny that day, and had dribbled on her
apple? Would she clench it over her head,
hurl the faultless fruit down? Looking at
her now, I knew she was not as bad as
I wanted to make her. Simply going through
the day, marking what was hers, as did
the first hunters with their prey.

I noticed the line ending, like a cataract
bending past the cashier. Matter-o'-factly,
I left my boss with some small advice:
that sometimes it's fine to get
a peach instead of the apple, and to
throw in some cigarettes as well.
And as she looked ready to shove
that red delicious orb down my throat,
I told her it might give her
a turn for the best: that a little sweetness
wouldn't kill her.

Michael Lambert, Age 16
Alabama School of Fine Arts
Birmingham, AL
Teacher: Anne Wyman Black

A TRAVELER'S JOURNEY
For Romey, whom I never met

Months after my return from France, I awoke from a most vivid dream. I had been sitting upon a rock ledge, my bare feet dangling into the sea, the water gently lapping my ankles. I had flown in to Marseille for mere hours, to sit by the Mediterranean once more, only to depart at sunset. I found a peace by those waters that I could find nowhere else on earth. The following day, I wrote an email to Rachel, describing my dream. "Never before this particular dream had I realized I dreamt in color," I remarked. "In my dream, the sea was so marvelously blue, now I am sure."

⚜

It was with passion and insatiable curiosity that I left the United States for France on that beautiful June morning. As the airplane slipped through silver moonlight over the Atlantic, I enthusiastically slipped into the mindset of the foreign tongue that I would communicate in for the next three weeks.

I was traveling alone, without the support of a student exchange organization; I was to abandon familiarity and fully become a part of a French family. There would be no fellow Americans to comfort the expected feelings of isolation and homesickness. I would be forced to process culture shock on my own. In my naivety and desire for adventure, I saw this challenge as entirely thrilling.

I drew great comfort in the fact that I had corresponded so much with my family-to-be in past years. In fact, my own family in the United States hosted one of the family's daughters, Elsa, several years before my own voyage to France. Elsa and her parents, Philippe and Rachel, and her fourteen-year old sister, Solène, were eager to welcome me into their home.

Weary and euphoric, I arrived in Marseille, carrying with me a journal of bare pages begging to be filled with stories of my travels. It was my hope that this once-blank notebook would be filled with my experiences so that I could read them again and again, relive them again and again. There would be a touch of the sacred in that journal, penned by my own hand in the immediacy, authenticity, and rawness of my experiences. With this journal, I felt prepared to face this adventure alone.

She, in fact, proved indispensable.

Marseille is a dynamic and beautiful port city in southern France. Formations of rocky cliffs extend from land and rise hundreds of feet into the sky. These *calanques* characterize the shorelines of southern France, sheltering fishing villages along the coast, accenting the skyline in their splendor and magnificence. Fickle shadows dance upon them as the sun's waning light is swallowed into the sea.

It is said that the sea brings the spirit to Marseille. I was immediately struck by the exoticism and beauty of the *calanques* and the Mediterranean Sea. On my third day in the country, I biked along the sea with Philippe. At first, I was nervous to share the road with cars. The streets were crowded, and we dodged motorbikes and cars and cyclists. But it was only a matter of moments until we escaped the congested lanes of Marseille, only moments until the soft breezes from the sea were freely sweeping over us. "*Suivez la mer*," Phillipe smiled, nodding for me to follow the sea.

We coasted through tiny fishing villages, past children playing with watering hoses in narrow alleys, above young lovers frolicking on the rocks below. Occasionally we would stop alongside of the road to take in the beauty of the setting sun, the glowing metropolis of Marseille spread in the distance. How stunning it was to weave between towering rocky cliffs and a shimmering ribbon of sea. I was invigorated beyond belief. I was incredibly full of life. Yet how sharply contrasting was my blissful afternoon in that Mediterranean paradise to that of another young girl.

Fully contented and exhausted, Philippe and I returned to the house. We entered the living room. Solène's eyes were red and swollen from her tears. Rachel embraced her and rocked her gently, back and forth. Elsa sat opposite them, her head in her hands. In the moments that followed, they related to us the nightmare that had descended upon the day.

Elsa's summary was concise and alarming. They had a cousin, Romey, who lived in another town in the south of France, closer to the Italian border, not too far from Marseille. Earlier that afternoon, Romey had been hit by a car, and was in critical condition in the hospital. She was fourteen years old.

Though Romey's condition was indeed serious, Rachel assured me that everything would be okay. I sank into a chair and tried to quiet my mind. I was at a loss for words. We waited in silence for any news. Several minutes later, the phone rang. Romey was hemorrhaging. The doctors were doing all that they could to save her. Upon hearing of her daughter's condition, Romey's mother had collapsed.

We were understandably shaken and very scared. Rachel suggested we make a run to the video store to rent something as a diversion from the grave mood of the evening. "*Bon courage*," she said to us, over and over again. I was unbelieving of Rachel's façade of composure, yet I followed Elsa and Solène to the video store.

We chose a movie and returned to the house, where several relatives had arrived in the meantime. We sat around a table beside the lovely flower garden to eat a meal together. I consumed food and drink, yet I tasted nothing. I heard voices, yet I did not listen. Beneath the darkening sky of late evening, my mind whirled in anxious bewilderment.

Some time later, Philippe and his brother returned, and told us of what had passed that afternoon. Romey had spent a day on the beach with her friends. On the way home, she and her friends tried to dart across the road, Romey advancing first. She was hit by a car and struck in the head. Her friends were spared from injury.

Philippe paused for a great length, and then continued, his voice as distant and flat as the line where the sky meets the sea.

There was nothing that could have been done for Romey. She was gone.

In that moment, I did not comprehend the tragedy. I was in utter shock. Because every word was foreign, perhaps it was easier to pretend the message was not real. To locate the English equivalent of *mourir*, "to die," on a matching section of a French History exam is an entirely different task than to comprehend the true fate of a young life taken too soon. I honestly did not process and comprehend that *la mort* was reality.

Months have passed, yet even in my mother tongue of English, I cannot coherently articulate the true turmoil of my heart and soul in those moments. It was very difficult to sit as a stranger, a guest in a home, and watch anguish of that intensity wash over a family.

That night, we watched *Ocean's Twelve*, in English with French subtitles. I cannot clearly recall a single detail of the film. My mind was elsewhere.

I did not write of death in my journal that night. I wrote of the captivating beauty of the sea.

The funeral was arranged to take place in the rolling hills of Bourgogne, in central France. Though Romey lived in the south of France, along the sea, she preferred and adored the region where her grandparents lived. I discovered it to be a lovely region of the country indeed; in contrast to the dry landscape of the south, lush pastures dotted with cattle and sheep dipped into deep valleys of soft green.

After a six-hour drive, we arrived at the grandparents' home in a tiny village in the countryside. I remember the eyes of Phillipe's sister, who sat on a stool by the rose garden, waiting to welcome us upon our arrival. Her eyes overflowed with the most sincere sadness I have ever seen. I remember the innocent eyes of Romey's young cousins, who were lying in the soft grass of a pasture, preparing some words to read at the service in the church. The sky was gray and the air was dense, weighed down by a tense emotion of deepest grieving—I could feel it in every person's presence, read it in their faces, and most deeply, in their eyes.

We gathered on a patio by the garden to eat a light lunch. The baguette felt coarse and rough against my tongue. I did not wish to speak to anyone, and so I chewed as slowly as possible. One by one, flakes of the bread slid down my dry throat. Cold winds swept over us in cruel, muted whispers, bringing chills to faces damp with tears.

The family then proceeded to the funeral. The first stop was a sort of town square where the family embraced relatives. I stayed in the car with an elderly man named George, Romey's great-uncle. George spoke no English. He was friendly and kind, and we relieved our minds of the truth that had brought us both to Bourgogne that somber day. He was very interested in where I was from, and my family, and my pets, my hobbies, and my hopes for the future. These were topics on which I could speak effortlessly, and I was strangely comforted by this facility in a foreign language.

The second stop was a beautiful church, where a brief service occurred. I did not attend, but rested on a park bench by a river that flowed through the town. I felt intensely numb and intensely empty. Swans graced the surface of the gentle current, birds sang in the trees above, roses flowered along the riverbank.

The church bells began to ring. There were two different pitches, and they slowly and steadily alternated, resonating for miles. They say a picture is worth a thousand words. If so, then a mere interval of sound is worth a million. It was the most heartbreaking sound I have ever heard in my life. A solemn declaration to the entire town; our hearts are overflowing with sorrow, let us grieve.

Romey's casket was carried from the church into a van, and family and friends gathered around to watch. Men carried beautiful flowers into the van, arranging them in the rear window. The flowers surrounded a large photograph of Romey. It was only through such photographs that I knew Romey— her laughter silenced, her dark hair stilled. I gazed into her eyes and fought back tears.

We proceeded to the cemetery. I did not leave the car, but rested again with George, who was too fatigued to walk the distance to see the burial. I asked George if he enjoyed the sound of a violin. He was very interested, and I rummaged in my bag for my CD player. I placed my headphones over his ears, gracing him with the lush melodies of Saint-Sean's *Havanaise*. George's eyes gently closed. The soaring music contented him fully.

I leaned back in my seat and stared out the open car window. I let my thoughts drift to the bucolic calm of the pasture across the road; cows nestled themselves into the grasses, colorful butterflies hovered above them. Vibrantly red flowers swayed along the roadside, and wandering honeybees periodically buzzed over them.

I remember the sound of dirt being thrown on top of dirt as Romey was buried. It was a wretchedly hollow and empty sound. Sometime later, a somber line of mourners emerged from behind the stone walls of the cemetery. They stood in clusters, clutching to one another. I remember the pulsing rap music that blared from a car. Romey loved rap.

The final destination of the day was an intimate gathering hall for Romey's relatives to be with one another before departing for their respective homes throughout France. Four cousins sat on a bench beneath a tree outside of the gathering hall. I sat on the ground beside them with Rachel. Her sister-in-law leaned against the tree, a cigarette balanced loosely between her fingers. Rachel's hand shook as she too lit a cigarette. "I need this," she said to me softly. We passed around photo after photo of Romey and her cousins: innocent infants dressed in festive holiday attire, giggling girls at birthday parties throughout childhood, and blossoming young beauties on the beach.

As the family conversed, ate, wept, and shared laughs, I floated from table to table. I was an unseen presence, nibbling hesitantly on bread and cheese, sipping juices. Until the hour of our departure, I vicariously grieved. Is that possible? What unimaginable circumstances I had found myself in! It was perhaps the strangest experience of my entire life.

It was past midnight by the time we were home, in Marseille. What a joy it was to see the familiar and beautiful sea again, even in her cloak of black. The dark Mediterranean reflected the brilliant skyline. I envisioned ballerinas gracefully pirouetting on the water's glassy surface, spiraling infinitely into the black expanse of peace beyond.

The following morning, the sky was once again a deep and vibrant blue, the sky of Marseille. The sun, casting her light on the swells of the tide, brought out a sparkling spectrum of distinct blues and greens; emerald, jade, cobalt, sapphire. Like a mother, the sea held, encircled, and embraced Marseille, cradling her city, cradling her children, cradling us; the same waters that had cradled Romey just days before.

As the sun rises and sets, and the sea rocks in undulating rhythms, life flows on. Darkness had fallen upon the land, yet we rose to greet the dawn. We rose to let the sun kiss our faces and dry our tears.

❧

And so began my summer in France.

It will take a lifetime for the experiences of that summer to settle in my heart. It was an overwhelming and powerful journey for me. Through it all, my heart was stretched—to empathize with a grieving family that I had become a part of—and was torn by the sorrow I witnessed. In the end, my heart was deeply changed. Perhaps it is that I breathe more purposefully, I watch the sun rise and set with heightened curiosity and wonder, I pause for an extra moment before crossing a road—and each time, I think of Romey.

Reflections and memories of my time spent in France have haunted, inspired, and challenged me relentlessly since my return. There are moments when I cannot fathom the experiences of that time, and so with curiosity I open the pages of my journal, letting my fingers fall over words written in moments of intense pain, intense confusion. The voice captured and preserved in those pages is the voice of a young girl in the midst of an immense internal transformation—a young girl finding peace in the beauty of her world despite tragedy. Time and again, I realize with wonder that the young girl's words are my own.

Upon stirring and awakening, I lay quietly in bed, contemplating the simplicity and haunting beauty of my dream. In the dream, as I sat along the sea, I fluidly conversed in French with Rachel and Solène. The content of our conversation I cannot recollect, beyond the fact that I felt a sense of closure, a sense of finality, and an overwhelming sense of peace.

There was another young girl who sat upon the rock ledge by the sea with us. Her long dark hair danced in the wind. I did not see her face, as it was turned away, towards the sun. Perhaps it was Romey.

Maya de Vitry, Age 16
Hempfield High School
Lancaster, PA
Teacher: Wanda Richie

CONFESSIONS OF A TEENAGE MASCOT:
MY LIFE AS A BEE

The corner of Maple and Orchard is a bustling hub of commerce in the otherwise sleepy northwest suburbs of Detroit. Stylishly dressed matrons converge there in search of goods to fill their larders and feather their nests. And in the midst of this strip-mall Shangri-La, a rather jarring figure appears, upsetting the balance of tree-lined avenues and awninged boutiques: a yellow and black winged insect, standing nearly six feet tall, and toting a perpetually perky bouquet of plastic daisies. He wears a maniacal grin on his furry cheeks that never seems to waver, rain or shine. This fuzzy, overgrown bumblebee serves as the walking billboard for our neighborhood florist; and for one honey-sweet summer, it was I who donned that striped suit and mammoth smiling head.

My transformation from mammal to arthropod began when I observed the original bee looking lifeless and lethargic, as if bloated with nectar. He seemed to be suffering from that little-known syndrome, "buzzing burnout." Drastic times call for drastic measures, and I knew I had to act decisively. I quickly stormed into the quiet, fragrant shop, and demanded an application on the spot. The manager inquired as to my career goal, whether it be floral delivery or working the counter. I responded "nay" to both. Channeling mad Prince Hamlet, I spoke those familiar words, there in the middle of the rose-tinted shop: "To be, or not to be," and then added, as if possessed, "You're looking at your new bee." On the application, I wrote convincingly of my talents, which I noted were "flying, dancing, buzzing, and fake-stinging." Apparently, these esoteric talents sparked their curiosity, as they promptly called me three months later.

With high hopes, I bounded onto the sidewalk, my antennae scraping the sky, my stinger pointing heavenward. As glamorous as the job appeared from a distance, after ten minutes of breathing stale, hot air within the heavy bee head, I felt utterly woozy. With every hop, skip, and jump of my frenetic bee dance, the thick plastic skull bopped menacingly against my head, as if I was being assaulted by a billy club. Yet despite the pain, heat, and wing-flapping fatigue, I made a decision. Not wanting to carry on the blighted tradition of my burned-out predecessor, I felt determined to find the joy in the job. What I did not know then is how much joy I would bring to others from my curbside pulpit.

When teenagers cruised by, windows open and music blasting, I picked up on the beat and my Van Gogh-yellow legs followed suit, pollinating the pavement with funk. I was rewarded with riotous honking and boisterous shouts of appreciation. Blue-haired grannies on their way to lunch blushed as I gallantly bowed to them, paying homage to their queen-bee matriarchy. Toddlers mobbed me, jockeying for position in order to high-five my golden wings. All the while, I was becoming keenly aware of the delight I was spreading on this otherwise ordinary day in my hometown. Anonymous within the cavernous head, I felt a tremendous sense of freedom and abandon, and the more absurd my antics became, the more mirth I elicited from passersby. These merry exchanges made the first hour buzz by (pardon the pun), yet as I glanced at my watch, I couldn't believe that I would be held hostage for seven more hours in this sweltering suit.

This bee business took a bitter turn when I took my life in my hands trying to fly across the busy parking lot to take my well-deserved five-minute break. As it is impossible to see anything clearly through the massive head (especially speeding soccer moms in the middle of an emergency juice box mission to the supermarket), I lifted the costume top slightly in order to save my young life. Hiowever, this prudent behavior was met with scorn by my floral superiors inside the shop. One particularly incensed scarlet-cheeked employee warned me never to lift up the head again, even if my life was in peril. After all, she said, "Many children love our bee and believe he is real. We would not want to disappoint them, and have them discover the bee's true identity." Hmm. Did she not think that a six-foot tall dancing bee would also induce freakish nightmares in the minds of impressionable tots?

After quite a few days of nonstop prancing and pollinating, I decided to hang up my plastic wings for good. I had fulfilled my ambition to make of the bee a spirited ambassador of gaiety and goodwill, unlike the depressive drone that now graces the intersection. My apiological alter-ego reaffirmed my philosophy that a curious mind coupled with a creative and lively spirit can elevate any situation in which it finds itself. In the words of poet Robert Southey:

> *The solitary Bee*
> *Whose buzzing was the only sound of life*
> *Flew there on restless wing*
> *Seeking in vain one blossom where to fix.*

In my case, the *blossom* was that bustling crossroad of Maple and Orchard, which for one precious moment in time became a heavenly hive for this wannabe bee.

Michael Yashinsky, Age 17
Frankel Jewish Academy of Metro Detroit
West Bloomfield, MI
Teacher: Elizabeth Platsis

ACROSS THE UNIVERSE
(EXCERPT)

I hate the Beatles. I really do. It's not just because I prefer the Stones, or because I like offending old people. I just really hate them. I hate the eleven thousand choruses of "Hey Jude," I hate their stupid haircuts, and I really hate that preachy "Imagine" song.

So when I tell you that my teacher is wearing a Beatles T-shirt in class, you understand why I'm not listening. First of all, what kind of teacher wears a Beatles shirt to class? How mid-life crisis is that? Why doesn't he just have a giant sign on his chest reading, "I am trying to reclaim my youth?" It's not even a warm-and-fuzzy liberal arts type class, where teachers are allowed to be a little flaky; it's biology, which is insufferable even when the teacher isn't wearing a giant picture of Ringo Starr on his chest. Mr. Howell and I have a great rapport going—he prattles on about mitochondria or whatever and I stare out the window. Sometimes I draw angry clowns on my binder. Once he kept me after class to give an obviously rehearsed concerned chat about how little interest I was showing in life sciences. Who is he kidding? Most people I know would be shocked if I showed interest in life.

Mr. Howell makes two fatal mistakes today. First of all, he wears the shirt, and then he has to go and arm us. I don't know why anyone blames me for what happens next. You don't give high school students knives and tell them to "have fun." Doesn't this man have cable? Okay, he calls them "scalpels," but whatever. They're pointy, and shiny. Kendall, my lab partner, is using hers to carve "Nirvana Rox" into the greasy black tabletop. We're supposed to be dissecting a frog, whose formaldehyde-laced smell is even more disgusting than the concept of actually carving it up. Naturally, I would be more than happy to twirl the gleaming scalpel between my fingers like a tiny baton for the rest of the period, maybe play a game of darts, but Mr. Howell comes and hovers over me and Kendall like some kind of papa buzzard.

"Having trouble?" he booms.

I find myself staring into the giant, English teeth of George Harrison. "I don't really know where to start."

He takes the scalpel and traces a delicate line down the frog's belly, hands it back, and warns me that if I didn't hurry up and find the kidneys, I might never catch up with the rest of the class. I grimace my thanks and start poking around the inside of the frog with the scalpel point. Kendall, suddenly afire with scientific inquiry, wonders aloud what happens if the frog was about to take a crap when it died, and I decide I will kill her with my scalpel. Around me, people shriek with the joy of discovering science. One girl scoops up a handful of tiny white lumps and runs over to our table. "What's this, Mr. Howell?" she asks, voice squeaky with excitement.

Mr. Howell frowns and pokes at it with his pencil. "That appears to be fat, Jenna." Jenna squeals in delight and waves it in front of my nose so Kendall can get a good whiff.

"Could you, like, make soap out of it?" Kendall asks lethargically. I try to ignore them and focus on my frog, which I've decided to name Yoko. Specifically, I focus on sawing her legs off. We are supposed to be finding organs, but bones are simpler. I want to pace myself. Besides, it would be awesome to leave one of these things right behind my dad's car—he's always running over small animals, supposedly by accident. Last week he crushed a chipmunk. I didn't even know we had chipmunks in North Carolina. Dad said this might be the last one and laughed really hard. Sometimes I worry it's genetic.

I am preoccupied with the thought of how many cumulative tons of dead animals people must hit every day on the roads when Jenna yelps, "Oh my God!" Jenna does this a lot, so I ignore her and keep cutting until I feel a sharp sting on my thumb.

"Oh, my God," I agree distantly. I must have sawed through the leg and kept on cutting, because my hand is covered in blood. The meaty part between my thumb and forefinger is drenched a dark, sticky, red that is an entirely different shade than poor Yoko's.

"Why would you do that?" Jenna demands impatiently. "Oh, my God. Are you okay?" I hold my hand up to the light, turning it this way and that, waiting for the pain to subside and admiring the way the blood seeps into the crevices around my fingernails. Mr. Howell smiles bravely, lifts my hand, and assures me, "It doesn't look like you severed any blood vessels. As long as you didn't get too much formaldehyde on you, you should be fine." He leads me over to the sink, where I stand blankly until he sticks my hand under the faucet and turns the water on full blast, like I'm four years old. I resent being condescended to by a man with frog fat on his shoes. Kendall creeps up behind me and pries the scalpel out of my un-mauled hand, whispering, "Before you do any more damage."

Mr. Howell quickly ushers me out of the room along with Kendall, who is supposed to escort me to the nurse. This means that either Mr. Howell worries that I'll faint in the hallway, or he thinks I'll make a break for it. Either way, I can't imagine how he thinks Kendall will be any help. As the door swings closed, I catch a good parting glance of Mr. Howell, looking slightly shaken, surrounded by students robotically clutching dead frogs.

Kendall tries to make small talk on the way to the nurse's office, while I try equally hard to ignore her. Usually, Kendall ignores me in favor of writing her boyfriend du jour's name on her sneakers, but now that I've mutilated myself in front of an audience, I guess I'm cool. The pain in my hand, which has made the ambitious leap from stinging to throbbing, distracts me too much to think of something glib when Kendall asks, "So, you're really dark, aren't you?"

"Excuse me?"

"You like, just cut yourself. In front of the entire class."

"I didn't actually do it on purpose, you know," I say tiredly. My head begins to ache as I envision a bright new future as Cutter Girl.

"I saw you, Gracie, you were, like, hacking away. It was like you didn't even feel it," Kendall insists, gesturing emphatically like she's waving a plane to land. "No, I mean, that's a totally legitimate lifestyle choice. I mean, it's your body, right?"

I try to work up some feminist ire about self-mutilation. "Yeah, totally. Do you have any Tylenol?"

It turns out that Kendall, shockingly, has a wide variety of painkillers in her car. We take a field trip to the parking lot instead of going straight to the nurse like good girls—where, after downing three Tylenol and wrapping my hand with an ace bandage Kendall mysteriously produces from her glove compartment, I find myself sitting shotgun in Kendall's '93 Plymouth. "You should get some sugar," Kendall explains, pulling out of the parking lot and heading toward the interstate, "You know, to cushion the shock to your system? Besides, the nurse isn't here on Thursdays." It occurs to me that this is a very bad idea, but I stay silent and stare out the window. I never want to be in school in the first place, so now that I'm on my way out, it seems silly to turn around and go back.

Kendall rolls down the window and steers the car with one hand while gesturing wildly at me with the other. I cringe a little every time one of her ring-laden hands swoops near me. "Hey, did you ever read that book where the girl's in the insane asylum, and then she, like, sticks her head in the oven?" Kendall twists her face into what she imagines someone dying of gas exposure would look like, which looks sort of like a narcoleptic chimpanzee.

"Um. Do you mean *The Bell Jar*?" I ask cautiously, worried about where this might lead.

"Yeah. You sort of remind me of that girl. You seem really deep, you know?" I stare at her blankly, so she adds, "Not that you're some kind of brain or anything, because I copied off your paper the first time we had a test in biology, and I should have just written down the names of the seven dwarves or something. It was sad."

"I was personally embarrassed for both of us," I murmur.

"But you're, like, really real, you know? There's just this—this honesty. You're in pain, and you don't try to hide that like most people do. I totally respect that. I mean, screw politeness, right?" She stares deeply into my eyes to underscore her point, a technique our seventh grade math teacher taught us to help seal business deals.

I'm unsure how to explain that I'm not really some kind of rude, misery-loving freak, so I stare mistily out the window and murmur, "Esther doesn't kill herself at the end, Sylvia Plath does." Kendall is sincerely impressed.

We miss the turn for Dairy Queen and wind up in a dollar fifty theater, watching some starlet run through the woods, somehow managing to lose bits of her clothing while simultaneously fleeing an axe-wielding madman. Except for the old man in the front row talking to himself about samurai, we are the only ones in the theater, so we feel perfectly guiltless talking through the entire movie. It turns out that Kendall always thought I was "really unique and stuff," but she thought I was prissy in middle school, so she never spoke to me. I confess to having a crush on her eighth grade boyfriend when we were in third grade ("You know, before he turned into a delinquent"), which makes Kendall gasp in mock outrage and pelt me with popcorn. She tells me a story about the time she got kicked out of Girl Scouts for organizing a game of Spin the Bottle with the boys' camp across the lake; I tell her a story about how I got busted for shoplifting eyeliner at Walgreens. She giggles, "Me too! How stereotypical is that?" She's so proud for being self-deprecating, and all I can think is, "People actually do that?" But the air shifts in the darkened theater somewhere between the murder of the sidekick and the closing credits, and I look over at her profile, which is shaking with hiccup-like silent laughter, and suddenly I want to...I don't know, paint her toenails and gossip about boys or something. I haven't actually been friends with a girl since third grade, and she moved to Bermuda. I'm just not equipped for this sort of situation.

EIGHTY PERCENT WATER

They found these little once-wood ships
Marking explorers' landings
on the Andes mountaintops.
They say before conquistadors
brought their guns and words to stay,
the ocean rustled up to kiss the sailors,
wash their feet, and run away,
stranding the boats up high,
fossilized oars forever pointing,
forever pulling down the sky.

This modern water is not so shy.
Someone hooked it up with chemicals.
On soft days it gets wistful, remembers being clean.
Now it's American busy, dashing itself against windshields,
or slumming it in drainpipes
among the dead animals and languages:
trust, for one. I will never run to meet the sailors,
then slip silent into the woods, to be a myth—an image,
a tourist attraction. To be silent is to be shaped and tailored
into pretty words by the children of invaders,
seeing all the ways that they could wash away,
learning that history is eighty percent water,
and twenty percent shame.

FOR SARAH,
ON THE DAY SHE TAUGHT ME TO OPEN MY EYES UNDERWATER

Maybe eight or nine, in the gray
backseat of your mother's brown car,
a Volvo, I think, something uncrashable,
smelling of French fries; your brother's toy
dinos littered the floor.
We made them kiss, speak Italian.

Your family had country club memberships
and we'd been unjustly expelled from its cool
suburban ocean. (We loved each other
because we pretended to be mermaids
and because we didn't admit we were
too old to play the fun games.) I imagined
the chlorine was saltwater burning my eyes.
I'd never been to the seaside. It was so hot
the seats burned and clung at our thighs.
Sit on your towels, said your mother, who
looked like Vanna White. That's what
they're there for. Don't ruin my seats.

Too late. We dripped processed water,
little puddles pooling around the puckered
seats of our swimsuits, raspberry and blue
to match the popsicle rings around our lips.
The radio was tuned to NPR. It was all talk,
never music. We couldn't dance to Madeline
Albright like we could the Mentos jingle.

This was before God had a British accent,
when the BBC was less ineffable than your
father. The detached voices in the airwaves
were talking about a town that I knew
was a flower in a state we hadn't reached yet—
there was a map, remember, and once a week we
colored in a state. The Midwest went pink
in one fell swoop, the South turned aquamarine

bit by bit. We knew where we were.
Your mother pulled into the steeply
slanting driveway of your beautiful house,
and said, these children are killing each other.
She cried all backwards. Her makeup
smeared and trickled down her face,
loud and ugly, but her sobs were small,
dainty, silent. Shoulders shaking.

I'd never seen a grownup cry
outside of movies, where it was tragic
and beautiful. There were no cellos weeping
in the background, just news breaking
and a tennis ball bouncing off a window
down the street. I thought we'd be trapped
in that car forever.

If it were a movie you would have unbuckled
the seatbelt that in reality you never
wore, slipped open the steel-laced door, and hugged
your mother tightly; you would have comforted
your mother and gone in to face your brother
with a new understanding of the world and how you
fit into it. Maybe you would have, if
I wasn't there. It's possible: we watched a lot of TV.
While your mother collected herself, our eyes met
and we knew that if we held still
enough we would be allowed to catch
minnows in the creek with red plastic cups,
on the sole condition that we ease them back
into the muddy water.

Denise Rickman, Age 18
Southeast Raleigh Magnet High School
Raleigh, NC
Teachers: Quincey Hyatt, Elizabeth Kaulfuss

SHE THINKS SHE LOVES HIM

Stewart has short feet. Wide and short. Marilyn doesn't know. She watches his torso and round greenish face (she bought her TV at an estate sale) with the closed captions on and imagines he sounds like a pineapple. When she was four years old, she signed to her step-dad to ask what sound carrots made and he playfully stuck one in her ear. Now she doesn't ask. But since fruits and vegetables are small and don't make any vibrations like trucks or rock concerts, she likes to think that pineapples make a light and floaty sound, like a cloud. She likes to think this about Stewart the TV psychologist, and she wouldn't want to know about his feet.

Stewart stares past the cameras as he talks and waits for the cue to end the show. It's coming slowly tonight and under these bright, bright lights his voice sounds flatter than it should, like sheet metal or paper. He wants to get home. His secret indulgence is children's books. He reads them sometimes with a glass of brandy in his hand (which he usually drinks) and wants to write a storybook of his own.

The only problem is that he's humorless.

His throat is drying out and his paper-flat voice is going through a shredder. His short feet are kicking around under his chair (below Marilyn's TV screen) and he's ready to take off running. But a wave of tingly stillness comes over him, and nothing happens for a few moments until he stretches his round lips into the Gaelic words "*Maidid glass for cach lus…*"

Marilyn understands that his lips are saying something other than the words rolling across the bottom of her screen. She moves to lift her iced tea from the green coaster, but suddenly there's a waterfall coming off the coffee table. The coaster floats a little. Marilyn looks back at Stewart, wondering what to do.

She remembers the storyteller at the library this morning. The image of his hands had drawn her away from the romance section and over to the back of the crowd, where she let people assume she was the mother of one of the children huddled up front. Stewart reminds her of the storyteller, the way his hands curve and shape the story he feels. The way he teeters at the climax, as if on the edge of a cliff. How, in the end, his eyes dilate to take in the happy ending he sees.

A happy ending is what the network producers had in mind when they hired Stewart for the job of post-11:00 news psychologist. They hope to convey the impression of a corporation who cares. After broadcasting their video clips of bombings, screaming mothers and those frightening passive children, KVTV hopes to revitalize its audience with a psychologist who makes them forget how depressing the world is. Humorless Stewart wonders if it's possible. All he wanted was a job—the actual idea for the segment was proposed by the CEO, who as a boy was scared by ghost stories and always felt better after making gingerbread with his mother.

Only tonight the CEO happens to be sleeping on a billowing featherbed while Stewart recites the poem he memorized in college when he wanted to marry the Scottish girl. His voice keeps going loud and strong, growing deep green. He doesn't know entirely what the words mean, he just lets them become his frustration, his not knowing how to act alone in front of the entire world. The individual behaving differently in various group settings and the individual becoming anonymous within a group is straight textbook. But this, Stewart's terrible aloneness while everyone watches, his studies never hit on. There's nothing for Stewart to refer to and he doesn't know how to act. "*Suanaid ler lonn liac/foling iach brec... brec... brec...*" What is the next word?

Marilyn fills in the gap with a hungry stare. If Stewart did an analysis of Marilyn, he would tell her that her need for love was high. Stewart's need is relatively low (he's a Scorpio), but that one time got to him.

The far right bank of studio lights explodes. Stewart jumps out of his chair in surprise and fear. Those damn light bulbs are like a wolf pack of gaping mouths with translucent fangs. Open mouths, just like he couldn't open his when the time came to say, I love you. Couldn't for the fear that if he exposed himself, there wouldn't be anything there—just a hole in his chest that the wind whipped through when he stood on a dry, grassy plain. Indoors, she'd be able to look through the hole and watch TV.

Stewart can see himself on the monitor. He sits back down, and his pupils swell to adjust in the relative darkness. He wants to cocoon himself in a soft, deep lack of light. He needs a purpose, and the Scottish girl isn't it. "Close your eyes," he says in English, reluctantly picking up the job he was hired to do. "Think about the news," he says. "What's the first image you see? It's the one your subconscious has been brooding over. Look at it. Ask yourself why it's important." A triangle of broken light bulb drops to the floor with an innocent plink. "Who in your life is it?"

When Marilyn closes her eyes, it's Stewart's round, caring face she sees. She didn't watch the news tonight, never does. Still, she's the only home viewer who watches Stewart's segment regularly. His skin's greenish tinge makes him seem otherworldly, like he might be perfect. She fantasizes about them having their own silent language. A kiss on the hand will mean we're out of orange juice. Looking into each other's eyes is I love you.

Stewart no longer feels like the cameras are microscopes. He no longer feels ashamed that he couldn't function under their glare, that he hasn't owned a TV or watched the news since the girl with the heather-scented hair smashed his Sony three and a half years ago. He realizes he's been seeking refuge in her words and she's not even coming back. He starts to laugh at the absurdity of it all; the sound is lopsided and unrehearsed.

By the end of the show Stewart is swaying, but his feet are planted firmly on the ground. He's spent the last twenty-seven minutes talking to himself and to her, and he's fine. Tomorrow, when Mr. Provine tells Stewart that his show has died, Stewart will have already said his good-byes. As he swerves homeward in a taxi, he will chuckle as he imagines a character who floats among the clouds, a pineapple-yellow parachute doming above her.

Marilyn will start wondering if Stewart ever existed at the same moment that Stewart writes the first sentence to his children's book. If he and Marilyn ever cross paths in the aisles of Powell's before a book signing, Marilyn will focus in on Stewart's odd-shaped feet and disregard him before she even sees his face, which he will cover when he sneezes at such a critical moment that he won't see her, the woman on the other end of his conversation.

Margaret Hayertz, Age 17
West Linn High School
West Linn, OR
Teacher: Bret Freyer

IT'S JUST TOO SOON

The first plane hits, and suddenly a distraught woman is running through the rubble and dust, trying to find her son. As the burning building begins to fall, gallant firemen drive toward the chaos and confusion, bravely willing to risk their lives. Flashes of sobbing families, falling bodies and...the trailer ends. A commercial for toothpaste begins, and I'm left trying to grasp the images that have just faded from my TV screen—scenes almost identical to those which played, over and over, on that same television five years ago.

Except I don't remember Maggie Gyllenhall running through the streets downtown, her flawless face perfectly tear-stained as she searches for her husband. I don't understand why Nicholas Cage is making his classic frustrated/serious expression, looking properly distressed in his artfully soiled fireman uniform. My memories from that day are less crafted, less perfect and yet much more vivid. The television continued to show the same footage, on every channel, without pause, without time to understand, and without intermittent movie ratings and critic reviews.

I don't need to write about the feelings of wonder, uncertainty and confusion that filled my mind—it happened to us all. And it's impossible for me to write about my experience that day, because it still generates unexpectedly strong emotions. Just thinking about September 11 is painful, and suddenly, it's being re-created and splashed across movie screens around the world.

As the Class of 2007 graduates this spring, the only remaining grade present at Hunter when the terrorist attacks occurred will leave. Perhaps it will be easier, next year, or in ten years, when the painting that hangs in the auditorium will not remind students of the memorial day we held one month after the attacks. Maybe in fifty years, when the event is another page in history textbooks, a story we tell our children, it will be easier to watch a re-creation of that day. But I truly doubt it. Just as Holocaust survivors argued against *Life Is Beautiful*, and those present on December 7 expressed anger at the creation of *Pearl Harbor*, it will never make sense to me that a movie studio hire actors to play out a scene that is already burned into our minds. *World Trade Center* director Oliver Stone's commitment to authenticity and realism is somehow supposed to comfort us all. True, an unimpressive representation of that day would be pathetic. But how will top-grade actors and multimillion-dollar visual effects make us deem this movie acceptable? How can our society allow a movie studio to make a single cent of profit from the indescribable suffering this day caused?

People who lived through Hitler's dictatorship do not want to see Roberto Benigni acting as if he has suffered in a concentration camp. Men who lost their fellow soldiers in Pearl Harbor cannot possibly see the point in Josh Hartnett looking brave in front of a green-screen bombing raid. And anyone from Manhattan finds little satisfaction or comfort in seeing a well-acted version of a nightmare they already witnessed. We were already there. We already saw it, played out with no rehearsals, with no breaks or editing or corny lines.

Someday in the far future, it will be necessary to begin showing these events to a generation who never witnessed them firsthand. In the same way that we watch *Glory* in history class to further understand the Civil War, a film of September 11 will one day help students to understand the first decade of the 21st century more thoroughly. Today, however, designs for the future of Ground Zero are not even finalized, the current administration is still wrongfully using "9/11" to justify their actions abroad, and investigations into whether or how September 11 could have been avoided are still incomplete.

And yet, while the release of *World Trade Center* is upsetting, it is hardly surprising. Filming this movie only five years after September 11 is not only inconsiderate and callous, but also characteristic of America today. How typical of the United States to market its own tragedy, working to profit off any possible angle. A wealthy corporation *would* disregard the emotions of offended Americans in order to sell more tickets. After all, haven't we shown the world that our version of capitalism is based on exploiting others and reaping the benefits? In fact, many believe that a major motivation of the terrorist attacks was the United States' exploitation of the Middle East for oil. Perhaps the release of this movie is merely an extension of the very phenomena that makes us an inviting target for terrorist attacks. We seem to exploit all: oil, the Third World, even our own tragedies, and thus make more tragedy inevitable.

Monica Klein, Age 17
Hunter College High School
New York, NY
Teacher: Lois Refkin

WOODNOTE

The mellow lanterns in the evening
spelled home, that hushed
somnolence where barn swallows
nestled in the slatted wood and thatch.

At night I was a thrush set loose
to the wind's soft pummelings,
climbing to cambered altitudes,

eyeing the night's inheritance.
I saw my grandfather hunched down,
planting a young oak tree
near the water, redolent

of sandpipers and rush.
"Remember this," he gently said,
"when you are standing in city streets

and see only dim windows."
So, like Odysseus, I kept
this olive-tree remembrance
with clarity in its nook,

our secret mainstay growing past
gravity's world-bent inclinations.
When I left the farm I broke

an umber sprig to bear
as a little shelf-bound keepsake,
some unasserted miracle
plucked from the ordinary.

Years later, I lifted it from
its given space to blow off dust
accruing on it. And when

I blew, my breath struck
its fluted, furrowed bark,
and a clear note sounded from
the verified wood. So, like a man

born deaf, now sensing tremblings,
I walked away affirming the cures
of happenstance and woodnote.

David Pederson, Age 16
Pederson Home School
Edina, MI
Teacher: Jonathan Pederson

MAPPING THE STREETS OF CHINATOWN

Our house is the cream-colored ranch, easy to miss with its pruned hedges, flagstone path and chemically green lawn blending with the rest of the neighborhood. In the two-car garage is a green minivan, the car that Mom had always wanted. Its three-row seating and wide trunk are convenient for carpools, instruments, backpacks and gym bags. It is reliable and efficient—the everyday car of a family in suburbia.

On weekends, we sometimes drive to Chinatown to eat and shop for groceries. The minivan is big enough for the bags of food and it handles well along the narrow curves and slopes of the neighborhood roads. The tree-lined Merritt Parkway flies past its tinted windows, and the roadways grow wider, the traffic heavier. The blue framework of the Henry Hudson Bridge marks the passage into Manhattan. Looking out the right side window I see chiseled crags and foaming ripples. On the left, concrete and stainless steel catch my eye, perpendicular to the horizon line, reflecting opportunity, haze. My father maneuvers the van through the side streets, swerving and stopping for the pedestrians, as I watch the movement of the city.

As the car turns onto Broadway, the demographic of the pedestrians begins to change. Old Chinese women with tight perms pull metal dollies filled with red plastic bags. Wizened men in windbreakers speak loud Cantonese. The younger ones talk on cell phones in English and thumb text messages. Perhaps it is the minivan that makes the pedestrians stare, or our clothes, or our Eurasian family. Perhaps the characteristics that set us apart from the true Chinese are indefinable. They lie within our mannerisms, our way of life. In this way, I know Chinatown only by the names of the streets and the restaurants, the novelty of its gift shops and grocery stores, the Lunar New Year parades and the tales of Mom's childhood.

We walk six blocks from the parking garage to the restaurant. Two lion statues guard the vestibule, and we join the end of the queue, waiting for a table. It seems as though our trips to Chinatown are centered about food—dim sum for lunch and grocery shopping in the afternoon. For my sister and me, the language has been reduced to the names of different dishes, the culture truncated to the ability to eat with chopsticks. Even inside the restaurant, the waiter tosses a fork at each of our place settings. He is doubtful that we have retained the ability to balance the bits of food precariously upon the thin bamboo sticks—the ability to grasp slippery things, never letting go.

Over lunch Mom looks past the forks on our table, at a young girl whose black hair is tied with red barrettes. These small observations—in combination with the familiar smells of the streets, seasonings, and dim sum—have a way of jogging her memory. Throughout her childhood, Mom accompanied her parents to Chinatown every Sunday for a meal, grocery shopping and a movie. They wanted to buy Chinese language newspapers and the ingredients and cuts of meat that were not available at the A&P. They wanted to enjoy a prepared meal—something too hard to make at home—a whole fish or Peking duck. Mom recalls the guttural ring of loud Cantonese and the hollow click of the beads of an abacus as the shopkeepers tallied the bill and called out the price. After lunch, they went to Chinese movies—double features: gung fu and courtship in a faraway land. As my grandparents watched, transported by the language, old-style costumes and martial arts, Mom fidgeted. She was unable to understand the language or appreciate the costumes, and the sword-fighting scenes scared her. Averting her eyes from the screen, she saw rats scamper across the theatre floor and learned to keep her feet from touching the ground.

A crowd gathers in the restaurant vestibule, and Mom's recollections are interrupted. The waiters are clearing the table, brushing half-empty teacups and plates into a plastic bin with the backs of their hands.

Even rituals cannot withstand the push and pull of time, distance and growing disconnect. Mom left New York City to go to college, where she met an American boy. She married that American boy and lived the American dream:

Two children, a house in suburbia, and a minivan. Now she sporadically takes us to Chinatown to buy groceries and enjoy a prepared meal—anything, even simple dishes, because she hardly cooks Chinese food at home. Yet this deficiency is irrelevant because somehow, by upbringing and the flukes of DNA, I am aware of Chinatown's stories. If I open my eyes, I will know Chinatown not only by the street names but by the intangible losses and gains of a journey across the Pacific.

From the restaurant, I follow Mott Street, past the Transfiguration Roman Catholic Church and Aji Ichiban candy shop. In front of the fishmonger, water from melting beds of ice veins the cement. Behind the counter, the men wear yellow overalls and rain boots, though the splatter and reek of chopped fish guts are impervious to rubber.

Mom stops in the Fung Wang Bakery to buy coconut bread and moon cakes. In the past, I have only noticed the baked goods, golden brown rolls and red bean pies, molded into the shapes of the animals of the zodiac. Yet this time, I look above the display case and ovens, my eyes skimming the ceiling. An altar sits atop a ledge, porcelain statues of the household gods standing resolutely over our heads. Burnt joss sticks are propped against the statues. The wood shelf has been painted red, the color of luck. Alongside the statues are plump oranges, offerings to the ancestors for happiness and prosperity.

Taking the plastic bag from the woman behind the counter, Mom unfolds crisp bills from her wallet, pays. We continue up the street as the sky darkens and the first raindrops fall. Soggy confetti, left over from Lunar New Year, floats atop the surface of the dirty puddles. Plastic bags, crushed cans, and discarded orange rinds sink beneath the murky water.

On Canal Street, we duck into the grocery store. Dried fish, frozen dumplings, steamed buns, and boxes of chrysanthemum tea are stacked alongside microwave meals, Betty Crocker cake mixes and Nestle Coffeemate. Chinese women weigh fruits and vegetables in their palms, pressing their thumbs to the skin. A slight twitch at the corner of the mouth or a wrinkle of the brow means, "Too ripe, no good." An undetectable nod of the head is, "Okay." Tourists gesture at the fruits and vegetables with their outstretched fingers.

Carrying the grocery bags on Mulberry Street, I hear the squeals of children in the adjacent jungle gym and basketball court. Their parents call to them in Mandarin from the perimeter of the playground, and they answer in English. "Coming, Ma!" Standing between the park benches and playground, I see a cracked plastic sign: "Fried Dumpling." Following Mosco Street, halfway to the top of the incline, I come to the door. The linoleum is a shade of yellow-used-to-be-white, and five leatherette stools face the soy sauce–stained counter. Four women make dumplings with nimble fingers and flying wrists, molding ground meat into spheres. Their faces are damp with perspiration as they hover over the griddle, flipping the dumplings. The wrappers are folded into lucky crescents—the shape of golden ingots. Twenty handmade dumplings cost five dollars, yet they taste as though they were made by an auntie or grandmother, a recipe from a faraway land and a taste of home in a dirty, foreign place.

I often wonder what the Chinese think of Chinatown. As an outsider, it is a place that I perceive with a mixture of admiration, novelty, and disdain. In this way, I am struck by the heritage that I share with the residents, as well as our overwhelming differences. I wonder if their prayers have been answered in the littered streets and meager storefronts; I wonder if they have found what they sought in America. I cannot imagine that they had come to this country—the city where stainless steel reflects opportunity, haze—with hopes of chopping fish, folding dumplings, or working at a bakery. Yet nothing appears as it is. Perhaps it is better to risk losing all you have in a foreign land than to settle for what little the motherland has to offer.

Yet the physical details of Chinatown are only a backdrop this quiet strife—a mood that is omnipresent but too elusive for words. It is the lurking threat of losing everything, and the manifestation of how necessity governs circumstance, that make Chinatown special. My grandparents brought Mom to Chinatown to get groceries, enjoy a meal in a restaurant, and watch a double feature. They brought Mom to Chinatown to maintain their connection with the motherland—the language and foods of their childhoods.

Today, the push and pull of cultures remain, visible in the park and grocery store. Displays of American food merge with Chinese groceries, as do the cultures. As Mom eventually gave up regular pilgrimages to Chinatown, the children in the playground speak English to their parents, who doggedly keep speaking in Mandarin. English, Mandarin, English. They do not want their children to lose their heritage to the sound of foreign syllables.

The rain begins to let up. As I peer from Mulberry Street running parallel to Mott Street, my gaze stops at Mosco Street. I begin to realize that I can get dumplings anywhere—frozen at the Kamman grocery store or the May May bakery. The popularity of the "Fried Dumpling" shop is beyond flavor or cost. It is the grit of the four women standing in a dirty storefront, where good fortune blends with tainted luck, tenacity filling the breaks in the brick, blending with the sounds of the city. In this way, the ambiance of Chinatown is not predicated upon the potentiality of loss, or the aches of loneliness and hard labor. The ambiance of Chinatown is defined by the ability to hold on to what little individuals possess—jobs, apartments, and the culture itself.

I wonder if the waiter is right. I wonder whether we have indeed lost the ability to balance the bits of food precariously upon the thin bamboo sticks—the ability to grasp slippery things and never let go. As we drive back into the suburbs, the need to hold on to a job, comfort and culture fades with every row of colonials and pruned hedges, every minivan and sports car on the Parkway. Yet having listened to my mother's stories and having seen the losses and gains of a journey across the Pacific, the sight of our cream-colored house and the chemically green lawn holds new significance. It is not only a symbol of the good life—having achieved the American Dream, now concerned only with landscaping. It is a foil to the fragility of the human condition, the limbo between reaching and holding. In the shadows of early evening, a dim light, left on since breakfast, glows from the kitchen window—a beacon of appreciation and possibility.

Kathryn Llewellyn, Age 16
Staples High School
Westport, CT
Teacher: Christine Radler

FINAL GRADE

Natalie's feet pounded against the school's white tile floor. Her breathing came in heavy, labored bursts and her mind was racing a mile a minute. *No, no, no,* Natalie cursed in her thoughts. She turned a sharp corner and almost lost her balance, her feet sliding on the polished tiles. After some arm flailing and more inward cursing, Natalie continued down the labyrinth of hallways. Much to her relief the next turn gave way to the door she was searching for. The doorway to the classroom was constructed completely of glass and engraved with the words *Class 2A*. Even as Natalie neared the door her pace did not slow. Seconds before her body made a messy impact with the glass, the door's motion detectors slid it open. Natalie entered the room just as a bell sounded throughout the school.

"Safe!" Natalie whooped triumphantly, punching the air. The entire classroom of students turned around to stare at her. Natalie felt her neck grow hot as she shuffled to her seat.

The teacher at the front of the classroom sighed, "Natalie, what's your excuse this time?"

"Sorry, Mr. Rowe, um…my dog ate my E-Chip?" Natalie joked, referring to the portable chip on which the students saved their homework. Her classmates shared a small laugh at Natalie's reference to the tired cliché.

Her teacher, on the other hand, was not amused. "I thought I wouldn't have to deal with students like you in an "A" class."

Natalie had the decency to look slightly chagrined. Her parents had been so proud when they received the news that Natalie was being placed in classroom 2A for the next year. At exactly 8:05 A.M. the intercom system sparked to life and a computerized voice instructed all teachers to turn on their EVB, or Electronic Viewing Board. Mr. Rowe walked up to the long, blank wall that the desks were facing. He entered a code on a digital keypad and the wall flickered on to show the morning news.

"Please take out your AECs and record any important information for your test on current events," said Mr. Rowe, as he settled behind his desk. The classroom began to buzz with noise as the students rummaged through their bags and pulled out their only school supply. The Apex Electronic Computer was a handheld supercomputer with a wireless connection to an advanced form of the Internet. Natalie flipped hers open with a flourish, proudly displaying her new electric blue cover.

"Nice cover," said Caleb, and grinned. Natalie smiled a thank you at her friend. His coal black hair was slightly tousled and his tinted contacts made his eyes look bluish-purple.

"Is it just me, or have the teachers been going crazy with the workload recently?" Natalie asked as she vigorously typed notes on her AEC.

"Yeah, the teachers have been going manic lately. It's probably that new school curriculum the government is implementing," Caleb shrugged.

Natalie looked over at Caleb with a raised eyebrow, "What new curriculum?" Both of Natalie's parents held high positions in the government. If an important bill had been passed they would have mentioned something.

"It's something about a momentous test that will decide our futures, blah, blah, blah," Caleb said, rolling his eyes. "Like they haven't been shoveling that down our throats since we were five."

Natalie snickered at Caleb's nonchalant demeanor and regained her focus on the Viewing Board. It was all the same old stories: The new brand of hydrogen technology would help the ozone to heal, scientists were working on methods to refreeze the lost ice caps, and the world's still expanding population had swelled prodigiously to over 25 billion people.

Natalie's mind began to wander. She scanned the room assessing her classmates as they pored over their AECs. The classrooms were organized by the students' standardized test scores. The students with the highest scores were placed in classroom 1A. The next highest went to classroom 2A, etc., etc. Natalie was probably the most laid-back person, compared to the rigorous workers she had to spend eight hours with every day. Those hours seemed to drag by as Natalie sat and typed notes. When the sweet sound of the lunch bell rang, Natalie wasted no time bolting out of her seat. The lunchroom was big enough to accommodate all the students of the school and Natalie looked forward to seeing her "B" and "C" friends.

When it came down to it, the students rarely segregated themselves: cliques were so two centuries ago. Natalie found her table at the center of the enormous cafeteria and sat down.

"Hey hon." A beautiful, platinum blonde girl waved to Natalie. She had been drawing an elaborate landscape on some classic tree paper.

"Hey Gianna…why are you still using that ancient stuff? Don't artists just use graphic computer programs to construct art nowadays?" Natalie pulled out her lunch and began to eat.

Gianna snorted. "Ha, those programs are just an excuse for people with no talent to make art. This is the only way to truly make beautiful pieces." Gianna lifted up her paper, which showed an amazing picturesque scene.

Natalie had to agree the traditional look was the best. She glanced around the table at the variety of people that surrounded her. Gianna was in 2C; Chloe, a petite girl with glasses, was a 1A genius. Caleb was in 2A with Natalie. Peyton, an aspiring music star, was in 3B.

In a flurry of dramatic movements, Peyton whipped out his Vibration DrumSticks. He began to tap the edge of the table in a fast, sharp rhythm as the sticks recorded the sound on their E-chip.

Gianna rolled her eyes. "Don't you ever leave those at home?"

Peyton laughed and tossed his brown hair out of his eyes. "Nope, babe, I keep these with me at all times. You never know when inspiration might strike."

Caleb motioned to the group to settle down. "Listen, they're going to announce the whole new curriculum thing now," Caleb nodded knowingly.

Sure enough, their principal, Ms. Kennedy, walked up to the front of the cafeteria and the students grew quiet. Ms. Kennedy cleared her throat and began to speak: "The government has instituted an exciting new program for schools across the country. When you turn 17 you are obligated to take a standardized test so the government may adequately place you in the proper future field. If there are any students who have already passed their 17th birthday, please come to my office immediately so we can schedule your test time. That will be all."

A strange silence fell over the room, followed by a low chorus of voices. Peyton looked just short of outraged.

"Since when does our government tell us we are *obligated* to do anything? And they think they can place me in a career field based on test scores. Um, what about our *dreams*, you know, *our* plans for *our* future that don't involve the government's input? Yeah, well, they are on drugs if they think they can make me take that free-will killing test," Peyton crossed his arms over his chest and slouched down in his seat.

Gianna burst into laughter. "You are such a drama queen! Don't worry, I'm taking the test in like two weeks so I'll tell you how it is."

That reminded Natalie. "Caleb, you turned 17 last month. Aren't you going to the office?"

Caleb nodded with the stark realization. "Yeah, I guess I had better head down and check it out. See you guys later."

Caleb didn't show up for school the next day. Natalie looked at the empty desk beside her and felt a wave of loneliness. When she got home from school she headed to her room to contact Caleb's AEC.

"Hello Natalie." Natalie's mom, Charlotte, blocked the stairs. She was cradling a huge stack of books in her arms and her glasses were slightly askew.

"Hey mom, did you know about that bogus test thing they are forcing everyone to take? I mean, what is *that* all about?" Natalie placed a hand on her hip.

"Honey, it's not bogus, it's a very important assessment of your skills. You'd do best to study hard for it. Here are some books to help you prepare." Charlotte handed the books over to Natalie, who trudged up the stairs with the load. Natalie dropped the stack of books on her bed. *I'll study those a little later...like the next millennium.* Natalie flipped open her AEC and scanned her contacts list. *What the...?* Natalie sat confused. Caleb was missing from her list. That's not possible. AECs are always connected, all the time.

A soft knock on her door pulled Natalie out of her daze. Her mother stood in the doorway, her eyes darting frantically.

"Mom...is something wrong?" Natalie stood up from her desk.

"Honey, I know you don't want to, but please, for me, look over those books. It's very important that you are prepared," Charlotte asked, almost pleading.

"Yeah mom, I will, I promise," Natalie gave her mom a small embrace and closed the door. Natalie's eyes drifted over to the stack of books. *What's the big deal?* Natalie sighed and opened the first one.

The next day at school, Natalie entered her class and her eyes immediately found Caleb's crazy black hair. She squealed and gave him a tight bear hug.

"It's good to see you too, Natalie," Caleb laughed.

"What happened? What, did you take the test? Why was your AEC disconnected? Details man, details!" Natalie rambled on like a maniac.

"One, nothing happened. Two, yeah, I took the test. Three, they took away our AECs, to prohibit cheating. But Natalie, something strange is up. I don't think the test was a career test at all." Caleb glanced around nervously.

"What are you talking about?" Natalie asked, sensing his discomfort.

"Well, it didn't ask any questions about likes or dislikes or career fields. It seemed like any ordinary IQ test. It had questions about math, English, history, and science. The proctors said that once we get our test scores, we aren't going back to school." Caleb looked away.

"Wh…What are you talking about? Where are you going?" Natalie stepped back, shaking her head in disbelief.

"I'm not sure. I think we are just going to some post-high school learning centers, like college. Except…I guess they choose where we go," Caleb revealed his uneasiness with a quivering smile.

"This is crazy! How can they tell you where you have to go to college? Can't you just say no?" Natalie's voice rose an octave.

"I tried to tell my parents that it didn't seem right, but they just kept going on about my future and how important the test was. They weren't even listening to a word I said." Caleb buried his face in his hands.

The intercom flickered to life and an announcement blared throughout the school.

"All students who took the Future Assessment Test yesterday, your results are in. Please come to the front office. That is all."

Caleb rose from his seat and gave Natalie one last smile before disappearing out the door. A few minutes later Natalie's AEC received its last message from Caleb: *I'm leaving. Goodbye, friends.*

"No. No," Natalie whispered fiercely as the tears blurred her vision. She flipped open her AEC ready to write him back but she saw the Caleb's AEC was disconnected again. She quickly typed a message that she sent to Gianna and Peyton. *We need to talk, now.*

After school the friends met together outside the school. Natalie relayed the information Caleb had told her. Peyton and Gianna stood in shock for a few moments.

Then Gianna cleared her throat and shifted her weight uncomfortably. "My parents are making me take the test next week. They feel the same way as Caleb's parents." Gianna looked desperately from one friend to the other. She then burst into loud sobs and pulled her friends into a group hug. "I don't want to leave you guys."

"Shh, Gianna, it will be okay," Natalie released herself from the hug.

"We're tough, we'll make it."

"Yeah, babe, if they think they can make me take that test, they are sadly mistaken." Peyton grinned.

Gianna sniffed and wiped her tears away. "You guys are right. Everything will be okay."

Gianna was gone by the next Friday. Peyton and Natalie both received the same message: *I'm leaving. Goodbye, friends.*

Peyton still remained strong in his resilience. "My parents are on my side. They sent the school a letter saying that they refuse to let me take this test. So we'll see how the government takes that one."

That was the last time Natalie spoke to Peyton. At breakfast the next morning, her mom informed her that Peyton and his family had moved.

"What do mean they moved?" Natalie paused, her fork halfway in her mouth. "They weren't planning on moving. Did they say something to you?"

"Well, no, but their house is empty so I assume they decided on it at the last minute." Charlotte sipped from her coffee mug and dropped her eyes to the newspaper.

"Mom this is *crazy!* Our school is almost empty. Everyone takes this test and leaves. Where are they going?" Natalie demanded, slamming her hands down on the table.

The dramatic movement barely registered with Charlotte. "Honey, calm down. There is nothing to get worked up over. It's just to decide your future." With that Charlotte dropped the conversation and left the room.

What is wrong with everyone? Natalie rested her head on the table, thoughts swirling around in her mind.

It was sunny when Natalie's test day came. It was almost as if nature was also trying to fool her. *Don't worry Natalie, nothing is wrong,* the blue sky and songbirds seemed to be reassuring her. The room she entered was plain white with compact little desks. The air was thick with tension and nervousness. The proctor passed out a thick booklet and a digital answer keypad. Hours passed of testing with question after question making Natalie brain throb.

Then the proctor signaled them to turn their keypads off and ushered them from the room. With a cheery smile the woman informed them that they would receive their test results by tomorrow. Natalie turned to leave when the women called out her name.

"Natalie, someone wishes to speak to you."

Natalie turned and re-entered the room. She stepped back in surprise at who was standing there.

"Dad?" Natalie's jaw dropped in shock. Natalie's father, Garrett, was a member of the Bipartisan Libertarian Superior Court and rarely was home during the week.

"Hello Natalie." Her dad gave her a tight smile. The gesture made Natalie more uneasy. That was his politician face; he was here on business.

"What's going on, Dad? Do *you* know what this test is all about? What happened to all of my friends?"

Garrett turned and touched the Viewing Board. It displayed a familiar picture. Natalie recognized the news footage from class. It was a story about the growing population problem and what the government was doing to relieve it.

"Population inflation. Big deal, what does that have to do with this test?"

"This is the answer, Natalie. A test." Garrett gave her that politician's smile again. "A test to find the most intelligent people, the most…useful to society. So that the government may properly relieve the congestion."

The realization came down on Natalie with a sickening thud. "You don't mean…you're choosing who lives based on a *test*?" Natalie felt bile rise in her throat.

"Resources are thin and stress on the world is extreme. We needed a quick fix, a solution. The people who pass the test will go on with their lives, those who do not…they will do their part to make this world better." Garrett didn't blink.

Dark spots blinded Natalie's vision. She gripped the desk next to her to steady herself. "What makes less intelligent people's lives any less worth living? What about the people with other talents…like athletes and artists and musicians…" Natalie paused, choking back sobs at the thoughts of Gianna and Peyton. *Wait…Peyton…* "What if they refused to take the test! Peyton refused." Natalie smiled triumphantly.

For the first time Garrett's smile faltered. "Rebels are dealt with swiftly."

Natalie's legs gave out and she slumped to the floor. "Isn't there any other way? Please stop this. Why isn't anyone stopping this? Why isn't anyone doing anything?"

"The plan has been set into motion and people are beginning to understand the reasoning behind the method," said Garrett. "There is no stopping it. Don't worry about all those other people. Once they receive their results they will do their part for society…just like you will. You passed, Natalie. You and Caleb both passed."

Garrett handed Natalie her AEC. Natalie opened her AEC and a message popped up, emblazoned in dark red letters: PASS. As she stared at the large red letters, the message's digital code wormed its way into her subconscious. Natalie's pupils dilated and a lazy smile crept across her mouth. *How could I not have seen the logic before?* Natalie thought cheerfully. *This is a good idea, a good solution.* She sent one last message to her mom and her friends: *I'm leaving. Goodbye, friends.* Then she closed her AEC and walked out of the room. Her feet tapped against the school's white tile floor, the sound echoing off the long, empty corridors. Her breathing was even and her thoughts were calm. However, a small voice seemed to whisper a resounding thought from the back of her mind: *No…No…No…*

Erin Guty, Age 15
Trinity High School
Camp Hill, PA
Teacher: Robert Casey

THE COTTON CLUB

I jerked up suddenly from my sleep as the car gracelessly went over yet another pothole on 116th Street. Resigned, I looked out the window to my side. Before me lay the incoherent sprawl of Harlem—the usual broken-down brick buildings, the shattered glass, the boarded-up storefronts. Once the jewel of the U.S. art scene, Harlem had finally and obviously succumbed to middle-class flight. My father, ever the nostalgic poet, had dragged me out here once again to wax sentimental over the days of Langston Hughes. One only had to turn one's head, I thought to myself, to see that there was nothing left here. The passion and the beauty were gone, given over to the pulsing hordes of the desperate.

The usual crack smokers huddled along the sidewalks, right out in the open. One or two leered at me with blackened teeth. A little girl sat with them, huddled up in a blanket against the wall. I *guessed* it was a girl—she had long hair that blew in the cold wind. I averted my eyes and fiddled with the radio. At a stop sign a hooker made a few tentative steps toward us. Dad waved her on, looking at me surreptitiously, clearly hoping I hadn't noticed. I pretended I hadn't.

We had no particular place to go that night. Dad just wanted to drive past the shells of buildings that might themselves recall some lingering note of Duke Ellington, some enduring word of Ralph Ellison.

The car crunched to a stop in front of the sad remains of the original Cotton Club. I stepped out onto the street, pulling my jacket tightly around me. Dad's shoulders were slumped as he stood mesmerized by the wall of graffiti. It was too bad, I thought, that this was all there was left for him to look at.

I looked around at this travesty of society. Unlike my father, I didn't see the pain of reality, but rather the pointless expression of what wasn't. Perhaps that is the only defense available to those who witness such things in the early 21st century. It is said that we only see what we wish, so maybe it is also true that what we wish not to see, we absorb as a lesser reality, less deserving of our concern. In any case, what I felt, though I am ashamed of it, was not pity but boredom.

I wandered around a bit as Dad held his hand up to the cold brick. I looked down toward Spanish Harlem, then back up the street. There just really wasn't anything to focus on. Then a shifting movement to my left caught my eye: a blind beggar sitting on a street corner. At least he seemed blind. He didn't focus on anything I could see. He scraped his jingly soda can across the gritty sidewalk and smiled. As the occasional person went by, the beggar never changed his oddly contented appearance. I pulled a dime out of my pocket and dropped it in the can. He kept on smiling. I dug around and found a quarter, dropped that in, too.

A group of businessmen turned the corner onto 116th Street. Seeing the three of us—Dad with his hand on the wall, me loitering on the curb, the smiling beggar on the pavement—they closed ranks, avoided eye contact, pulled their long coats around them. As they passed, it struck me that the scene had becoming mystifying and almost poetic—a beggar surrounded by the billowing black cloaks of rich white businessmen. The men each glanced at the beggar and then walked on, at a quickened pace. They scurried in that puzzling way we humans use to run from the rain even when there is no shelter in sight—as if to comfort ourselves from the face of the inevitable, from the fact that we are indeed running.

I watched the businessmen recede toward downtown. I could hear their conversation start up again, loud and opinionated. Looking back to the smiling beggar, I noticed that he'd managed to get to his feet. He glanced at me once, barely meeting my eye from under his knit cap, then shuffled off slowly. The wind blew. Leaves and trash gathered in the spot he had sat. I watched him go. Dad was saying something, but the wind blew it away.

The beggar hobbled past the crack smokers, now sitting on a stoop. He stopped in front of the child, still huddled in her blanket but obviously awake now, playing with some scrap of something. He dropped the can in her lap. She looked up. And then he just kept walking, evenly, slowly, probably with that same smile, until he turned the corner and I couldn't see him anymore.

As we worked our way through the snarling traffic of Manhattan, it occured to me that I had just witnessed something profound. I try not to think about it too much, not to read too much into it. But it's a nice memory. It takes the edge off an otherwise blank and disappointing evening. It makes it not quite so awful that Langston Hughes is dead and that Duke Ellington doesn't play at the Cotton Club anymore.

Eugene Stockton-Juarez, Age 14
Carlisle High School
Carlisle, PA
Teacher: Susan C. Biondo-Hench

FAMILY REUNION: CHINA, 2005

The bus is crowded.
Men try to steal my seat,
jump over luggage.
Outside smudged windows,
gleaming rice patties lap at
the oversized doors of two-roomed houses.
My grandfather's house looks like a stable.

I perch on a jagged wooden bench,
leaning my wrists against
the table's crude edge.
My pants pick up mud and filth
congealed on molding wood.
I wave away flies hovering over my dinner.

Our family shares a room.
The bamboo mat's coarse weave
catches at my clothes, scratches my arms.
Mosquitoes fly in through open windows.

I have to wash my clothes in the river.
Duckweed coats its murky surface.
Scattered refuse clings to crumbling banks.
I dip my fingers into chilled water.
Its smell is pungent.

I've found a frog in the cooking water.
It's splashing inside the wooden barrel,
sunlight illuminating its gray-green back.
I scream.

"I want to go home!"
I yell in English,
then Chinese.
My parents shush me,

glancing at my aunts, uncles
and grandparents.
My cousin pretends not to hear.
We're all going fishing,
on the little bridge.
I decline.
My cousin takes my hand.
"Come," he says.

Boys in straw hats
line the bridge.
Slippery silver fish
swim around and around
in plastic buckets.

We're quiet.
The river is mottled with light.
Fish draw steel circles in the water.
I hear their splashing, our breathing,
the sighs of bamboo groves
leaning in the wind.

My cousin hands me a fishing pole.
And a worm. I squeal.
He sighs, sticks the wriggling body
through the hook,
hands me the rough hewn pole.

I lower the homemade line.
It twists in the wind.
The worm smacks
against my bare leg, plops
into the water.
My cousin laughs and rolls his eyes.
We wait.

My eyes are closed.
Wind combs out my hair.
Its smell is wild.
I feel a tug and drop the pole.

My cousin lunges,
grabs it, hauls it up.
He places a fish in my hands.

The fish's body is
a bar of smooth muscle.
It flips between my fingers.
Glistening slate scales
scrape my skin.

I smile.
The fish slips
through my hands
into the bucket.

Lisa Pang, Age 15
Thomas Jefferson High School
Alexandria, VA
Teacher: Mary O'Brien

CHURCH PEOPLE

Part I – June 24, 2003, 5:30 P.M.

5:27 P.M., an hour far from the sun's early-summer retirement, welcomes a blinding ray of light through the uppermost stained glass window (its stately, vibrant appearance puts on the airs of utmost sanctity, yet *I* can see the missing windowpane in the top right-hand corner, where, last year, some angst ridden teen trick-or-treater hurled an innocent rock). The light teasingly bounces off of whatever it can reach—eventually, even the hand-carved maple pews and tarnished chalices are awash in golden hues. With three minutes before the precious hour, the air is virtually devoid of any sound. I hold my breath—and in an instant, a steady stream of churchgoers flows in like the mystical "Holy Water."

The old veteran, considerably shrunken since his days at the Bulge, is the only one I have seen who can muster the power to transform a walking stick into a regal scepter. His wife, careful to take him by the arm ever so gently (using her well-played guise of, "Now don't let go, Charles, I would hate to be alone."), allows her eyes to sink into the surroundings. Inching towards their habitual home in the first row, the pair gruffly sighs with old age as they begin to kneel, crossing themselves as men and women of their upbringing would.

5:28 P.M., with only two minutes to spare, *he* enters. The man of indistinguishable origin, age, and intent takes his customary seat in the second-to-last row. Second-to-last. *I see.* The location is far away enough for him to decline involvement and mindlessly mouth the words to the hymns, yet not so distant as to land him in the apparent realm of the "guilty." The sun delights in his bare, shining head, and manipulates it as a considerably effective mirror. Yet, per usual, he does not seem to notice. Nor does he seem to care.

5:29 and forty-two seconds P.M. In the nick of time, as they always seem to be, the little one with the bow bigger than her head and her exhausted caretaker (Babysitter? Nanny? Distant cousin from Peru? It is difficult to determine) burst through the door. Unlike the veteran couple and the oblivious man, they are not blessed with a choice selection of seating, yet Nanny always makes it her business to attend Church—or else. As the guardian clumsily slides into the last remaining seat, the little one (blind, as most children are, to awkwardness) climbs onto her lap, gargantuan brown eyes surveying the hanging lights above. I can sense a strange, curious wisdom lurking within the small girl. The protector brushes a stray lock of hair out of the child's eye, and proceeds to wipe her own forehead in relief and prayer. They made it.

5:30 P.M. These three "families" (if Mr. Unknown qualifies as a family) comprise the motley group that is the subject of tonight's observation. All that is left to do is sit back and watch it happen, in the usual 15 minute increments. Perhaps I should take notes.

15 minutes into Mass: Charlie and wife have proceeded to immerse themselves in the staunch, Catholic world of yesteryear that they know and love. Mrs. Charlie's gaze lowers to see the vet's finger outstretched, at the ready to tap her hand. Although she believes that speaking aloud on such holy ground is pure irreverence, gestures are just fine. So she allows this mini-conversation to slide. She shrugs subtly. Charlie motions at the guest priest, a mild-mannered man I have come to know as a reserved Pakistani missionary.

"Bad enough they don' even say it in Latin 'nymore. Now we can't even have it in plain ol' English!" Charlie quietly huffs, noting the priest's thick accent. Blasphemous spoken word has ensued.

"That's my Charlie," Mrs. Charlie reluctantly whispers through clenched teeth. Yet she gives his hand a quick squeeze, as if to say, "I still love you, even though you'll never change, you stubborn oaf." And their attention is turned once more to the homily.

30 minutes into Mass: Mr. Unknown in the second-to-last row. Would you look at him? The local male "youth group" awkwardly seated near him regards his closed eyes with a holy reverence. ("Is he talking to God?" one asks) I know better. I suppose those vulnerable young men also believed that it simply must have been a conversion experience when Mr. Unknown began spontaneously emitting a polytonal version of the Hallelujah Chorus during the Gospel reading. What a fitting all-in-one organizer/cellphone ring for such a devout man. Now, eyelashes fluttering, mouth agape, graying nose-hairs drifting in and out with each semi-snore, he is little more than a statue in the pew—perhaps an insult to the alabaster, saintly sculptures positioned around the perimeter of the Church.

45 minutes into Mass: Bow-girl and Peruvian cousin/nanny/general caretaker begin to stir. Scratch that. They have been stirring for 42 minutes. For the first three minutes, the almost- four year-old was in her usual state of silent...awe? Fatigue? Contemplative constipation? Yet the onslaught of Biblical "stuff" soon filled her ears like the drone of belligerent bumblebees. She wanted her animal crackers (despite the fact that the only ones her mother allowed her to consume were those of the nutritionally sound variety, aka "the gur-oss wheat ones."). She wanted Mr. Googles, the stuffed purple monkey whom she dragged everywhere by his single leg, his one remaining limb. Remarkably, unlike most of the adults present, she did not mind being in this new home for an hour or so. Just as long as she could make it her own. Her Peruvian cousin/nanny/caretaker, on the other hand, wanted nothing of the material sort. She simply wanted to understand the foreign-sounding syllables of the priest. Yet, language barriers aside, she now finally feels at peace in this place (at least *someone* does). She ponders this for some time before the little one pokes her. She wants her hair bow. Which, by some act of God, found its way to the hook on the light above the child's head. (*¡Dios mío!*)

The hour is up. Mr. Unknown, thankful to restore power to his Almighty Blueberry (or whatever those useless gadgets are called), races through the doorway with a sense of urgency that one only sees in the queue for a particularly crowded ladies room. He has fulfilled his weekly duty, and can now go forth to spread peace...and the evidence of his church-going devotion, so as not to be deemed "religiously impaired," as he was by his former girlfriend. The vet and his wife leave the same way they came—slowly and steadily. Mr. Charlie refuses to shake the priest's hand on the way out. ("Damned immigrants," I can hear him loudly remark from outside the door, "looks like they let just about 'nyone proclaim the word of God these days.") Bow-girl and her nanny are nowhere to be seen. They left ten minutes ago, right after communion. Yet, for all that can be said, the little one was the only one thoughtful enough to shift her gaze towards me on the way out. Thanks for the acknowledgment, blessed child.

Part II – December 24 (Christmas Eve), 2003, 5:30 P.M.

4:27 P.M., an hour absurdly close to the donning of night's cloak, looms with the prospect of frigid air. Mother Nature has sent her armies of snow, sleet, and hail in full force for the past week, and presently, a renegade snowflake and her pea-sized partner hailstone fly through the crack in the familiar window, stopping only when they reach the aging "patrons only" balcony pews. The stained glass, its distinctive colors once wholly apparent in the mid-afternoon sun, now appears eerily monotone (at least, from my indoor perspective), a homogenous, "dark sky" hue. Looks a lot like a crayon color, in my opinion—"regal blue cloudy sky with a hint of puce." It would be just perfect for doodling on the hymn books. With an hour and three minutes before the precious moment, the air is devoid of any sound, and rightfully so. I hold my breath—and, as expected, they begin to silently enter.

The shriveled veteran and his wife, Mr. and Mrs. Charlie, are the first—nothing new there. I have seen them every Saturday, give or take a few, since the past June 24. Apparently, something has changed...what was it, again? That's right. Mrs. Charlie mentioned something—Charlie had a heart attack two months ago. Perhaps he will have a change of heart (please, no pun intended) on this blessed eve...towards a certain, unassuming clergy member, I hope? The king clutches his scepter for dear life as he slides into the first pew, customarily reserved for the video camera–toting parents of the annual Christmas Pageant children. (I remind myself that, although technology seems to clash with this sacred setting, capturing little Louise's acting debut as the Virgin Mary is a golden opportunity, and, as such, it really is not all that sacrilegious. Besides, I would much rather see cameras than scraps of technology with fruit and berry namesakes.) Charlie glances at his watch, which, as I have heard his wife remind him all too often, stopped working three years ago.

"Beat the crowds, again! Eh, what do ya think of me now, Muriel? Wasn' I right? Wasn' I right?" Muriel—that's her name. Mrs. Charlie's gloved hand pats Mr. Charlie's knee.

"That's right, dear," she says. I detect a hint of sadness in her voice, yet perhaps I am just prone to tuning into nonexistent emotions. Charlie opens the missal to the Christmas Vigil readings, though he knows them by heart. Mrs. Charlie follows suit. They don't speak until the Mass begins, in approximately one hour.

Fast-forward to 5:06 P.M. The heavy oak door swings open with a cringe-inducing groan (I can remember the days of its youth, when creaking was out of the question), ushering in the crisp air and her snowflake entourage. As far away as I am, the wind still manages to numb my bare toes. Like an emperor entering his palace, Mr. Unknown swaggers over the threshold. Yet, wait, what is this? He has brought his ultimate prize, the ex-girlfriend, perhaps in an effort to demonstrate his true religious fervor.

"See sugar, told you so. I'm no C and E, twice-a-year Christian, that's for sure," he boasts, pulling out his Raspberry. "I even made sure that we could get here early so you would get a seat." Ex-girlfriend's makeup laden features tighten—the female signification of incredulity. "I know *that* look, and I was prepared for it!" Mr. Unknown holds his Blueberry/Raspberry/Strawberry high. "I catalogued each day I've been to Mass. Go on, see for yourself!" he prods, shoving the digital organizer in her face. Her plump lips break into a smile showing flawlessly white teeth.

"Oh, Harry!" she coos, running her manicured fingers over his bald scalp. "You aren't so morally ambiguous after all!" From her lauding, one would have assumed that he had attended Church three times a day, every day, plus a few hours of adoration thrown in for good measure. For your sake (and mine), I won't reveal the true number of Masses that I counted. Hastening to the front pews, Mr. Unknown and girlfriend (no longer an ex, as of two minutes ago, I assume) shun his usual second-to-last row. It is Christmas Eve—time to be good Christians, after all. Like synchronized skaters, they sit down, greedily grab the missals, and bow their heads in simultaneous prayer.

I silently hope that, perhaps next week, and every week after, he will change, and sit where he sits tonight. I am reminded of Dickens's *A Christmas Carol*. People can change, right?

5:24 P.M. The little one enters, six minutes early, flanked by mother and father. Her Peruvian guardian is nowhere to be seen. Nose and cheeks red with frost, she begins to whimper upon realizing that there are no more seats. Poor child. I would invite her up to the altar, if she wanted. Mother and father, wearing some assortment of inhumanely acquired furs, continue to whisper with one another. Little one, clad in so much velvet and tartan that she looks like she should be a present under the Christmas tree, breaks away from the conversation. Eyes wide, she sits down in the front, with the Christmas Pageant children. No one seems to object. Her parents tiptoe to the back of the church, safely away from the priest's gaze, where they can titter about the nearby community center's Christmas party. "She'll be just fine by herself in the house of God," they sheepishly, unconvincingly agree. I emit a silent, unnoticeable sigh. The little one contentedly swings her legs back and forth—I can already see a run starting to form at the knee in her white stockings.

Tonight, things are different. Tonight, things are the same. Tonight, Mr. Charlie will listen to the thickly accented words of the missionary priest with his usual incoherence, yet he will manage to smile, and shake the foreigner's hand on the way out. Tonight, Mrs. Charlie will tell her husband, again, just how much she loves him, despite his little quirks. Tonight, Mr. Unknown (aka Harry) and his girlfriend will pretend to immerse themselves in the Mass, all the while thinking of the glorious Caribbean vacation on which, as he informed her during the homily, they are embarking tomorrow. *At least they tried*, I like to think. Tonight, the little one will not mourn the absence of her parents, as they dream of growing tipsy on eggnog at the holiday party next door, yet she will vaguely remember her good friend from Peru. (For the record, she has become a nun in her hometown. Yes, I was surprised too when she told me—yet she always did strike me as a particularly rigid, holy woman.)

Tonight, each of these men, women, and children, of every size, shape, and color, will listen. They will reflect—some more than others, yet they all will attempt to do so. I have seen them when it is not one of the most important Christian holidays of the year, when they enter God's house clad in patchy jeans, baseball caps, and post-picnic mustard stains instead of winter finery. I have seen them when they doze off and daydream, rather than listen fervently as they do now. Yet, does it really matter? Anyone, everyone, can change. And, perhaps, some don't have to.

The Vigil has ended. The children of the Pageant are hugged and kissed, as their parents shower them with bouquets and whisper secrets of tomorrow's glistening presents. The Church empties...more quickly than usual. The little one is left alone, standing beneath me (her parents have already snuck away to the community center). She looks up.

"I wish you could have stayed," she whispers. "Why did you have to leave? Tomorrow's your birthday, 'member?" Her vocal pitch heightens considerably at the end of the sentence.

I left for your own good, I think to myself, assuming that she is speaking to me.

"Oh. That was awful nice," she replies, shuffling her burgundy, patent-leather shoes. "But I got a question."

Shoot. Fire away. I carry on in a haze, without a care.

"Do you get lonely up there? Ever? Does it hurt, bein' hung up like that all the time?" I pause. It is a long time before I can gather my thoughts. By then, the quizzical child has been whisked away into the blizzard of the century. Now that I am alone, I finally know what I want to say.

Sometimes, I answer, to no one in particular. *But not now. Things can change, right?*

Katharine Eisenberg, Age 16
Convent of the Sacred Heart
Greenwich, CT
Teacher: Mary Lee Rafferty

SO OLD SCHOOL

The girl loomed before me, lithe, tanned, highlighted and Hollister-jeaned.

"Hey," she chirped, startling me. I languished in shady solitude on a park bench, waiting for our summer writing class to begin. She cocked her head and blinked curiously at me: I knew she could tell I was of another species. I stood to face her. At just under five feet, my head barely reached her shoulder. My hair fell in exhausted ringlets halfway down my back, the same red-brown that I was born with, not even enhanced with artificial highlights. My heavy ankle-length black skirt wilted in the summer heat, as I nervously pawed at the ground with a booted foot.

"Cool, you have an iPod," she said, groping for some shred of commonality. Without warning, she grabbed for it. "Can I see what's on it?"

I gulped. She saw no Black Eyed Peas or Justin Timberlake, no Keith Urban or Sarah McLachlan. All she could find were ancient English ballads, ragtime, traditional Scottish music, Irish jigs, Nordic folk rock, audiobooks of mythology, poetry and Sarah Vowell. She stepped back, looking slightly perplexed, as if I had just spoken to her in Icelandic. She didn't know it but she had just had an encounter with the "dead."

The dead walk among you. We are the ghosts, otherworldly entities, not from the grave, but from the distant past. You might not recognize us by our appearance as we sit beside you in classrooms, offices, on the bus. If you examine us closely you might find subtle clues: an unfashionable hairstyle, old-fashioned eyewear, odd tastes in clothing, eccentric behavior, or strange reading material. Though we share your space, we seldom share your time. We are historians, writers, re-enactors, performers of traditional music or dance, fans of outdated literature, military enthusiasts, and devotees to the *History Channel*. We are the misfits that draw succor from a departed era while we painfully endure the travails and indignities inflicted by the modern era; not the mere "buff," but those so swept up and enthralled by the past that it has become an alternate reality.

You might know us better in our natural habitat. We stand in patient watch in living history museums, quietly glide through the aisles of archives, sit half-hidden by relics in antique shops or peer through the bowing shelves of musty bookstores. No one pays much attention to us, except when we are called to entertain listless children or enthusiastic tourists by carding wool, thrumming a dulcimer, clustering about a mildewed tent to fry bacon and boil coffee over a smoky fire or, engaging in mortal combat and dramatic buffoonery at a Renaissance Faire. Sometimes the contemporary hoi polloi sense our difference and lash out, labeling our kind *dork*, *nerd*, *geek* or even *goth*, but often we are left to wander alone, invisible in our self-imposed temporal exile.

I don't know if the dead have a congenital compulsion to ignore the conventions of their own age or hear some clarion call to the shrouded mists of another era. I suspect it is a latent defect that when triggered by a benign stimulus, metastasizes into an obsession with moldering things, suffocating reason and overwhelming the sensibilities. Regardless of whether it is nature or nurture that leads the victim astray, parents ignore the signs in the young at their own peril. Beware the kindergartener who refuses to part with the tricorn hat that he was asked to fashion from newspaper, the lost classmate found in a deep trance beneath the dinosaur skeleton. Be alert for strange imaginative stories, an obsession with comic books or biographies or abnormal tastes in clothing and music; though I fear that your best efforts to nip the disease in the bud will be in vain. It might be more kind and beneficial to the contemporary social order to consider a stake through the heart.

My own demise began when I was eight. I was casually frolicking in the wonderland of my beloved public library when I picked up a book about Queen Victoria's wedding to Prince Albert and her notoriously isolated widowhood, accidentally releasing my nascent inner-Victorian. I suspect that I already had a genetic predisposition for my ailment.

My grandmother was born into a wealthy Philadelphia family in a fine house on the Main Line with servants and a chauffeur. Photos portray my relatives in silk dresses, playing croquet on their expansive lawns. In an effort to build my good character, my grandmother claimed that she was never affluent as a child, insisting that her father would not even buy her a pony. I later found out this was a lie—she had two ponies!

The Great Depression and the war scattered my ancestors, and the estate was replaced with a shopping mall. By the time my mother's family moved into their modest ranch house on Cobblestone Drive in the suburbs, only the elegant family crypt in a dreary Philadelphia cemetery stood as proof of their legacy of power and privilege. In her retirement, my grandmother took up residence in an imitation Vanderbilt mansion for the elderly that sadly re-created her halcyon days. The sprawling rooms were elegantly decorated with ornate gold molding and wallpaper with brocade and grandiose fleur-de-lis patterns. A grand staircase led to a parquet ballroom and ostentatious dining rooms, including one called the "Hunt Club", adorned with bugles and paintings of foxhunts. In the tearoom, an authentic Edwardian gown hung in a glass case. I was so smitten that my grandmother physically pulled me from these rooms and scolded me for making a public spectacle of myself with my gawking. Safely sequestered in her apartment, I quietly perched on her sofa in my requisite frilly dress as she taught me to arrange her antique silverware and deport myself like a proper lady.

I recall that these visits were never especially fun, so my newly awakened interest in the stifling Victorian world was surprising. Things became even stranger when I discovered that I had been possessed by an old woman with a rather stuffy British accent who, without invitation, assumed the role of life coach. Like my grandmother, she began to sniff out and smother the thoughts and behaviors that she felt were, in her words, *scandalous*. I was urged to be repulsed by cars, planes, pants and hormonal birth control; forbidden to swear (aloud); and encouraged to champion traditional gender roles. Without warning, I found myself frowning at my contemporaries' immodest attire, provocative and uncouth behavior, and vile tastes in entertainment.

My prim advisor's ideals clashed with my own values, beliefs and upbringing. I was born to liberal parents and raised in an unconventional environment with a working mom and a pioneering stay-at-home dad. I was the kid who went to kindergarten with mismatched braids and thrown-together outfits; the one who once broke my mother's guilt-ridden heart when I proudly told her that Dad had taken me to the lake to see "the daddy ducks and their babies." I was raised to pursue a career—yet as my inner Victorian emerged, I secretly pined for the days when a woman's proper role was as the guardian of the hearth, helpmate and spiritual uplifter. I was raised to love and respect animals, yet I was called by the romance of the hunt—moved by the rustic images of dead stags strewn about the lawn and yapping hounds clustered in the parlor. I abhor materialism, elitism, and bigotry; I champion equality and tolerance but am helplessly beguiled by the elegant country estates, the pursuits of the English aristocracy. I have a strange fascination for the age of colonialism. Watching the movie *Gandhi* or reading Irish and Scottish history leaves me reeling with mixed emotions.

The most profound impact came in the realm of taste. I suddenly craved romantic literature, poetry, and art. I devoured the works of Tennyson, Burns, Keats, Shelley, Ruskin, and Sir Walter Scott. I first read traditional English ballads then began to load ballads, folk songs, and folk music by native performers and revivalists on my iPod. I leisurely ambled through the painted greenwoods and meadows of the Pre-Raphaelites and John Waterhouse, studied Anglo-Saxon history, archaeology and folklore of every era, and greedily consumed every popular and scholarly book and article I could find about Victoria and her milieu.

I can't explain why I began to identify with Her Majesty. I suspect that not many of today's *Fergie* fans, with a slightly different idea about the meaning of *London Bridge*, would adopt Queen Victoria—the dour black-draped widow whose very name is synonymous with prudery and repression—as a role model. It shocks and frightens me that I see so much of myself in Victoria. I even resemble her—she was my height, four-eleven, had the same color hair, and was left-handed. I console myself with the knowledge that the old queen was misunderstood and her image was unjustly distorted by her many enemies. She was far less conservative than the era in which she lived. She shared my love of animals and was responsible for enacting the animal cruelty laws in Britain. She had a good sense of humor and loved to dance and listen to the old ballads. Victoria appreciated romantic art and literature and was especially fond of the funloving Scottish Highlanders and their rugged homeland.

I also confess that I am strangely enamored of her beloved husband, Prince Albert, the 19th-century version of Al Gore. Today's lads suffer in comparison. It's hard to find a boyfriend when your ideal man is a 19th-century German prince, though I'm willing to compromise—the pale guy at the pizza parlor does sort of resemble an 18th-century "Jack Tar" sailor…I wonder how he'd look with a tarred pigtail, a striped Guernsey, and bell-bottomed trousers? If the prom isn't Regency-themed and I can't convince Lord Byron to go with me, the pizza boy just might have to do.

My best friend since first grade has become my sextant to measure how far I've drifted from the mainstream. Once I would have sworn she was numbered with the dead as she patiently took part in my elaborate Victorian fantasies, even though an earlier age called to her. She made me watch the musical *1776* over and over and claimed to have a crush on Thomas Jefferson, once distastefully uttering, "I want to dig him up and marry him."

When she entered middle school, she had a Lazarus moment and temporarily joined the "living." The pimpin' quarterback, the class clown and the rebel suddenly held more allure than the desiccated powder-wigged dandies of her prepubescent fantasies. But, alas, the perceptions of youth are keen and when they caught the scent of must and decay that still clung to her, she retreated to the comfort of the tomb. This time her tastes were so repellent that even I recoiled in horror as she became enthralled by the *Brat Pack*, *New Kids on the Block* and other relics of the Reagan years. She is in love with Jonathan Knight of N.K.O.T.B.—now a forty-something real estate developer—and plans to name her first child Tiffany after another '80s icon. While I am very accepting of the weird habits of the dead, my internal queen is not amused and finds my old friend's new interests especially scandalous.

America is a bleak realm for the dead. The country was founded as a haven for those seeking a fresh start and became independent by throwing off the bonds of a land where tradition is revered and cherished. We prize innovation and invention and are enticed by shiny fads and fleeting fashion. Most Americans agree with Henry Ford, the man who did so much to destroy our rural heritage, that "history is more or less bunk." Tradition is stifling, gum in the wheels of progress: uncool, old school. We tear down old buildings, ignore or ridicule our rich musical traditions (until foreigners make money with them) and ignore the lessons of the past until we've repeated the folly.

By chance, or by choice, the dead do care about the past and our unpopular interests set us apart. We are in many ways like minorities; some of us hide our differences in the closet and "pass," pretending to enjoy the things of this world; some live in self-imposed isolation; and many band together with like-minded people in clubs, regiments or societies or participate in events like fairs, festivals and re-enactments to bring to life, preserve and celebrate their esoteric interests. I often tread this age feeling alone and unappreciated, but when I meet a fellow time traveler it is a rare and special gift.

That day at writing camp, just a few minutes after my iPod collection was rudely examined and dismissed as "so old school," another classmate stopped to chat. She had a slightly elfin look and seemed to have stepped out of a painting by Dante Gabriel Rossetti. She was forthright, kind, confident, and very different from the other students in the class. That day we talked about our strange interests for nearly four hours—French chivalry, the Byzantine Empire, the Roman emperor Constantine. I nearly fainted from surprise and delight when she said that the person she would most like to invite to dinner was Vercingetorix, the man who led the Gaulish rebellion against the Romans. We even had the same Pre-Raphaelite painting on our computer desktops.

I hope that college will be different, that I will find others like me hidden among the bleak stacks in the library, far from the roar of the football stadium, or reading Rimbaud in the lounge while roommates frolic at the frat party. If not, I will try to fit in and chat idly about TV, hot guys, or the weird professor. I will grit my teeth and get my driver's license. I will master my fear of flying and travel to England and Scotland in hopes of finding a more hospitable clime, where the dead are very alive and where I can at last be unapologetically old school.

Elizabeth Motich, Age 17
Motich Home School
Dillsburg, PA
Teacher: Mark Motich

BOUNCING BACK:
LONGTIME FRENCH TEACHER BRINGS IRON WILL TO THIRD BOUT WITH CANCER

As she awakens, she carefully removes the surgical cap from her head and peers inside the lining to check the day's contents. It's a fairly good day, so the cap has only captured a few locks of her crimson-brown hair.

She rolls out of bed and downs a few pills. As she catches a glimpse of herself in the mirror, she can't help but notice her hairless face—no eyelashes, no eyebrows, and no makeup to conceal the nakedness, a direct result of intensive chemotherapy treatments.

French teacher Ina Rubin didn't lose as much of her hair to chemo the first time around. When she was diagnosed with Hodgkin's Lymphoma just after Memorial Day ten years ago, she was ready to fight back—and she did. Come the next Memorial Day, though, Rubin was out of remission and facing Hodgkin's once again, this time in need of a more aggressive treatment. After a summer of treatments, a bone marrow transplant, and a year off from teaching, she was in the clear.

So when she strolled into her oncologist's office this past August for her annual check-up with nine cancer-free years cushioning her confidence, Rubin didn't think she had too much to worry about. After a routine PET scan, she left for a weekend away with friends. Her asthma acted up a little, but she blamed the intense heat wave.

When she got an unexpected call from her oncologist saying that she would need to come in the next day, Rubin knew something wasn't right. Before the doctor said more, Rubin took out her calendar and began planning when she could schedule treatments that wouldn't interrupt the coming school year, her 26th at South. She knew that she had cancer again.

The next day, Rubin met with a thoracic surgeon and her oncologist. The surgeon would perform a tissue biopsy on Monday.

After the biopsy, as she was rolled towards the recovery room, her mind still fogged by anesthetics, the surgeon confirmed the presence of a malignancy. After nine cancer-free years, she had developed a new, independent cancer.

"It was just 'here we go again,'" she said.

Since Rubin had already been through two bouts with cancer, she knew the routine. When she was diagnosed with stage four Hodgkin's ten years ago, she went through an initial period of denial but managed to accept the diagnosis. She took one year off teaching and returned to South part time for two years, until she recovered and resumed her full-time job. This time, there wasn't that same period of denial. She accepted the diagnosis and braced herself to fight an aggressive yet treatable cancer.

"Before, the whole time I'd just thought 'this can't be so' and this time I didn't have those questions anymore because I knew it could be so," she said. "It was so. And that was all there was to it. I just do what I have to do."

Without the "why me" questions pinning her down, Rubin prepared herself for intensive rounds of chemotherapy treatments, which would start immediately.

Rubin was both shocked and devastated, though, when she learned that the circumstances were a little different than she had anticipated. When her oncologist of ten years told Rubin that she wouldn't be able to go back to school to teach this September, her world came crashing down.

"She said to me 'Look, you can't work and do this. You have to be out one day a week for your treatment. You don't know how your body is going to respond. And you can't be explaining to kids that this is what you're going through, and then you're out one day. Plus you can't be exposed to kids like that.' She was very clear that I wasn't going anywhere."

As Rubin left the hospital room, her oncologist gave her "a great big bear hug," but the thought of not going back to school in September was unsettling.

Her oncologist said Rubin would need at least half the school year to recover, and as of now, she is looking forward to finishing chemo in the third week in January and returning for the start of the third term.

The treatments, Rubin says, are going well, and everything is moving forward as planned. Unlike her second encounter with cancer, that required a bone marrow transplant, radiation, and chemotherapy, she is currently only receiving weekly rounds of chemo.

While Rubin tries to take everything as it comes, her friend Nancy Bloom, a South special education teacher of 20 years, had a difficult time handling Rubin's diagnosis, especially after Rubin had been in complete remission for so long. When Bloom came back from Africa this summer and Wheeler housemaster Kathy Daviau told her that Rubin had cancer again, Bloom "flipped out."

"I felt so angry thinking she was so sick again," Bloom said. "I tried to be really strong for her, but I couldn't."

As tears of frustration and anger rolled down Bloom's face, she said Rubin actually ended up comforting her.

Bloom considers herself a very spiritual person, but at the same time, she can't help but ask herself how anyone could deserve to go through what her friend is enduring. Nonetheless, Bloom admires Rubin's level-headed approach.

"She has such an invincible spirit. She said she was going to beat it," Bloom said.

And still, Rubin strives to maintain that same spirit and fighting mentality, as well as a sense of humor. To answer the "why me" question, Rubin often jokes that she's a perfect target for cancer because she does so well with chemo.

"Evidently, chemo really likes my body," she said. "I'm thinking that I got this so somebody else didn't have to go through it. They just said, 'Look, try out those drugs on Ina Rubin because, you know, her body really likes chemo.'"

The battle hasn't all been smooth sailing, though.

While drawing in her eyebrows isn't very fun and the constant fatigue is an inconvenience, the worst side effects by far are the "gastric disturbances," especially since before she got sick she "had a stomach made of iron and was never sick a day in [her] life."

Still, the hardest part of the ordeal is not being able to do what she loves: teaching French to kids.

"At South, it's French everyday, and I'm living the love of my life," she said. "This isn't like being on one long vacation. It put a stop on my life this time around. It takes control of your life."

Rubin is on medical leave and is grateful to be a part of the accommodating school system, but it's not just the health coverage that makes her so glad to be a part of the South community.

On the Thursday in August when she began chemo, the door to her hospital room opened and in walked "the three musketeers," world language teachers and longtime colleagues Becky Block, Lise Elkind, and Marla Wiener.

Fellow teachers drive her to and from treatments, and over the years her colleagues have also cooked for her, helped her move to a new apartment, and even stayed overnight "babysitting" her after some of the more trying rounds of treatment.

Her colleagues and her sisters have been her support throughout this, she says through the tears.

"It overwhelms me because they aren't just colleagues. They're friends."

Even with such a solid support system, though, cancer has taken its toll on Rubin.

When she thinks back to the last time she went a day without hearing the word 'cancer,' she laughs.

"It's been a while. A long while.

"It can't be off your mind entirely when you're living it, but at the same time, you have to stop dwelling," she said.

For now, Rubin is eagerly anticipating her return to South, her home away from home for the last 25 years.

The germs that she will face when she returns to school in the heart of cold season make her a slightly nervous, though, since the chemo has significantly weakened her immune system. The answer to avoiding all the sicknesses? A little Purell and a lot of luck, she says.

She remembers returning to school nine years ago and how often she would get sick.

"That first year back was basically one long respiratory infection," she said. "The only times I was well were December vacation and April vacation!"

Although she was surprised that she got cancer again, she always knew the risk existed. With Hodgkin's, all of the treatments and therapies make patients susceptible to an entire list of new cancers, so even when she thought she was well, the idea of cancer returning was always in the back of her mind.

For now, she's doing her best to beat cancer once again, and she wants students to know that cancer doesn't rule her life entirely. Even when she was diagnosed this summer, Rubin immediately checked her calendar to make sure that she'd still be able attend the Eric Clapton concert she had wanted to see for months.

"You can't be scared of life. Okay, yeah, it's not fun, but at least I can be grateful that I'm not a parent having to watch my child go through this," Rubin said.

Six months ago, if she had the chance to make one wish, she says she might have wished to see a Clapton concert or to go back to France a few more times. Now, though, her wish would change.

"If I had one wish in life, right at this moment, I would say to beat this thing—get some more years out of it. I mean, I really feel like the last ten were pretty much a gift. I got those, but I hope to get another ten anyway," she said.

"After all, I haven't taken my last trip to France yet."

Kaitlin Sanders, Age 17
Newton South High School
Newton Centre, MA
Teacher: Brian Baron

THE WITNESS

Discovered last Tuesday,
the "dirty" book I stuffed
under my mattress as a kid.
The Human Body
with the red back and binding that were too much,
hissing the word like my mother
every night after 5:00 Mass: *Sin Sin Sin.*
It was a serious thing that held some weight
when pressed against a bare hungry stomach.
But back then, to my aggravation, it taught me nothing.

School had been too thorough,
and whatever I'd thought I'd find
when I stole the thing from my brother's shelf
was not there after all.
No new outrageous facts of life.
No surprises except that there were none.
I shoved the thing away one night and forgot it,
disappointed or bored
with the mundaneness of life,
and there it remained for years.

And, though trite, I do wonder what it thought,
lying there, thing of wisdom that it was,
listening to the rhythms of a real body:
my 13-year-old thighs toning themselves
endlessly with exercises I had learned
in other books and magazines,
and not forgotten so easily,
sick for the slight physique I knew
would bring me something like enlightenment
which did not need to be explained.

Silent witness to everything, including the year
my brother moved out to live with our father
and for the first time it was just my mother and me
and the twenty-six pound mutt
that ate more than the two of us put together—
the year she quit religion and became sure someone
had planted taps in the TV and phones and computer
that she eventually took to pieces
but found nothing. How was she to know
it was the book listening all along?

In any case, now that it's well out of hiding,
it's shame, more than anything, that gets me—
never escaping old sin. So that
some days I want to bury my book where I'll never
have to see the thing again. Because who can say,
really? Any day now, that cover could easily
open the big fat mouth it's been hiding
and tell the other books, the furniture or worse,
observations about human paranoia,
perversion, obsession:

A woman, triumphant, carefully pulling the last green chip
from the back of a keypad of the security system
she bought to replace God, and saying Aha!
Or a girl shoving a popcorn bowl of vomit
under her bed and feigning sleep
until the life is low enough in the house
to dispose of her evidence properly;
tracing each rib with the anticipation
of someone still uncertain
of what it is they're looking for.

MENU PLANNING

At thirty-five hundred dollars a week and roughly the size of my dorm room, it is a thoroughly unimpressive place. A table sits exactly in the center of the space with six chairs spread out around it—there's a rocking chair, an armchair, one wooden with a straight back, one metal with cushions, one computer chair that squeaks when it turns, and a tall, red, plastic one without any arms. Two of the walls have observation windows that look out to the hallway. Because the room is on the main corridor, not in the shelter of the in-patient ward, the windows are covered to protect our confidentiality. A previous group has spread craft paper over the windows and decorated it with motivational quotes and practical bits of advice for anyone in partial hospitalization. It's become one part of the discharge tradition to add your piece of departing wisdom, *Today I choose to love these obscene freckles; Avoid bad habits!; Beware the pretzels, they reproduce like jack rabbits.*

There are cabinets on the two windowless walls filled with piles of convenient foods: small boxes of cereal, Nutri-Grain Bars, oatmeal, Pop Tarts, fruit snack race cars, little cups of peanut butter, Milky Ways, jam, frosted animal crackers, and the last of the twenty-count box of Paydays. Everything is in single-serving sizes, nutrition facts printed on the sides. There are four drawers: one full of individually wrapped plastic forks, spoons and knives that can't cut; a drawer of mayonnaise, mustard, honey mustard, and ketchup packets; a drawer of dressings; a drawer of cream cheese and salt and maple syrup. There is a microwave with a bowl of black bananas and apples sitting on top of it. In the corner there is a refrigerator stocked like the cupboards with milk boxes and juice boxes and yogurt and cans of vanilla Ensure, a freezer piled from one wall to the other to the ceiling with dozens of Styrofoam cups of ice cream, untouched Mighty Shakes (at least a year old) and exactly one sherbet cup, resembling a tub of Play-Doh.

On the walls themselves are charts of everything a person needs in life. Love, passion, self-respect, family, money, work, sex, education, personal possessions and other luxuries are not included. The sane world boils down to the same inarguable truth: one woman, three fruits, two vegetables, two milks, five meats, six starches, five fats, to repeat every twenty-four hours, despite the stress of work or men or taking care of cats.

Fruit:

The requirements of a fruit are as follows: one serving contains sixty calories and fifteen grams of carbohydrates.

An hour outside of the Twin Cities, farm country starts. While you're still very young, you and your mother pick berries in the summer, apples in the fall. You don't like the apples: they're small and sour and difficult to eat; the skin sticks in your teeth and irritates you to the point of tears; you get mad because you can never lift the full pretty barrels. But the berries are different. You eat them in great handfuls, cover the bottom of your basket and empty it again, fill and empty, fill and empty, fill and spill the berries all over the ground, sit down where you are and eat each one out of the dirt, until your belly bulges under your brother's T-shirt.

For your seventh birthday, during apple season, your mother brings home a brown tabby kitten from the orchard with a beautiful tan "M" on his forehead. She can't stand to have him fixed. "He's a farm cat," she says. "So you'll have to teach him all of your city kid tricks."

Vegetables:

One serving of vegetables contains twenty-five calories.

You hide food under your bed long before anyone starts calling it a disorder. One night your family is eating dinner on the back porch. You get a turkey burger and cooked carrots and spinach; you eat the burger and don't want to ruin the rest of the meal with the bad parts, but also hate to insult anyone's cooking. So, you attempt to feed carrots to the dog when no one is looking.

"She sure is hopeful tonight," says your brother, scratching the dog's ears while he takes another bite.

"I was just thinking that," says your mother, mid-chew.

"Uh-huh," you say. "She misses Minoux."

"Where is that cat?" They both ask, peering around the backyard.

"Beats me," you say, artfully discarding the last of your carrots into a napkin under the table.

Then: "Where's Dad?" asks your brother. A long pause.

"With his girlfriend," says your mom.

He says, "You're lying."

She says, "She's young."

But from below the porch, a painful feline moan takes the air space. Your brother looks at your mother. Your mother looks at her plate, the half-eaten burger.

"Hey, look what I ate!" you say, as the cat's crying grows louder.

Meat:

Meat contains seven grams of protein and seventy-five calories.

Maybe you should know that something is amiss when your father picks you and your brother up from school on time for the very first time since your parents' separation. Because instead of bringing you home, he takes you to the hospital where you were born to see your mother, tubed and tied to a mechanical bed. She tells you she just forgot how much medicine she had taken, and you have no reason not to trust her. You smile, point to her ID bracelet and say, "Dad, I want one like she's got there!" but cry when he refuses you, hurt that not even he seems to gather the necessity of such a matter.

The next day, your teacher tells you to eat lunch with her. She asks what your favorite subject is, *math*, if you have any pets, *one dog and my cat*. Soon the conversation dies away and she admits what she really wants is to say that she's heard what happened, that it must hurt to have a mother who cannot stand to live *even for her children*. Suddenly, the turkey sandwich you're eating doesn't taste right. You can't take another bite of it, say you're sick, and beeline to the bathroom. As your stomach lurches toward your throat she knocks and says, "Yoo-hoo, are you okay?"

"I'm fine," you say. "I have the flu. Please go away."

Milk:

One serving of milk contains ninety calories and thirty percent daily calcium.

There's a surprise waiting after your mother picks you up from school. When you walk into the kitchen a fat Himalayan lunges at you from the top of a wooden stool. It purrs and rubs its fur against your shins. "What's that?" you ask, startled. "Whose cat is that?"

"Her name's Sharma," says your mother, with an odd, eager smile. "Her owner's on a trip, so she'll be staying here a while."

Something about Sharma doesn't seem right. She keeps you up all night rubbing against you under the covers. If you ignore her she starts moaning, and moans for hours. In the morning, she only leaves you long enough to eat. As far as you can tell, she never sleeps.

After a week, the cat is driving your mother insane. She complains on the phone to her cat-owner friend, but there's no end to her torment. Finally at her wit's end, she picks up Sharma and throws her in the basement.

The problem is, this is where Minoux, your cat, lives. Sometimes he doesn't leave for days, driven crazy by infections from fights or early old age—you can't say. You live with your father except for the few hours after school and don't see Minoux often. But you know there's no good in sending Sharma his way, so you follow her downstairs. You hear your mother lock you in, and there, across the room, Minoux sits staring at you intruders. He's uglier than you remember, all bone, patches of dark raw skin showing where pieces of him have been bitten off.

Sharma gets low on the ground and starts to growl. Soon Minoux is mimicking the sound. You're afraid Sharma might finish him. Something must be done: you run upstairs and pound on the door until your mother lets you out, grab the milk and a bowl from the kitchen, then sprint back down, pour the milk until the dish is half-full, and set it on the floor in front of Sharma. Pig of a cat, she goes for that. You pick up the bowl and walk slowly back upstairs with it, Sharma following the milk closely.

Later that day, your mother announces that Sharma is nothing short of evil and should be put to sleep. She's taking her to the animal shelter. Sitting still in the basement, watching Minoux's breathing slow, you let her go.

Starch:

A starch contains eighty calories and fifteen grams of carbohydrates.

Your dad picks you and your brother up from your mom's house on a Wednesday in October. The month is almost over, cold moving in just in time to ruin Halloween. But you just turned twelve on the tenth, and try to act older, so you say there are better things to do than get fat on all that candy, anyway.

You sit in the back of your car picking at a bag of candy someone gave you at school. Your father gets in the front seat, turns the key, and puts both hands on the wheel. "How would you both feel," he asks, as you put down the bag and curl both arms around your gut, "about moving to Connecticut?"

You say, "What?"

Your brother says, "Why?"

At first you say you'd like the change, but when it sets in, you say that you'd rather die.

You leave first day of Christmas break. You cry, and straight through moving day, you beg to stay, you don't tell a soul you're moving. Your mother doesn't take your leaving well. She slips back into sickness like a leaf into a water well, snaking around the house to listen to your phone calls, convinced some days when you get home from a walk that you've been somewhere with older men, whom you see regularly. The accusations get to be too much and soon you and she stop talking.

So, standing in front of her house, about to head out east, you pick up Minoux and give all your attention to him, gladly ignoring your mother standing behind you, looking old and angry, cold and gray, and thin.

Fat:

One fat contains forty-five calories and five grams of fat.

So happy to be home again, you tell your dad that you've decided not to go back east with him. You're old enough to deal with the repercussions of your actions and your mind is made up. You're moving back to Minnesota to live with your mother to finish eighth grade. Minoux's as good as dead, some injury in his ear smelling like road kill, more black now than red. The last week of June, your mother schedules an appointment with the vet. Meanwhile, you try to get in touch with teachers from your old school to see if you can visit and talk about enrollment for the fall. But your computer's been collecting dust since the year your mother busted all the hardware, certain she'd found a hidden camera there, and you can't get it to work at all.

Luckily, you know a technology wiz from where your father used to work. He's an engineer from India taking classes for his America-recognized bachelor's degree. You've known him forever, and when you explain the situation, he's happy to let you come to work with him and use his computer. He insists on treating you to lunch. The college cafeteria staff think it's cute to see a little girl for once, and bake you special fries especially, the shape of smiley faces. You try to eat them daintily, so take most of them to go.

There's a Hindu elephant on the dashboard of his car. You can't help but think of it later when he won't let you leave his apartment. So much strength. So many arms.

Later, in your kitchen, you stand with the box of French fries in your hand. Not knowing what else you're meant to do, you open it and see ten sick brown faces smiling up at you.

And then, like a sin, your mother creeps in. "We had to put Minoux to sleep. There were maggots in his ear and the infection was too deep. He never would have gotten better. So, what do you want to eat for dinner?"

What are you supposed to say? You close the box and throw what's left away.

In that room where I spend three weeks counting carbohydrates and conjugating French verbs for hospital school, there is barely room to stand at my stoning ceremony. The head nurse takes a green rock from a bag and passes it between her hands. She tells us all about my first day, my stoic façade at intake, the strange combination of ice cream and fruit that I ate three times a day. She does not say how I shook like I had frostbite when the technician stuck the cups on me for my EKG, startled by my own bare chest. The nurse passes the rock to Dr. Levia, who draws more blood than the Red Cross, joking how I fought like hell to get out, mimicking me leaning over my blood work beaming, "Isn't my potassium good? Aren't I doing well?" because it would reassure them in a way I could not.

The others have comparatively less to say. Fellow patients hold the rock like a precious gem, say what a good job I've done, wish me luck, and pass it on, wishing it was meant for them.

Along the far wall, our menus are pinned up along a thin cork strip, each one planned like a budget. I want to say that the numbers still trip me up, that nothing is ever so precise, so nice and neat. That milk is more than milk, and meat is never just meat. I want to shout that there must be more than this constant filling and filtering out of patients and nutrients and thoughts, that some things just stick. I want to tell them that they're all sick themselves if they can't get it.

But the desire fades as easily as it came. And when everyone's been heard and the stone comes to me, I don't say a word. I copy a poem on the observation window, Muchado's "The Wind, One Brilliant Day," open the pouch on my backpack, and tuck the stone and the measures and the menus away.

SHARPENING

The truth is that
I don't get much rest.
At 3 A.M., my mother wakes me,
standing over my desk
pressing a pencil
into an electric sharpener.
She lets it grind five seconds
then pulls the pencil out,
examines the tip of the lead
like a syringe then
sticks the pencil in again,
somehow unsatisfied.

Unable to fall back asleep
or bring myself to close my eyes,
I watch her do this for an hour,
grind and check and
grind again until the pencil
is nothing, a stump,
a cigarette butt leaving indents
in her fingers from how tightly
she's been holding it. Then,
she is taking another
off the desk and starting this
old process over again.

Of course I will have dreamed
it all tomorrow,
my mother simply worked
late into the night.
And because of this,
I won't need to ask her
why she won't leave bed,
just set the glass of water down
beside her and close the door.
Nothing need be said about
the fifty pink erasers scattered like
empty bottles on the bedroom floor.

Anne Katherine Reece, Age 18
Interlochen Arts Academy
Interlochen, MI
Teachers: Michael Delp, Anne Marie Oomen

OBITUARY FOR AN *A*

Following a valiant battle with procrastination and neglect, Jack's A passed away over the weekend while Jack was busy playing Civilization IV.

Although his later years were marked by failing health and decreased strength, many will remember A for the bright blooming grade he once was, full of ambition and hope for the future. Jack's mother remembers the day Jack and A first came home together in Jack's kindergarten year—how in those days A's red ink was almost too bright to look at.

A was so vivacious, many thought he would live forever. But those who were close to A saw his health in heavy decline. He became reclusive, and in the last few months was rarely seen in public. Dignified to the end, A hid his rocky relationship to Minus as long as possible. Some say Minus drained A of his vitality; others say she slowed his decline. In the end, they were rarely seen apart.

A is survived by Jack's B, Jack's C, Pass and Exempt, and other grieving friends and family. A memorial service will be held when the report card arrives. Jack will be observing his grief from the confines of his house for weeks to come. Friends and acquaintances will not be allowed to call.

Jack Anderson, Age 13
Meridian School
Provo, UT
Teacher: Matthew Kennington

UNDERGROUND

Marguerite Johnson had every right to be there. The guard looked down at her papers, then back at her. The young woman ducked her head and waited. She had every right to be at the corner of Fifth and Browning, in the gateway to the Roughshod Sector: every right, but no reason.

"Shouldn't you be back at your dormitory, Miss Johnson?" he asked, flipping through her papers once again. They were all in order, having been signed and updated that afternoon in the factory where she worked. She was a metal worker, specializing in the inner workings of washing machines.

"I am returning from my Education," Marguerite said. Her dark brown hair needed to be cut back. Without the aid of a headband and a few motley rubber bands, it would be falling into her eyes. Dangerous, for a metalworker. He made a note on her papers.

"The Education facility is in the Industrial sector," said the guard. It had been placed there to spare young people such as herself a long walk on their way to and from their daily hours of compulsory Education.

Marguerite ducked her head. "This is my free time," she said. Her tone was deferential, her shoulders tugged inward as though to protect her core.

"Just so, just so," said the guard. "It's a rough sector, Miss Johnson."

"There are enough guards about to keep me safe," she said. He didn't like it, but there was nothing illegal about it. Frowning faintly, he added a second note to her papers. Her boss at the factory would see it tomorrow morning, and perhaps have a talk with her regarding a more efficient use of her time.

"Be careful, Miss Johnson," he said, handing them back to her. "And keep your curfew in mind."

She tucked them into her shoulder bag. "Thank you, sir," she said, and, without raising her face, walked through the gateway and into the sector.

He shook his head—he didn't like it. The Roughshod Sector had its uses, of course. The street laborers needed a place to release their frustrations so that they wouldn't spill into the other sectors. But when anyone could enter…he shook his head. The lack of control was troubling.

Fin was waiting for Marguerite by the back door of the gaming hall. He gave her a faint nod of the head and let them both in; as the door clicked shut behind them, he said, "You're late."

"I know." She ran her trembling hands through her short, dark hair. "The guard wasn't happy with letting me through."

"Did he hurt you?"

"Of course not, Fin. This is a city, not the crossroads."

"Come on, then." He led her down the hall. Marguerite squinted; the light was uncomfortably bright after the smoky dimness of the Roughshod Sector.

"He marked my papers," she said.

"We can make you new ones."

"Fin—" She stopped, and when he continued to walk, spoke to his back. "I don't want to do this here."

"Where else, then?"

"It's the first place they'll look for us," she said. "It's fine for you, you live here, but I can't keep coming in, and I can't—"

"Marguerite, this is the city," Fin said, finally stopping. "They won't notice one more girl walking in and out."

"But they will. You didn't grow up here, Fin—if I had…if a guardsman saw me with a leaf in my hair, growing up, I'd have a teacher lecturing me about climbing trees the next day. They keep records, Fin, records like you wouldn't believe—"

"Do you want to stop this?"

"I can't stop and you know it."

"Then come on."

"Fin, just because I don't want to do it this way doesn't mean I don't want to do it at all. We're not all so black and white as you."

"Marguerite." She looked up at him, small chin raised. He took her hand and pulled her along. She followed, reluctantly. "They won't catch us."

"They'd better not," she said.

They walked in silence for a few moments, then Fin said, "I found a new audience for you."

"New?" Marguerite said.

"Most have never seen this before. Never heard of it."

"And they all check out?" she asked.

"They're fine."

"But do they check out?"

"They check out."

She nodded, relieved. He stopped before a door, opened it, and walked away, releasing her hand. Marguerite looked at the small tin heart he had pressed into her palm and, smiling to herself, walked into the room.

The lighting was dimmer than that of the hall. A dozen faces looked up at her from the gloom; old, young, street laborers and factory workers and thinkers alike. She moved to the stool in the center of the room and sat. Her gift rose up inside of her, keen edged and forbidden.

She opened her mouth and said, "Once upon a time…"

Alyssa Fowers, Age 15
Mast Academy
Miami, FL
Teacher: Karen Sutton

THE LAST REVOLUTION

United States of America, 2006

I remember very clearly a strange afternoon when I discovered the pins. They had lain, forgotten, in a bottom drawer of my mother's dresser: twenty shiny, red and gold pieces pinned neatly onto a cotton handkerchief with roses embroidered in maroon. They were almost all identical, some square, some oval, some with a strange man's face on them, others with Chinese characters etched carefully into their polished surfaces. I lifted a pretty gold one from the others and pinned it to the collar of my shirt. My mother came in a moment later, and as I spun around in surprise I saw something unfamiliar flitting across her face, darkening the circles under her eyes and bringing the wrinkles around her mouth into sharp definition.

"Where did you get that?" she said, after a pause. I pointed wordlessly to the drawer, and she moved slowly over to me, ran her thumb over the gold pin, which was sparking faintly in the afternoon light. "Do you want it?" she asked me. The pin sent lightning streaks of brilliant gold over the walls.

"Can I have it?" I felt very small, very lost.

She sighed. "I would rather you didn't." Another silence. "Maybe when you are older." She gently twisted the fastening on the back of the pin and pulled it away, resetting it in the cotton. But she didn't put them back in the drawer, and I knew I would never look at them again.

Growing up, I loved to listen to my mother's stories of her childhood; she was one of the most spirited and mischievous children I had ever heard of, and though she got herself into trouble more times than she could count, she had the kindest heart, and everyone loved her. She had been the favorite before she was even born. While my grandma was pregnant with her third child, my grandpa, one of the most renowned and respected architects in China, had been called away to oversee the construction of a large new airport in a nearby city. "Send me a telegram if it's a girl," he told my grandma before he left. "If it's a boy, send me a letter." When the telegram arrived my grandpa was so ecstatic that he named the airport after her, Chang Lin, his little princess.

My mother grew up in Fuzhou, China. Whenever I thought of her childhood I thought of humid summer days thick with heat, the constant humming of cicadas, the wide, endless arc of fresh sky, white clouds like soft brushstrokes on rice paper. I thought of Japanese beetles in a porcelain jar, of a fortress of banana-tree leaves, of a tiny accordion wheezing softly in the distance. When she mentioned a new silk jacket her brother had bought her with his own money I did not think of bare feet freezing in a mountain stream, of the salty stench of blood. It was years before I learned what the pins had meant—and what they hadn't meant—to my mother, and how she had seen in me what she was afraid to recognize in herself. "People can be really blind," she once told me. "Sometimes…you just lose your mind." It was not until I had long forgotten the way the pins had shone in the fading orange light that I understood what she had meant.

People's Republic of China, Fuzhou, 1965

It never happened suddenly, was somehow never quite unexpected. I was barely nine or ten, and I only knew that somehow things were becoming tighter and tighter. Sometimes I felt as though I could not breathe, and in the streets, the market, at school, everyone wore a mask of twisted pain, as if they were slowly choking.

The Red Guard moved through the town, and the stillborn air was filled with the sounds of shattering glass, splintering wood. I thought the Red Guard had missed our house until one evening when I came home from school and found my mother sitting on the living room couch in the dark, silent tears glistening on her face. My brothers pulled me away, and I could not understand until dinner, when I realized with a sudden terror, like a cramp in my heart, that my father's chair was empty.

The next day Mother pulled the family albums slowly from her wooden cabinet, biting her lips so hard that they became stained bright red with blood.

She moved them all into the kitchen, and as lunch bubbled passively in the wok, she lifted each glossy photo carefully from its sleeve, staring down at it with quiet eyes before she slipped it, hands trembling, into the fire. For days and days we burned photos, books, letters; breakfast, lunch, dinner were all a feast of memories. Sometimes my mother would tear out pages by the handful, thrusting them into the shivering flames with aggression, and other times I found her kneeling on the floor, her skirts pooled out around her, watching as tears blurred the images in their black-and-white frames. Everything, everything was burned. The only object that survived was my mother's Bible, which we buried within the tall, brick and dirt walls of our house, in a shady corner overgrown with weeds. That was when my mother first began to teach us about Christianity, and that was when I first had a God that I could pray to—praying, every hour, every minute, that we would be free, and that my father would come home.

At last we received a notice that we would be allowed to visit my father. I rode with my mother on the back of her bicycle, a long journey to the government office in Fuzhou. We waited for him in a large office room, grey brick walls with unforgiving corners. A door creaked open, and my father, flanked by two officers, stepped slowly into the room, one foot wobbling in front of the other, as though he were not certain they were there. He walked with his head down, his chest sunken low, and his face pale and torn with worry. *Chang Lin, this man is a traitor. Your father is a disgrace to mankind. He is a spy. He has no honor. He has no morals.* They handed me a short story and told me to read it. It was about an evil man who betrayed his country and his family. *Your father is this man*, they said.

It isn't true! My father is innocent! I cried, and they only laughed at me. They pulled my father forward. *Is this true?* they demanded. *Is this true or not?*

In a very weak voice, and so low that I almost could not hear him, he whispered, *Yes, it is true.* He couldn't look at me, and I felt something clawing behind my heart, something ripping apart inside. It was the first time I had known despair.

Months moved achingly past. My mother was required to attend study camps—to cleanse her of bad thoughts against our country, to wash away the grimy fingerprints her marriage to my father had left on her. She was gone for many days, coming home only on weekends. I remember standing under the streetlamp at the end of the street with my brothers, waiting for hours in the streaming light, mosquitoes buzzing in our ears. After a while the familiar squeak of my mother's bicycle would reach us from the thinning darkness, and we would run forward to hug her, scratchy canvas on smooth skin, sunburned arm around paled neck. Mother pulled back and opened her fist, and several round things rolled over her palm, like glass beads. She let them tumble into my hands, and she closed her hands over mine. *Something for you to do while I'm away*, she whispered.

In a small square of mud at the back of our house I planted carrots, cabbages, eggplants, green peppers. I loved the days in spring when a fine mist of green blanketed the ground, loved to watch the long, delicate tendrils of snow peas trace gracefully up their wooden shafts, erupting into wide, white flowers like so many butterflies. One year we planted wheat and I remember hundreds of thousands of ladybugs: in my hair, in the folds of my large, bulky skirts. There were so many that they tinged the wheat a blazing orange.

I learned to plant flowers, too, and soon our entranceway was lined with bright, brilliant petals sprouting from the shallow confines of rust-ribbed cans. It filled me with a settled weight when I smoothed the dirt flat with my hands, and picked white, round stones from the garden beds. For some reason I kept remembering one of the last things my father had said to me before he had been taken away: *Possessions can always be stolen or lost, but knowledge is something no one can take from you.*

One year slowly bled into another. School began again. Our class took long trips to the countryside, where we learned to work in the fields and trained to be soldiers. Chairman Mao had declared that every citizen must be "a worker, a farmer, a soldier," and so the life I had lived behind our towering brick walls evolved into wheels spinning over spits of mud and grass, endless trains and buses that opened the doors to the furious hatred of a frozen rice-field. It was cold, colder than anything I had ever experienced, and the rice patties were filled with leeches and mosquitoes. I was crowded into a room lined with bunks, twenty girls to a room, two or three girls to each bed. On our first morning in the fields, I saw a boy climb out of a rice patty, his legs coated in leeches. I quickly understood that standing still meant bugs and worse, so I moved as quickly as I could through the rice fields, beating at the water with my feet so that the mud frothed between my toes.

At first each day stood apart: the day my math teacher was bitten by a cobra, the day I punched a boy who pulled me aside and told me to try to free myself from the shame of having a 'black dog' father. But there was too much mud, too many stalks of rice crippled by the weight of the grain—and each day, each week smeared itself into another until I had lost track of the time altogether. After months in the rice fields we were taken to another remote terrain, rugged with cliffs. We practiced air raid drills, dug trenches, learned basic military commands and the proper way to throw grenades. When we were introduced to rifles my officer was astounded; I had perfect marks with all kinds of targets, and was sometimes a better shot than he. It did not matter. I had already grown used to the weights of my father's name, always knew that I would never be promoted, never again be recognized in the blur of a billion faces—the way I had, once, the way I had been so many years ago, when I walked the streets of Fuzhou as if they were my own. That life had become background static, out of which I could only occasionally hear my father's voice, whispering into the faint obscurity: *Yes, it is true.*

News came slowly to the far-flung provinces, but we heard of revolutions breaking out all over China. Across a thousand mountains and a hundred rivers, I imagined people breathing for the first time in many, many years. The study camps were being shut down. Families were coming back from the fields. But the most important news I heard on a rainy, dreary day, while I was waiting with my classmates to be tested about rice. A boy from another class came into our room asking, "Is there a student in this class named Chang Lin? Has she heard? Her father has just been set free." I swallowed hard and leapt out of my chair, shouting, "I am ready to be tested!"

After a few questions I sprinted across the wastelands to our shack, screaming and laughing and crying all at once. On my bed there was a package from home filled with candies, and a letter from my eldest brother, Chuan-ru. Digging my hands deep into the package, I threw the candies into the air like confetti. My eyes ached with tears and I thought I would go blind, but I couldn't stop. I read the letter aloud in a hoarse, raspy voice that broke down into sobs again. The last few lines of the letter had been written by my father, in a shaky hand that staggered over the edges of the paper with excitement. *My dearest Chang, my little princess...*

Papa wanted to see me. It had taken six years, but Papa was home. I closed my eyes and tried to picture him. He must be very weak. Chicken soup would do him good. I ran outside again and went door-to-door in the entire village, asking if anyone would like to sell me a chicken. I didn't find one, but that night, as I restlessly pulled the sheets around me, I realized I would have readily sacrificed a hundred of my chicks to have him well again.

Gou Lou District, Hong Wei Factory, 1976

The heat is so thick that I feel it parting over me in waves every time I take a breath. The gun is empty, but it hangs wearily around my shoulders, and my back muscles are beginning to cramp. Thousands of eyes are fixed on a spot just above my head, but I won't look up. It is only a face, and one of a dead man.

The crowd shifts, and I see a child dressed in a smart red uniform move to the front, grasping her mother's hand tightly. She gazes up at the portrait of Chairman Mao, but there is no flicker of recognition across her face, none of the same fervor that veils everyone else's with a sheen of sweat. Maybe they had wanted him to die.

Her eyes shift over the famous profile, and then onto her jacket. When she moves the light catches on a row of golden pins, and at that same instant I can feel a row of round, hot irons blazing across the front of my uniform, identical to hers.

She meets my gaze. How many years ago had I wished to be her, to tie a red handkerchief around my arm and be given special 'duties'? I once thought I would never be granted that wish, that I would never be pardoned for my father's transgression. My pulse pounds through my upper right arm, where I have knotted the red band too tightly. I almost glance up at the portrait. *He* did it to my father. Instead I focus on the girl's eyes, large and admiring. *The gun*, her eyes are saying.

Yes, the gun. I lean to the right slightly. The gun is heavy. The straps are cutting into my neck and my shoulder blades. I blink sweat out of my eyes and imagine the gun is loaded. Perhaps I would yank the straps over my head, startling the crowd. Perhaps I would hoist it with both arms and tighten my finger against the trigger. Maybe I would point it straight up into the face everyone was staring at. Bang.

As our most talented worker and someone in great possession of leadership, Chang Lin has been chosen from our factory to guard the portrait of Chairman Mao in this factory's memorial service, the manager had announced. There was applause. I sunk lower into my seat. My friend leaned towards me in excitement.

Wow, what an honor! She exclaimed in a hushed whisper. *I used to always dream of doing something like that!*

Me too, I think, but I only whisper back, *I have to stand in the sun for hours without moving. Do you have any idea how boring that is?*

You will be dressed in the traditional Red Guard uniform, the manager continued. *You will also carry a gun to represent the service a soldier provides to our great nation. Don't worry, though. The guns are empty.*

The girl is glancing at the gun and then at me, and she's shrinking back into the crowd as the next row of people move forward to pay their respects. I look at her mother just before the two of them are swallowed into the mass of shuffling feet and curtailed whispers. I suddenly feel trapped, trapped by the uniform, by the heat, by the faces of the crowd. I am struck by how similar they look—the same brown, unblinking eyes, the same expression. There is an unexpected certainty; I know that I will never be like them. I think of the few language disks my brother Chuan-de has worked so hard to buy. He has a scar across his foot where it was impaled and broken by a sharp bamboo stalk in the wild mountains. He worked for a whole year to earn a mere forty yen, saving every penny, sometimes starving himself, to buy me a disk player. He knows I can do it.

I stand a little taller.

One day I swear, to all these thousands of people and the girl—and most importantly, God—I will leave China and never come back. I will learn English. I will free my family. I will free myself.

I look up at Mao for the first time. His uniform looks too stiff, too artificial.

And every man, woman, and child, will be a worker, a farmer, a soldier…

He is trapped forever in his heavy frame. He is trapped forever in death.

Naomi Funabashi, Age 16
Philips Exeter Academy
Exeter, NH
Teacher: Michael Golay

THE ROAD HOME

The cab smelled of feet left too long stewing. I didn't want to be here. We wound down the dirt roads, passing farmland, fences, and more farmland. I would've given my left arm for a cigarette. Then I saw the "No Smoking" sign hanging from the rearview mirror along with a pine-scented air freshener and I laughed a little. So much for that.

The bright red mailbox wasn't as bright as I'd remembered. It was now more of a burnt orange from too much Iowa sun. It was standing a little lopsided, too, as if someone at some point had run into it. Even the mailbox is melancholy, I thought to myself. The house wasn't in too great shape either. It hadn't aged well. In the four years that I'd been gone, three shutters had fallen off, and the rest were on their way. The siding sagged and slouched, as if the house was giving off a big sigh of exhaustion. The poor thing just couldn't get up the energy to breathe in again.

"Thirty," the cab driver grunted. He didn't make a move to get the bags from the car, so I got out. I lugged my baggage from the trunk and dropped it in the dust. Walking to the front of the cab, I handed the man the money.

"Yeah," he said. "And thanks for raising gas prices." He rolled up the window and sped backwards down the drive. I looked down at my camouflage uniform and smiled wanly.

"Just doing my civic duty," I replied to the settling dust as I carried my bags onto the porch.

I stared at the closed door. I could still run. There was still a chance that I could somehow make it out of here alive. I'd catch a bus to Des Moines and beat it the hell out of here. I hesitated, looking back down the long drive.

Screw it, I thought. I have bags to carry.

I could hear the bell like nails on a chalkboard through the door. Home sweet home.

Thumping down the hallway.

The scratch of a key turning in the lock.

A man was standing there, at least sixty. He casually held one hand on the doorway, as if to look comfortable, but I knew better. His fingertips were white. He held a pipe in his other hand. A long scar ran from the center of his shin to the very top of his knee. He was a big man with a dark complexion and white hair. His jaw was set incredibly hard, and it clenched up even more tightly when he saw me. His blue eyes were wide with fear, excitement, or pain, maybe a combination of all three. I couldn't tell.

"Hi Dad," I said, as casually as I could.

"What the hell are you doing here?" he asked, trying to conceal the way that he really felt, the way that we both felt. I laughed nervously.

"Visiting," I said.

"Visiting? Well it was nice of you to call!"

I smiled. "Surprised?"

There was a long and awkward silence as he inspected me from head to toe: my uniform, my black boots, my luggage, and then my face. "You know, that uniform doesn't look half bad," he said. "You look real mature, which was more than I ever expected. Really sharp." He looked at me again. "Well what are you standing out there for?" he said. "Get in here." He motioned for me to follow him into the house. I noticed how he pushed off from the doorframe in pain, limping down the hallway. He'd had knee replacement surgery. That was twelve years ago. I also noticed that he hadn't lost any weight. He looked worse.

"Gimme that," he said, exasperated with watching me drag my luggage inside. I refused his help. I just left it inside the door. "You sure are quiet," he said.

Yeah, you talk enough for the both of us.

"So, what've you been up to?" my dad asked me. I looked down at my uniform.

"Isn't it kind of obvious?" I said. He laughed.

"You hungry?" he asked. "All I have are cold cuts and peanut butter, but I'm sure we can find something." He tried to stand up and I saw his face clench into a painful grimace.

"Dad," I said. "Let me get it."

"Like hell you will," he said, but he sat back down. I pulled out the peanut butter, the jelly and some bread.

"So where's Carolyn?" I asked. My dad was silent. "Oh," I replied. "I'm sorry."

"Yeah, she's dead," he said bluntly. My dad never saw the point in beating around the bush. "I thought about calling you, but you two never did quite see eye-to-eye."

I shrugged. He was right. We didn't. Carolyn didn't like me, and I didn't like Carolyn. I didn't like Carolyn because she was a hypocrite. She wasn't honest and she treated me like extra baggage that she had to carry around. At least my father treated me like useful baggage. She had wanted to marry my father, but I was more than she'd bargained for.

I opened the cabinet, searching for a knife. My dad always kept things so neat and tidy. I was surprised that I couldn't find one.

And then there they were, in that same orange bottle: those little white dots. I pulled them from the shelf.

"Dad," I said.

"You leave them pills alone," he bellowed sternly, the way he used to do when I was little. "They're for my corroders." I laughed in disbelief.

"Dad, I'm not a kid anymore," I said. "This is the reason I came back." I paused. "Part of it anyway." I put the bottle between us and sat down at the table. "You need help."

My father shook his head and swept the bottle off the table before I could get it. "Oh, I don't need any help." He limped over to the cabinet and put the bottle back. I noticed that he was trying to hide three others behind the wine glasses.

"I don't think you understand," I said. I was angry. "You're not just hurting yourself, you're hurting everyone around you: you hurt Mom, Carolyn, me, Daniel, and everyone else who's ever given a damn about you!" There was a pause. "Why did you think I left?"

"Because of Daniel," he said quietly. "Adrian, you can't tell me this wasn't about Daniel." My anger shriveled.

"Yeah," I said. "Yeah, it was."

"I guess you can stay in your old room," my dad said. "I haven't moved anything." I nodded.

"Thanks." I finished my sandwich and went to take my bags upstairs.

"Need any help?" he asked me.

"No," I replied. "I'm fine, thanks."

My window. It was a perfect view of the barn, which made it less than satisfactory. I wouldn't know until I was up close how much it had changed, but I was guessing not a lot. I didn't want to see the barn. They should've torn it down when they had the chance. Then maybe Daniel would still be alive.

I pulled myself away from the window and looked around my room. It was exactly the same, down to the blue comforter on my trundle bed. The pictures were all gone because I had taken them with me. They were still in my bags. There was one that I missed. It was a picture of Daniel and me, when we were young. He was bigger and he had his arm around my shoulders. We were sitting on a park bench somewhere. I looked at the photo, and then walked outside to the barn.

Daniel was older than me by three years. He was bigger, faster, tougher, smarter, everything that I wasn't. He was the perfect son. Dad liked him best, I could tell. It was obvious. I just always knew. I didn't hate Daniel for it. He was my brother and best friend. I loved him.

There was a high loft in the bar that you could reach via ladder. The mountains of straw on the barn floor made the perfect cushion for jumping. Daniel and I used to jump from the loft all the time until my father caught us one day.

"Don't you ever do that again, d'you understand?" He gripped us both by the forearm, leaving bruises. I understood. Daniel didn't.

He went back to the barn the next morning, and I was at his heels.

"Danny, we're going to get in trouble," I said.

"Don't be such a wimp," he replied. "We'll be fine."

"Well I'm not jumping," I said. He shrugged. I thought about getting my father, but losing Daniel's respect was worse than dying. I followed.

He was up in the loft, ready to jump. "You sure you don't want to go?" he said. I shook my head. "Whatever." He jumped.

My dad found me screaming in the red straw, a pitchfork knifing through my brother's back. The ambulance came later. Daniel was put on a big white stretcher. Then the funeral.

Dad and I didn't speak for days. The days turned into months. The months turned into the four years that I was gone. After Carolyn came, I didn't see any point in staying. I enlisted. Dad wouldn't have cared if I didn't make it through the war. He saw it fitting that I was off killing people, seeing as I got my start right at home at the ripe old age of nine. His addiction got out of control.

"It hasn't changed much, has it?"

I jumped.

"I didn't hear you come in," I said. He nodded.

"That's the point. I didn't want you to leave."

Fair enough.

There was a long silence.

"So," he said. I take it you came back to talk." I had to think about this. To this day, I don't know why I went back. I guess that something was just left unfinished.

"Sure," I said. "There are some loose ends that need to be tied." My dad nodded.

"Yeah, they're loose alright." There was another pause. "You know," he said, looking at me. "You're a pretty good kid. You're all right." I smiled.

"Thanks," I said, laughing slightly. "You're not so bad yourself, for an old cripple." He laughed at this, and then we both fell into silence again. Light was just beginning to stream in through the gaping seams in the wood of the barn. My father turned around.

"Where the hell is my pipe?" He limped back towards the house and I followed, closing the barn door behind him.

Margot Miller, Age 16
Padua Academy
Wilmington, DE
Teacher: Elizabeth Slater

SLASHED SKIES

The birds went first
when the sky wore through
like a pair of faded levis
with smeary clouds like grass stains
birds fell like bricks
up through tears of deep purple
in an otherwise cyan sky

The trees went next
uprooted, leaving enormous craters
where their roots once grew deep
their leaves rustled loudly as the wind
whistled through them
and they fell through the clouds and
up the immense rip

Confusion incarnate as men gaped
with starched shirts and pressed suits
through the sunroofs of limos
or paused with their hands
on ornate brass doorknobs
that led to thousands of stories

Our glass ladders to success went next
all eighty-six million stories
crumbling upward
and through the immense purple rift
their foundations close behind

Our comfort went soon after
three-story homes
on Hollywood Boulevard
Rolls-Royces were at last liberated
from their bondage to streets

It was just us
and the mountains now
but we came to feel the strain
and slowly but surely the attraction strengthened
and we found ourselves slipping through as well

Weightless
for what seemed to be eternity
we stared at each other with blank faces
and floated through outer space
like the asteroids do

Here's where I'd like to mention
just how overwhelmingly beautiful outer space is
all our thoughts were captured by it
like butterflies in a net
so much so, that we didn't even notice
when we finally hit the giant silver mass
that we used to call the moon

We bounced across the dusty surface
until we slid to a stop
and we got up
and built a new metropolis
with new glass ladders to success
and called it Earth

Eric Roper, Age 13
League Academy
Greenville, SC
Teacher: Teresa Blankenship

RISE UP

Sitting at my kitchen table, I opened the newspaper to find a headline in bold words:

**IN NAZI ARCHIVES, ONE NAME STANDS OUT—
ANNE FRANK.**

No doubt, Anne Frank has an amazing story of bravery, but she is remembered mainly because she was a young writer who did not survive World War II, who left us a legacy of letters about the person she could have been were it not for Adolf Hitler.

Millions of Jewish people died fighting for what they knew and loved. However, there are people who fought for their lives and religion and won.

I have come to love one woman of such courage, passion and selflessness, that she has changed my life forever. I have the honor to say that I am a friend with a Holocaust survivor who lives across the country, who is of a different faith than I am and who has lived a life filled with sorrow, courage, and dedication.

Alicia Appleman-Jurman was born in the Polish city of Buczacz, Poland. She was a child full of wit, laughter and pride. She had four brothers—Moshe, Bunio, Zachary, and Herzl—a strong, kind father, and a mother she loved dearly. She was nine years old when Hitler attacked her country. Russia invaded east Poland, where she lived, on September 17, 1939.

From that day on, Alicia Appleman-Jurman fought for her education, her religion, and eventually, her life.

⸙

One year ago, my teacher came across a book. *Alicia—My Story* was the memoir of a survivor of World War II. When my teacher gave me the memoir, I was preparing for National History Day. The topic was "Taking a Stand in History." I didn't have to think twice. I was going to write a one-woman show about Alicia Appleman-Jurman.

I e-mailed Alicia's publisher, who provided me with her home address. She lived in California. I wrote a letter explaining my feelings of admiration for this amazing person. Unsure of how she might respond, or whether she would at all, I mailed my letter across the country.

After about a month of waiting for Alicia's reply, I began to search for other National History Day topics.

One night in August, I was setting the table for dinner when the telephone rang.

My mom answered and her face lit up as she listened: "Yes, this is Alicia Appleman-Jurman and I am calling for Jillian Kinsey."

"Jill, it's Alicia." Excitement overwhelmed me, then nervousness. When I picked up the phone, my hands were shaking.

"Jillian, I've received your letter, and of course I am willing to help you."

I sat on my porch swing and talked to Alicia for a long time. We discussed my costume, the main stories I should cover in my script—she told me many more stories about her mother and her brother, Zachary. The sun began to set and a chilly wind tickled my feet. Tears filled my eyes, yet I could not stop smiling. Her last words to me that night were, "*Shalom*, dear Jillian. Thank you for telling Alicia's story." I was speaking to a hero.

Because of her Polish accent and the long distance static, I was unable to hear many of her responses to my interview questions. I later mailed Alicia a set of questions, which she sent back to me with handwritten answers in beautiful cursive, with a heart-shaped smiley face by her name. After so many years of heartbreak, love and happiness had finally found their way into Alicia's life.

⸙

Anti-Semitism first struck Alicia's family in 1938. Zachary, her brother, had warm blue eyes and was a strong, tall musician. On his way home from the conservatory of music in Lvov, a gang of Polish boys attacked and beat him terribly.

When Zachary returned home, his father decided he needed to learn how to fight. Alicia hid in the bushes as her father taught her brother how to stand up for himself. She felt the urge to learn as well.

However, learning to fight was not the education she truly desired. When Jewish children were banned from school, she climbed a tree outside of her classroom. She sat there for weeks just listening to lessons. Her teacher knew that she was there, but did not press the issue. One day, Alicia knew an answer and, forgetting she wasn't inside of the classroom, she raised her hand. She fell from the tree and her teacher came running.

"She slowly wiped the dirt from my clothes, and in doing so, her fingers brushed the yellow Star of David on my armband," Alicia told me. Her words were so meaningful and true.

The teacher knew Alicia was a girl who wished to be educated more than anything, a girl who would later strive to save the lives of others.

⌐✦⌐

While writing my script, I mailed Alicia several drafts. She sent them back to me along with letters on her own stationery, illustrated with a picture of Israel in the left-hand corner.

One part of my script made reference to Alicia wanting to give up after seeing an SS man shoot and kill her mother.

"You must take that out, Jillian, for Alicia never wanted to give up. Alicia swore on her brother Zachary's grave that she would speak for her family. She never even thought to give up. Giving up was not an option."

Her response stunned me, and I grew to respect this woman even more. She spoke of herself in the third-person in order to remove herself from the terrors of her childhood.

When my script was finished, I mailed a final copy to Alicia. After receiving it, she called me in tears.

"Jillian, you have told Alicia's story so well. Your writing style is very touching. I feel such a deep connection with you, dear heart."

⌐✦⌐

My first performance was for the competition at my school. I performed for my teachers and six judges. I felt myself trembling as I introduced myself and the title of my show, "Rise Up—The Bold Journey of Alicia Appleman-Jurman."

My voice shook as I said my first line.

"And now that you students have heard my story, please know that there were millions of people who died in World War II." My show began in the middle of Alicia giving a speech at a college. I wore a gray suit and hat, just like Alicia did when she spoke at Ricks College in Idaho. She had sent me a video of her speech, which I used to help craft my script. Not having the opportunity to meet her in person, I relied on this video to capture her voice and cadence. I watched Alicia's eyes, which showed her painful history.

As I performed at my school, I pictured Alicia talking to her audience. I was used to smiling people applauding at my performances. After my final line and bow, the crowd stared into space. Their faces showed fear and sadness, relief and regret. Alicia's story is one that has the power to leave any person speechless. At that moment, I felt Alicia's pain and also, her pride.

After winning first place at my school, I moved on to the regional competition at Messiah College. Two nights before my performance, Alicia called to wish me good luck. "You have worked so hard to tell Alicia's story. I know you will win, dear Jillian."

And I did.

Next was the state competition at Penn State. In order to prepare, I performed for my junior high school. More nervous than I had ever been with this show, I stepped out on stage. These were my friends and I was unsure what they would think. My hands were cold and my voice cracked, yet somehow both conditions were beneficial for the part.

Tears found me while singing the *Hatikvah*, the Eretz Israel national anthem, at the end of my play.

"As long as the heart of the Jew beats,
And his eye is turned to the East,
Our ancient hope still lives:
To be a free people in Zion."

The state competition clearly brought better actors and topics. Thirty-four other performers arrived that morning.

Alicia's words from the night before were still ringing in my mind.

"Thank you, dearest, for speaking for Alicia's family."

I stood in an empty room, warming up my voice. I could almost feel Alicia's family there with me. *This is for you.*

"Next." A judge called for me. With only five minutes to set up my scenery, I hurried out onto the stage.

"Whenever you are ready you may begin."

My words flowed and emotions overcame me. I felt Alicia's feelings taking over my mind and heart and it was my best performance yet. Then the judges began our interview.

Again, most questions were about Alicia. I shook their hands, cleared my set, and then the waiting began. I pondered what it would be like to tell Alicia the bad news. The thought really upset me—I didn't want to disappoint her.

Finally it was time to check the list. I entered the room where they were posting the results. I passed many students crying and a few that were shouting with excitement. I nearly ran to the list.

I made the top six and was scheduled to perform the next day.

My next performance was in a room much like the one before. The judges were younger and more alert. I felt the presence of Alicia and her family with me once again, and performed almost flawlessly.

After my performance was over I attended the award ceremony several hours later.

The third place winner was announced. The second place winner...

"Rise Up—The Bold Journey of Alicia Appleman-Jurman." I had won second place in the state of Pennsylvania and was advancing to the national competition. My journey with Alicia continued.

Before calling my friends and family members at home, I called Alicia.

"I won second place! I'm going to nationals!" I could almost picture the grin on her pretty face.

"Oh, Jillian, I've been thinking about you all day. I'm so proud of you!"

We talked for a long time about my performance, the judges, and the national competition. Knowing that our friendship was not coming to an end, happiness overwhelmed me.

Unfortunately, nationals were not held anywhere near California. Alicia would not be able to see my last performance.

The rush of the people around me was amazing and I suddenly realized that

I was competing with the best of the best.

Penn State's forum was long gone, and I expected a beautiful theater. After checking my papers and the number on the door many times, I realized I was performing in a small classroom. About 30 people crammed into the back of the room, including several of my family members and eight of my friends, who had taken a road-trip to Washington D.C. and then come to watch me.

The judges seemed impatient when they called my name. I nervously shoved my rocking chair through the door and hurried to grab my coat rack, podium, poster of Alicia, table and costume pieces. After all was set, I waited. I remembered the first time I opened *Alicia—My Story*. The beginning lines of the book wondered throughout my mind.

> *First they killed my brother Moshe...*
> *Then they killed my father...*
> *Then they killed my brother Bunio...*
> *Then they killed my brother Zachary...*
> *Then they killed my last brother, Herzl.*
> *Only my mother and I were left. I vowed that I would never let them kill her, that I would protect my mother from the Nazis and their collaborators for as long as I lived.*
> *Love and hate were what motivated my young mind and heart. Love for my dear, gentle mother—and hate for the cruel murderers.*
> *And this is my story.*

I thought of Alicia's warm, kind voice and smiled as I stared at her picture. I remembered all of my performances and the comments each judge made. And then it was time.

My show began and I felt every word and said every line as if it were my last. I sang the Eretz Israel national anthem loud and clear, and ended *I sang as a young girl searching for a home, later as a soldier in the Israeli army, and now as a woman who has stood up to Adolf Hitler.* The anger and sadness in my eyes faded and I smiled as I bowed. *I love you, Alicia.*

⁂

I didn't place in the national competition and avoided calling Alicia for several days. It seemed like the end of our friendship and I couldn't bear to say goodbye.

Finally I dialed her number with tears in my eyes.

"You have done so much for Alicia, dear heart. I am so grateful that you have come into my life. I love you, Jillian."

⁓✳⁓

Two months after my History Day adventure, I received a package in the mail.

I slowly opened the box. Inside were two silk scarves, a bag of caramel Hershey kisses, California nail clippers, and two gifts that I would treasure the most. One was a gold medal with an Israeli symbol for "Life." The other was a hardcover copy of *Alicia—My Story* with a note and Alicia's signature inside. This book was rare because Alicia instructed her publisher to only make paperback books so the children could afford her novel. Inside the book was a letter.

Many people ask me, "What will happen when all the survivors are gone?" I don't have to think hard to say, "We have Guiding Angels"—like you, dear Jillian— to tell our stories for us.

You had a very intensive school year. Telling my story requires a lot of energy and bravery. You have the bravery and you have proven it by standing in front of an audience and judges and pouring your heart out.

To me, dearest Jillian, you are a hero.

Before I start crying, I will finish my letter to you. Thank you again for coming into my life. God bless.

Always with Love and Friendship,
Alicia ♡

Jillian Kinsey, Age 14
Seven Sorrows School
Middletown, PA
Teacher: Dana Kinsey

DEFINING YOU

Victor busied himself in buttoning and unbuttoning his shirtsleeves. It was a habit he had acquired somewhere in the last two years and he wished desperately to be rid of it. Nervousness didn't become an explorer of such eminence as himself. For, he told himself, Victor Ferraney is not just an explorer, but *An Explorer*. And he had to be in top form for this speech. EverStrong Energy Drinks depended on him. They depended on him to stay a hero. Well, he would oblige.

As the previous speaker introduced him, Victor ran over the story he had to sell. He didn't remember it. Not really, not any more than the people who were about to hear would remember it. He'd seen the tapes, and he'd told the story often enough that he thought he knew exactly what had happened and what it meant. He thought he could tell it convincingly enough.

Which was important, because it had happened to him.

"I am proud to present Mr. Victor Ferraney, here to relate his experiences on the 2021 Valkyrie expedition to Mars."

The crowd cheered wildly as Victor came to the podium. Everyone expected that. Even though this was a scientific convention, half the people here had come just to see Victor speak. He raised a hand in a friendly wave, and a hush fell over the crowd.

"On June 17, Earth calendar, I left our Mars base to scout out the canyons alone. In hindsight, I was pretty stupid. But Mars is so empty, its solitude so total, that I couldn't imagine sharing it with anyone else—even my fellow astronauts."

His audience smiled indulgently. Yes, they could forgive him. He had been young and impulsive still, even after years of training,

"You should have seen it. Red everywhere. Red rock, crags jutting up into a red-pink sky and back down into red valleys. A thin layer of red dust on the ground, sticking to my boots as I walked. The static from my radio buzzed in my ears. The air tasted stale in my suit, and how I wished that the atmosphere had a little more oxygen. I was shut up like dehydrated biscuits. Did I care? No way. Not after five minutes under the Martian sky. I almost felt like I could imagine the feelings my suit took from me—the metallic tang of the air, the echo of my own footsteps."

Victor looked out into the distance as if seeing a Mars from those years ago. Some of his listeners sipped at their EverStrong drinks (At Special Discount to convention attendees). They would be seeing what he was describing now, bright and clear as if they were with him themselves. They would feel the serene strength of standing on the soil of another world.

"I started down into one of the canyons. Great walls of stone rose on either side of me. Enclosed in a tunnel, buried deep in the heart of the planet and delving deeper, I had to keep glancing up at the sky to make sure it was still there.

"Then the ground slid out from under me."

The crowd gasped. Every one of them knew what had happened, they knew he would be safe, but still they were carried away in knowing that he was there, close enough to touch, telling them about it.

"I slid down some ten meters of steeply sloping rock face. If I'd gone straight down, or if the spacesuit I was wearing hadn't been so expertly designed," Victor gave a magnanimous nod toward NASA's engineers. "That would have been curtains for me. As it was, I more rolled and bounced than fell, but my suit held firm. I reached the canal's floor sore and bruised, but in one piece. The pathway I'd come down by was completely blocked by rock fall.

"'No problem', I thought. 'I'll just radio for help. They'll send someone with a good, long rope.' But all I got was static. I reached up to adjust the antenna… and it was gone. Broken off by the fall. I was on my own."

He paused for a moment to let that feeling of utter aloneness (that he could not really remember but only imagine) sink in to those without the aid of the drinks.

"Luckily for me, I had EverStrong Energy Drink in my suit's water tank. Even on Mars, I won't leave home without it." Because he was hooked on it. Hooked as a baby unable to wean off his bottle. "I sipped, and I thought, and I figured that there had to be a way out. So I went looking for it.

"Half an hour later I found it—my best chance. A chimney carving into the rock on a slight angle, maybe fifteen meters up. It opened onto a ledge flat enough to walk the rest of the way—if I made it that far. But the holds looked large and firm. So I started up—no way was Victor Ferraney going to end his days in the bottom of a Martian canyon, not while there was a path up, be it a bare inch wide."

No, he would not, thought the crowd. They knew their hero. They trusted him to keep going, no matter what. Victor Ferraney wouldn't take death lying down. He'd give the reaper a run for his money. Maybe even win.

"Slowly, I made my way up. Took my time. I knew there was no hurry. I had hours of air left in my suit, and it was looking pretty good. Then I slipped on a pile of loose pebbles. I stopped thinking, just reached out by reflex. I caught myself before I went down the chimney again. Good, I thought. Then I heard that slow, soft hissing noise coming from a tear in my suit."

Like one creature, the audience held its breath. Victor held the moment, drew it out. He spoke very, very slowly.

"Well, there went my 'hours'. The suits are built to self-correct for safety—but at the rate my suit was losing pressure, I knew I had half an hour. Tops."

Victor leaned forwards, his voice low. His listeners started to breathe again, shallowly, to conserve air. The air in Victor's suit so long ago. They would help him make it last.

"I pulled myself up that chimney, fair near ran along the ledge up to the top. I started to feel faint from low air pressure and lack of oxygen. I made a dash for the base like a man possessed. That was my one taste of the Martian air, that I had wished for that morning. Sharp as I had imagined, with a stale edge to it. I never wanted to breathe it again. No sir! I'll take good old Earth air any day.

"With bare minutes to spare, I made it into the base's air lock. Hear that? Minutes!"

He banged the podium with a fist. One or two of the academics flinched, but the audience was spellbound. Freed from the harsh oppression of CO_2-heavy Martian air, they breathed deep.

"Let me tell you, it never felt so good to get a good lungful. Even recycled oxygen tasted like a good mountain breeze.

"But this is more than just a yarn. There's a lesson in all this. And I think that's why our esteemed scientists and engineers from NASA invited me here today."

His nod triggered polite applause from people who thought that anyone who didn't invite Mr. Victor Ferraney to an astronautics convention was a plumb fool.

"Space exploration is humanity's big chance. We can't afford to ignore it. Not with population the way it is, and not with us chewing up natural resources at our rate. And more than that, too. The pure need to explore is in humanity's soul, so deep that to wrench it out would kill us all, slowly but surely. My story, friends, and that of any astronaut's, is proof that we can do it. We can win the stars, because no challenge is too great to overcome with strength, intelligence, and straight-out grit. We have been reaching out and snatching victory from defeat for centuries. We have risked all for a dream of glory, to experience, to discover. Sometimes it may seem like we have lost. But never, friends, never, will we fail. Why not? Because we keep going, even when the future looks bleak indeed. Even when we anticipate only a shallow grave on some godforsaken rock. We can only fail if we refuse to fight. Will you fight with me, in whatever field you have chosen?"

Gravely, Victor stretched out a hand to the people. Once by one, they nodded. Yes. They would accept his covenant. They stretched their hands out in the air toward his, and Victor nodded.

"Thank you, friends."

He stepped down from the podium. There was a stunned hush. Then, thunderous applause.

Other speakers came and went, but the crowd was tepid at best. Many people left. How could they be expected to listen to phrases like "escape velocity," "artificial ecosystems," and "the speed-of-light barrier"? They had come to hear Victor Ferraney speak, and that was all.

Victor himself applauded politely after each speech. After the last speaker stepped down, Victor slipped quietly off to the side, where his wife wrapped him in a steady embrace.

"How'd I do, Sara?" he said into her hair.

"The more you give that speech, the less you believe it."

He stepped back. "How so?"

She shrugged. He didn't push it. She didn't need to explain any more—he knew that she was thinking about the EverStrong contract.

They walked along the narrow paths between convention booths. It seemed to Victor that they were visiting a bizarre fairground. If you squinted and looked at the booths just so, they could be cotton candy stands and shooting galleries: Pop three balloons and win an astronomy book signed by NASA's head geek and Victor Ferraney! And there, in the corner, was some sort of twisted carnival ride…

"Do you want to have a go in the g-force simulator?"

What was that? Sara had asked him a question. Now she was looking at him strangely. He shook his head, and the booths became informational displays again. The warped arms of the carnival ride snapped back into the smooth curve of the g-force machine, carted there for the convention.

"No thanks, dear. After you go up, it just isn't the same." Just this past year, Victor had been forced to admit to himself that rides gave him vertigo. He couldn't even go on the teacups if he expected to keep his lunch.

A small boy, ten or twelve years old, ran up behind Victor and his Sara.

"Mr. Ferraney? Mr. Ferraney!"

Victor turned around with a grin on his face.

"Call me Victor."

"Yes, Mr. Victor. Is it really you?"

Victor opened his eyes wide in shock and patted his face, arm, and chest. "Yes, I suppose it is. Go figure!" The boy giggled. Victor noticed the can he was carrying in his hand. "I see you drink EverStrong."

"Yup. I…I don't know why, Mr. Victor, but when I do…I almost feel like I'm you." He blushed a red as deep as the surface of Mars.

"Do you? I've never heard that before." But he expected it. That's what they were supposed to do, wasn't it?

"D'you think…that I could be as good an astronaut as you someday?"

"If you want to, you can be better. I guarantee it."

The kid ran off then, probably to find his parents and tell them that he'd talked to Victor Ferraney (*No, really!*)

Sara smiled at her husband. "That was sweet. I'm glad you encouraged him."

"I was being honest."

They left the convention then and drove home. It happened to be held in the Ferraneys' hometown, or else Victor would have found some excuse not to go. Or else travel by train for days. He couldn't bring himself to fly. Not after the EverStrong contract.

After dinner, Victor and Sara went through a bit of paperwork, putting things in order for the cruise they would take in the summer; the cruise Victor had promised they'd take as soon as he got back from Mars. It had been a long time coming, what with the money troubles. Three years, in fact. But here they were, set to go within weeks.

Only they'd have to take the hi-speed train to the port, since Victor wouldn't take a plane. Sara wasn't too pleased to spend so long just getting there, but she let it go. At least they'd get a good view of the countryside. And nowadays, the train didn't take nearly so long as driving. Some people were even beginning to give up their cars.

Victor remembered what had driven him to space in the first place— all the noise and crowded streets, and smog choking up the air 'til a body could scarcely breathe. Even recycled spacebase air was better than that. The government had caught on to the noxious air by the time he got back, though. Took them long enough. At least they were starting to deal with it.

He tried in vain to remember what it was like to be in space, to see the Earth spread out under him like in all the photos. To land on Mars after a quick stop on the International Space Station. To know that it's just you and your buddies alone on an entire planet. No smog, no stereos blaring, no rush-hour traffic…

And he realized that the thought of all that aloneness gave him the willies.

"You ok, honey?" Victor realized that Sara was staring at him again.

"Fine." He dropped the pen he was holding and stood up. "Just a little tired. I'm going to tuck in now."

Victor slipped off into his mindless evening routine. Nightshirt.

Mouthwash. Alarm set for 7:00 A.M. He put on his headset, barely wincing as the tiny needles pierced his skin. It was uncomfortable.

Not that he resented it, of course. Apart from the occasional speech, it was all that EverStrong asked of him. He'd been in a bad way when they called him up. His money stretched too thin, headed for bankruptcy. No way he could have afforded Sara's cruise without their contract. All they wanted was a sponsor.

Someone to wear the set every night. To let it pick up material while he slept. Dreams. Memories. Little flashes of brain-energy that they could copy and package and ship out in their TV commercials, and even in the drinks themselves. He couldn't very well refuse to let others share the wonderful things he'd seen, could he? It was a chance to spread the joy of space, of Mars, to everyone. At least, everyone who drank EverStrong. And it was a lucrative contract.

Of course, they never told them that he'd lose his own memories. Maybe they didn't know. Didn't know that although they could package 'em up and ship them off to kids like the boy at that convention, they couldn't give them back to Victor Ferraney.

But those kids were the wave of the future, and Victor was just the stuff of the past. So it was worth it.

Wasn't it?

Katherine Sedivy-Haley, Age 16
St. Mary Academy Bay View
Riverside, RI
Teacher: Marion Wrye

BRACE YOURSELF

Several years ago, before there were enough pictures of presidents to be used as dollars, teeth were used as currency. The most affluent cave men were said to be the ones able to hoard the most Tyrannosaurus teeth. It has even been documented that Adam purchased Eve's engagement ring with four bat molars, a lion's bicuspids, and a pack of Crest White Strips. Fortunately, society has changed significantly since the barbaric days of antiquity; we no longer participate in savage activities such as waging holy wars, detaining alleged criminals without a trial, or photographing naked prisoners of war in compromising positions. However, it remains overwhelmingly true in American society that the person with the most teeth is the wealthiest and most powerful member of society. Who is that person? He is known as *the orthodontist.*

Bad teeth have plagued our nation's middle schools like locusts for some time now. My own teeth were unfortunately no exception. Thanks to my parents' gorgeous genetics I was blessed with teeth bearing a striking resemblance to Stonehenge. My peers failed to see the historical significance of my pearly whites, and before long I was more than willing to submit my teeth to the *care* of Dr. Novak, the renowned orthodontist who my dentist enthusiastically recommended. (Note that I am using the term "Dr." very loosely. This man is a doctor in the same way Michael Jackson is a babysitter.)

Though I didn't realize it at the time, agreeing to get braces is the dental equivalent of signing over a blank check to an Enron executive. No matter what you do or say those shackles are not coming off until the orthodontist decides that he's finished straightening your teeth (or wrenching every last penny from the wallets of your reluctant parents). My *teethcuffs*, as I've named them, have been chaining me to the jail that is the orthodontist's office for about three years now. I've been brushing often, so I'm hoping to get off for good behavior within the next few months, but until then I'm stuck. I could look at my period of dental servitude in a negative light, but realizing that the only possible way to pay for my own braces would be to become an orthodontist myself, I have decided to glean as many tricks of the trade as possible.

First and foremost, to become a licensed orthodontist it's necessary to attend a school specializing in orthodontics for three years. However, most orthodontists don't stop there. Rumor has it Dr. Novak also found it necessary to obtain a *License to Kill*. This may sound like a hard license to come by, but most accredited dental schools offer it—and as with any medical degree, the Dominican Republic is a goldmine of easy opportunity.

Mastery of the art of awkward conversation is perhaps more important than technical skill when it comes to fixing teeth; in fact Dr. Novak majored in it in college. One good way to strike up the perfect awkward conversation is with the use of inadvertently malicious questions. Think along the lines of asking a three hundred pound boy which sports he plays, or the girl with dental headgear who she took to the prom. With the perfect vocal pitch and tone these questions can seem like friendly inquiries, while also serving their main purposes of cruelty and demoralization.

Nicknames can have a similar effect when applied appropriately, and with a creative touch. The boy with a surplus of cavities and a penchant for ballet dancing might receive the nickname "Tooth Fairy," while a girl with an unfortunately large mole on her face might simply be called "molar." The complexity of the nicknames can vary, as can the level of cruelty and political correctness.

Another strategy is what I call the *gag order*, a favorite of Dr. Novak, this is when the orthodontist sticks large tools in your mouth, making any oral communication aside from emotive grunts impossible—and then proceeds to begin an in-depth conversation requiring lengthy responses, which you are unable to give. Appropriate topics can include (but are not limited to): "What are your feelings on existentialism?", "Do you prefer Charlotte or Emily Brontë?" or "Do you approve of the way George Bush is handling the situation in Iraq?"

All of this is hard work, and of course Dr. Novak could not possibly do it all by himself. As the saying goes, "Behind every great man there is a great woman." Unfortunately, Dr. Novak couldn't find any great women, so he settled for seven moderately attractive and mind-numbingly unintelligent ones. I like to think of them as a modern day rendition of the seven Vestal Virgins of Ancient Rome, worshipping the God of the Teeth with their every action. They go by the job title "Dental Hygienists"—even though more of their time is spent gossiping about Jennifer Aniston and Brad Pitt than actually completing work that would deserve this title. As trivial as they sound, assistants are an essential accessory for an orthodontist.

It truly is a brilliant spectacle when all of these elements are brought together in one procedure, like a choreographed orthodontic dance. I was privileged enough to be a part of such a performance recently. My gums were deemed too large. Dr. Novak decided that it was essential to use a dental laser to burn off portions of them.

"What ever happened to accepting imperfection?!" I reasoned frantically.

These days imperfection gets burned off with a laser, I soon found out.

After dreading the appointment for several weeks, the day came for me to face my inevitable fate. I arrived at the orthodontist's office and was greeted promptly.

"Ah well, here's Dubble Bubble!" Dr. Novak exclaimed when he saw me.

"Excuse me?" I said.

"You know Dubble Bubble, like the brand of bubble gum. It's twice the size of normal gum."

"Yeah, yeah I get it. I'm Dubble Bubble because my gums are too big. That's a really good one," I responded apathetically, sliding into the chair in which I would undergo my operation.

"Yeah well hopefully after this we can cut you down to Chiclet size—get it because Chiclets are a traditionally small type of gum…"

"Yeah, that's very funny."

No one but an orthodontist could get away with this.

"Ok, well, Sandy is going to get you ready. I'll be right back." He said, taking a bow and walking off stage.

Silicone Sandy sat down next to me, and asked me to open my mouth. She began prying at my braces with the gentleness of a woman prying her firstborn baby from the jaws of a Bengal tiger. After she had finished removing the brackets from my braces (and I had finished screaming in terror) I was ready for the main act. Dr. Novak returned and told Sandy to go prepare everything else while he checked what she had already done to my teeth.

He decided to start a conversation. "So prom was last week; who did you go with?"

I was in shock! I knew the kind of people who got asked this question, and I was offended. Luckily after a few grunts he dropped the subject, and Sandy came back.

"Ok Sandy, why don't you give the laser to Cathy and let her do this."

I looked behind me and saw Cathy stomping over. She was significantly more corpulent than any of the other assistants, so I figured she must be at least relatively intelligent.

I was wrong.

Her greeting to me was, "Hey, I'm um, new here. So I don't really know how to do this. But it can't be that hard to figure out, right? So, *brace* yourself!" She giggled at her impressive wit, then began numbing my gums, and after a few minutes lifted the laser into my mouth.

I was in a panic. I had been expecting one of the Vestal Virgins to gently tend her eternal flame near my gums, but now somehow I was stuck with Mrs. O'Leary's cow lighting the Great Chicago Fire inside my mouth. Tooth and nail I fought the urge to spring from the chair with my Double Bubble gums, before too much damage could be done. Fortunately I didn't, and I am sitting here today with normally sized gums. I have not yet noticed a difference. In fact, the only noticeable change in size occurred in my parents' bank account.

Fortunately, through this whole process I have found my calling in life— and that calling sounds a lot like the terrified shouts of middle-school children with Stonehenge teeth.

Thomas Renjilian, Age 16
Abington Heights High School
Clarks Summit, PA
Teacher: Cyndi Page

AQUARIUM

"Gender is not about males and females, courtship is not about persuasion, fashion is not about beauty and love is not about affection."
—Matt Ridley on Lewis Carroll's ***Through the Looking-Glass***

Alligators and Chrysemys

In humans, it's pretty simple. The X chromosome hooks with the Y, and you have a boy. If the X hooks with another X, than you have a girl. This occurs in humans, your dog, your cat, the line of birds on the power lines you notice on your morning jog. Anything warm-blooded really. It's more complex with cold-blooded animals. With most reptiles, the sex of the offspring depends on temperature. This can be found in alligators (genus *Alligator*) and the painted turtle (genus *Chrysemys*). The alligator and turtle make a nest out of sand and other materials, mostly sand. The animals lay their eggs, then bury them. While the eggs mature, the temperature is the deciding factor of the nest's sex. If the sand is hot, the litter will be all males. If the sand is cooler, all females.

Niche

Randall welcomed me with the spinning of a large black salon chair. My friend Jarred stood nearby. Jarred had known Randall for over two years now. They met in a club in Charlotte one summer. The club was holding an amateur night, and Jarred had only been doing drag for six months. He had never done a show until then.

I didn't go with Jarred on his first trip to Charlotte, but I had made numerous trips to thrift shops with him the week before. He bought a lot of women's clothes. I spent most of the week trying to convince him that gold and red weren't his colors. Most of the clothes he bought were from the seventies. He corrected me every time I called them old and ugly. "It's vintage," he'd say, holding up a short gold-sequined dress to his small shoulders.

After Randall studied me for a moment, he ran his fingers through my hair. He teased the shaggy tips of it. There was a moment of silence among us while Cyndi Lauper played in the salon. The silence was broken by the sound of clippers turning on, then Randall brought them to the back of my neck.

While I watched pieces of shaggy auburn hair fall to the floor, Jarred and Randall talked. I heard names of people I didn't know, drag names, code names. I found out that Randall was sometimes Amanda Blake. I had helped pick Jarred's name: Vivian Blake. He had idolized Amanda since the night they met. While Randall clipped around the edges of my ears, he explained the bond they shared. Amanda was Vivian's "drag mother," meaning Amanda found Vivian clueless and alone one night at a club, and took her in like a child.

Randall spun me around in the chair by degrees. Soon I was facing a wall lined with hundreds of bottles, all different shapes, sizes, and colors, with names like *Bedhead* and *Dirt*.

Finally, Randall asked me, "How old are you?" He pulled the scissors away from my hair and waited for a response.

"Seventeen," I said. Randall looked at Jarred and Jarred smiled, winked at Randall, and turned his head toward me.

"When do you turn eighteen?" He began snipping at my hair again.

"Not until January," I said while he moved my head into position.

"You have a fake?" he asked.

"No," I said. He looked up at Jarred again.

"You know, they probably won't even card him if I say he's with me," he said, raising his eyebrows.

Amphiprion percula

The *Amphiprion percula*, or clownfish, lives within the coral reefs of Australia. This fish is able to live where most cannot. The clownfish covers itself in a layer of mucus. This protects the fish from the anemone's sting, which could kill the clownfish.

The Cove

The Friday night after my hair appointment with Randall, I carried things into the back room of a small gay club. I toted in clear Rubbermaid containers full of hair products, makeup, and accessories to match the drag-glam attire Amanda and Vivian would be wearing that night. Jarred helped me with a few of the boxes. I waited behind Jarred while he spoke to the bouncer sitting behind a sheet of Plexiglas. Jarred stepped back and I heard a faint buzz. A black door opened.

Holding the containers, we walked through the small club. Jarred warned me to keep my eyes ahead, and whatever I did, not to look over at the bar.

Mirrors covered the walls. Glitter was scattered on the black floor. Queens gossiped as they put on layers of blush, eyeliner, and lipstick. They walked back and forth with large wigs, some in short dresses slipping on long white gloves. Jarred made his way to an area beside Randall, and we put the containers down.

Randall was applying green eye shadow, leaning into the mirror, watching other queens walk back and forth out of the corners of his eyes. Some of them had curlers still in their wigs; one was looking for a pair of high heels. She accused another of stealing them, and they argued for a while. Randall rolled his eyes in their direction and began to apply even more lipstick.

I sat between Jarred and Randall and watched while Jarred took things out of the containers. He pulled out makeup case after makeup case, a blow dryer, hair brushes—the sight of his surgical tape made my eyes widen and my forehead wrinkle. I watched queens practice lip-synching the songs they'd perform. The songs ranged from Ella Fitzgerald to Blondie to Britney Spears. I found out later Vivian would be performing a Kelly Clarkson number.

Dominance of the Amphiprion percula

When the dominant female clownfish of the school dies, the next biggest fish will take its place. Thus the male will become a female and a juvenile will turn into a male. This will happen over and over again in the school.

Transformations

Jarred took over an hour to become Vivian. I watched him as he put on his makeup. He worked slowly, deliberately. Randall sat nearby, giving him pointers. *Not too much, you'll look cheap*, was one. Too much? It took ridiculous amounts for them to cover their male features. Five o'clock shadows were hidden by large amounts of foundation and blush. It amazed me to see that with every fluff of Jarred's makeup brush he became more Vivian.

"Why Vivian?" I asked Jarred. He closed the tube of lipstick and blotted his lips on a Kleenex.

"Because it's what I want to be. *Vivid*. It's where I got Vivian from. I didn't tell you at the time." He tossed the Kleenex into a small trash bin and stood. "Are you ready?" he asked Randall.

"I've been waiting on you," Randall replied. I followed them down a short hallway into another room, the wig room. Wigs lined the shelves along the walls. Wigs of different lengths. Short hair wigs, long hair wigs, and there was every shade of hair color. They rested on mannequin heads. When I saw the wigs, the fakeness finally set in. I felt like I had walked into the Revlon color-testing room. Randall took pride in the wigs. He explained to me that he had styled them all perfectly, spending hours on each one. He showed me a few that he had made himself. I stood in the doorway, letting the fake blue eyes rest on me.

I stood behind Amanda and Vivian while they dipped their head into the wigs. Amanda adjusted the mass of long, brown locks on her head, and explained to me that you never slip a wig on like a ball cap. Vivian put her head between her legs like a person getting nauseous. Then she dipped her head into a short blonde wig and pushed it closer to her forehead. They did one last makeup check and both applied another layer of pink-glitter lip gloss.

An older guy walked around with a headset and a clipboard. He frantically flipped through pages and crossed things out with a pen while speaking loudly into the mouthpiece.

"Vivian! Vivian! You're on in ten!" he shouted toward the mirrors. He crossed out something on the clipboard again and walked back into the club.

Beta splendens

The Siamese fighting fish (genus *Beta splendens*) is one of the most commonly owned among fish lovers. Betas come in a wide range of colors. Although they might be beautiful, their seductive shimmer gives them a misleading reputation. Betas are very territorial, and a pair should never be in close proximity. Betas use a defense mechanism called *flaring*. The act of flaring, or "puffing out" involves stretching out the fins and gills to appear more impressive. This behavior is used to either intimidate other fish or to attract a mate. Flaring is a behavior found mainly in males, although the behavior can be found in females.

To see this firsthand, you can take a small mirror and place it in front of the beta. When the beta sees its own reflection it will swim in place and begin to flare out its gills, and its tail will grow almost twice its normal size. This shouldn't be done too often, however. It creates in the beta a sense of panic.

Self Portrait as a Beta

While I waited on Vivian, I studied the beauty supplies on the table. I wondered why, why they did this. I noticed Vivian's eyeliner. I picked the tube up and pulled off the cap. I noticed how identical to a colored Crayola pencil it was. I ran my finger over the tip of it. It left a charcoal-like streak on the soft pad of my thumb.

I pulled the lower part of my eye down and exposed the pinkness under my eyeball. I brought the tip of the eyeliner closer. When the tip of it actually touched my eyelashes, I blinked and my eyes began to water. I tried again, bringing it to my eye again, slower this time. My eyes still blinked uncontrollably. I sat there in front of the mirror with the eyeliner still in my hand.

A few moments later Vivian came back in and saw me sitting in her chair. She saw the eyeliner in my hand and grinned.

"Were you putting that on?" she asked me, breathing hard, sweat on her forehead from the heat of the spotlights. I wasn't going to try to deny it.

"Yes. Maybe," I said to her. She pulled off her wig and set it down on the table.

"You don't know how, do you?" she asked, mocking my attempt at the eyeliner. "You've seen me put it on how many times and you still don't know how to do it?" I didn't say anything back. Before I could put the eyeliner back on the table she was behind me pulling it out of my hand. "Turn around here." She sat next to me in Amanda's chair and studied my face. She ran her fingers under my eyes.

Vivian worked quickly. She pulled down the skin under my eye, brought the eyeliner to the pink part. I was forced to trust her. Any jerk of my head or unexpected movement could cause her to jab me in the eye. I trusted Vivian.

The eyeliner made me look tired. Vivian told me it wasn't a good look for me. She tried removing it with a Kleenex she dampened with her tongue. While she rubbed the under part of my eye, I felt disappointed. I had never imagined myself in drag, and Vivian's comment somehow made me self-conscious. I noticed the feeling and wondered why I was disappointed.

After all, Vivian wasn't real. I began to understand that saying Vivian looked bad in that dress would probably give her the same insecure feeling. Vivian was a part of Jarred. Vivian might be someone Jarred wants to be. I began to understand that these queens were still the same person, that Amanda was still Randall, who had cut my hair earlier that week. After the eyeliner was removed I was still myself, backstage at a drag show.

I picked up a tube of hot-pink lip gloss. I squeezed a pea sized amount onto my finger. "Here, let me show you," Vivian said. I waited while she pulled another shade from a makeup bag. She began wiping the lip gloss from my lips. "That's a bad color on you," she said. "Let's try this one."

QUICK MONEY

After Ray was fined over two thousand dollars in noise pollution tickets, he sold all of his roosters, paid the fines, and purchased over 132 Siamese fighting fish. The owner of the pet store made a special order for Ray a week before, and the fish were shipped from Thailand to California, then across the country to Little Switzerland, North Carolina. Ray didn't mind that the cost for shipment was almost twice the price of the small fish themselves, and as soon as he opened the box and saw the shimmering tails of the betas, he knew this was a good investment.

"You know not to put two of them together, right? They're all males," the owner said.

"Yeah, I know that," Ray said.

"What are you doing with so many anyway?" the owner asked, hesitant to hand the box over.

"I'm doing a favor for the hospital. They say that watching fish swim can help heal patients faster. Since we can't put real aquariums in the rooms, we're going to put a beta in each room, you know? In those set-ups you see in offices and such. The ones where you have the plant, then at the bottom of the vase you have a little beta swimming around," Ray lied. He thought of this two days before as he was ten feet off the ground, cutting off cable to a home that hadn't paid their bill in two months. Ray worked for the cable company, and always needed a little extra money here and there.

"Well that's nice. Is it a church group doing all of it or…"

"Yeah, it's a church thing. Some people are getting the plants, and the rest are getting the vases." Ray took the box from the counter, walked out to his work truck and sat the fish on the floorboard.

Ray and his friend Danny stood in Ray's basement, putting the small clear plastic containers on a shelf above a large toolbox. They watched as the fish flared their tails and stretched out their gills. Their color intensified, and this defense mechanism occurred nonstop, but Ray still didn't separate them in hopes it would make them more ornery.

"So, you're going to let them fight?" Danny asked.

"Yeah. It's quieter than those roosters, and I don't think much of two dogs fighting. They're just fish, and they cost hardly anything," Ray said.

"Where're you going to let them fight?"

"Well, down here. I'm going to set up a table over there," Ray said, nodding over to a corner. "Then just take bets like I used to. Really, there's money to be made."

'Why can't you just breed them instead of letting them fight? Just go out and get a few females, and set up an aquarium. Sell the eggs as caviar. Sell them back to the pet store."

"That takes too much time. This way, the money's quick," Ray explained.

The following Friday night, trucks lined the side of the road across from Ray's house. The neighbors found this strange, considering they couldn't hear the sounds of men shouting, and feathers and beaks rustling and clashing. They couldn't see the men standing in a circle in Ray's backyard, their quiet silhouettes bracing the soft glow of cigarettes.

In the basement the men shouted, and Ray struggled to keep up with the bets on a legal pad. They stood around a round table, watching a blue beta and a red one nip at each other's tails, thrashing in the clear Rubbermaid container. The fish would stop for a few seconds, swim around one another, flaring, then the blue moved in on the red, and the water slowly turned a shade of rust. Ray cashed the men's bets and Danny walked over to the shelf and grabbed two other fish, then the men shouted out wagers and Ray took them down all over again.

By now Ray had a favorite beta. It was a white fish, with specks of burgundy on its tail, and it managed to win Ray over three hundred dollars in one night, without too many tears in its tail. After the fight, Ray scooped up the fish in its small plastic cup, and held it eye level. "You're a tough one," he said. "I think we're going to call you Cut Bait."

After that night Cut Bait earned a place next to the television. When Ray came home from work, he'd sit next in his recliner next to Cut Bait, eat his dinner, and usually fall asleep watching the eleven o'clock news. Ray never kept in mind the unfair advantage Cut Bait had over the other fish, being almost twice their size now. Ray also failed to mention this to the men that placed bets.

There was a man who came every Friday night to the fights with a friend of Ray's. His name was Fernando, and Ray didn't know him very well, but as long as he was placing bets Ray let him stay in his basement with the other men. All Ray knew about Fernando was that he was the co-owner of the small movie theater, and that he spent a lot of his free time at the shooting range.

That night Ray kept Cut Bait next to him the entire time. Ray would always let the other fish fight first, saving Cut Bait to fight last. That night the bets kept coming through the air, and Ray would cash in and out. Finally, Fernando stood across from Ray at the table.

"I hear the white one's the best," Fernando said. He was wearing a white button-up shirt, sleeves rolled up halfway from his wrists to elbows, and had loosened his tie at some point in the night.

"Cut Bait's tough," Ray said.

"I bet you five hundred dollars he can't fight two." Fernando folded his arms, and Ray thought about the offer.

"Cut Bait could take two of them," Ray decided. " I'll even let you pick two from off the shelf."

"You want to put money on this?" Fernando asked.

"Go pick two off the shelf."

Fernando walked over to the shelf, and returned shortly with two purple fish, darting around in their containers.

"Put them in," Ray said. Fernando poured the fish into the Rubbermaid container on the table, and the men began shouting bets again. The table rocked slightly, and small amounts of water splashed and fell onto the floor. The two purple ones circled each other, then before they started into it, Ray dumped in Cut Bait. At first the fish spent minutes flaring at one another. Seconds later it turned into a free-for-all and the water turned a familiar slight orange. Five minutes or so into the fight one of the purple fish began floating away from the others, and Ray scooped it out, leaving it in its container on the table. Cut

Bait and the remaining purple fish flared again. Suddenly there was a flurry of torn silky fins, and like its counterpart, the purple fish slowly floated away from Cut Bait.

The men made nothing more than a soft murmur, then went silent when Fernando shouted, "You cheat! You're a cheat!"

"How did I cheat you? You even picked the fish," Ray said, scooping out the dead purple fish.

"You cheat!" he shouted. He leaned over and examined Cut Bait. "Look at the size of this one!" The men standing around the table leaned slightly in, but said nothing about Cut Bait in particular. "That one's almost twice the size of the others. You're a cheat."

"You heard before you came here tonight that Cut Bait was stronger than the rest," Ray said. "I don't see the big deal. You even wanted to put five hundred dollars on it, not me."

"I'm not paying a cheat. You don't fight fair. I'm not paying," Fernando said, still leaning over Cut Bait, a vein in his temple bulging.

"Fine. Don't pay. Just leave and I'd appreciate it if you didn't come back," Ray said, stepping closer to the table.

"I won't be coming back. Neither will that fish," Fernando said. Before Ray could jerk the Rubbermaid container away, or scoop out Cut Bait, Fernando knocked the container on the floor. Ray bent down to fetch Cut Bait as Fernando raised the heel of his boot.

BIRD WATCHING
(EXCERPT)

When Hubble realized that Dee's pain would keep her from enjoying her only hobby, Hubble went out every other Saturday night and got another tattoo. Dee had been diagnosed with Multiple Sclerosis two years ago during a time when another man was in love with her. Hubble was never interested in bird watching. He would rather spend the days in his body shop, or in his usual evening bar defending Jeff Gordon's heterosexuality, or cleaning the gutters of his home, or pressure washing his small walkway as if he might actually have company coming. Then Hubble met Dee.

He met her one evening in Bello's pub. Dee was leaning into the jukebox with red, yellow, green, and blue lights hitting the sides of her face, and long dark brown hair falling past her earlobes. She selected a song Hubble didn't know, then turned and noticed him, and his greased stained jeans. She walked over to the stool next to him.

"You look like you work hard," she said, eyeing the jeans over.

"I try," Hubble said. The bartender came over and asked Dee what she would like to drink.

"Ginger ale. Three cherries, please."

"Nothing harder?" Hubble asked.

"I don't drink," she said.

They talked until last call. They talked about people who didn't bother to read the directions on a variety of products at the drugstore she worked at, about the countless tire rotations he did everyday. Later, they stood in the parking lot beside Dee's older white Buick, and Hubble found out she was having troubles with another man.

"He keeps begging me back. I don't want him," she said.

"I can see why he keeps begging you back," Hubble said, winking. "You can't blame the man."

Hubble didn't know the '87 Ford Pickup belonged to Fernando, until he found Polaroids of Dee wearing a hot-pink bikini, laying out on a beach towel, under the front seat while he did a routine inspection that came along with the oil change package. He put the pictures in his back pocket, checked the tire pressure, put the hood of the truck down, then walked into the waiting area of his body shop.

The man he found out was Fernando stood next to a rack of air-fresheners, smelling the difference between the scented cardboard pine trees and the yellow and orange floral scented bouquets.

"Excuse me, sir," Hubble called out to him. "I can total you up here at the register." Hubble walked behind the counter, punched in the twenty-five dollars for the oil change, then tossed the Polaroids down on the counter. Fernando looked up from his wallet, then let the money fall on the counter at the sight of Dee in the hot-pink bathing suit.

"You went through my truck," Fernando said, brown eyes widening, then narrowing as he leaned closer toward the counter.

"No, I didn't go through your truck. I just happened to notice these under the seat."

"I could sue you for this. You don't even know her. Why—"

"I know her. Dee. I met her a week and a half ago at Bello's. We had dinner last night." Fernando began to ease off the counter, then grinned as Hubble pushed the money drawer shut, then ripped off a receipt.

"It's pointless, you know. Trying to date her," Fernando said.

"Just because she doesn't want you doesn't mean she can't have anyone else," Hubble said, putting his hands on the edge of the counter.

"She can't have kids. But, she probably hasn't told you that yet."

"What?" Hubble asked.

"Multiple Sclerosis. You know, MS. That's why she left me. She always felt so guilty that she couldn't have kids," Fernando explained, still grinning, making his way to the door. Hubble didn't say anything afterwards. He let the bells tied to the door break the heaviness of this discovery, then watched Fernando drive away from the large front window.

That evening Hubble and Dee sat in the parking lot of a McDonalds, eating French fries and plain hamburgers. Hubble was quiet that afternoon. They let the country music from the radio mediate the silence between them, and Dee wondered what might have been bothering Hubble. Finally Hubble said, "Fernando needed an oil change. He came in today after lunch."

"He still driving that pick-up?" she asked.

"Yeah. Still has some pictures of you under the seat too," he said, crumpling up a hamburger wrapper. She bit a few fries in half, and chewed slowly.

"Those are so old," she explained. "They're from two summers ago. I don't understand why he still has them."

"I bet I could tell you why," Hubble said, a slight smile on a face.

"Oh hush!" Dee said, smacking his arm softly. They finished off the fries, and Hubble turned down the radio before turning the ignition. He went to put the car in reverse, but instead his hand rested on the gear shift.

"Why'd you leave him?" Hubble asked. She rolled down the window, and hung her arm out.

"I think you already know," she said looking at him. "I think you know."

After six months of Hubble knowing why Dee had left Fernando, he managed to buy a small house not far from the body shop and Dee moved from her one bedroom apartment. The ideal love Hubble had for Dee become more domestic. While they unloaded Dee's things from the back of a small U-Haul trailer, they both thought of how this would work out. Hubble would get up every morning at seven thirty, eat breakfast, then Dee would come in still in her baggy tee shirt and look out the window by the table in the kitchen. She'd sip her coffee and do a routine headcount of the birds that showed up at the large red wooden feeder that was already posted in the yard the day they moved in. Hubble would leave for work before Dee, and they would reconvene every night for dinner, except on weekends when they would go to the movies, or the occasional camping trip.

One Saturday night Hubble found himself sitting in a tattoo parlor getting a yellow finch engraved on his left shoulder. Dee knew there was nothing she could do at this point but hold his hand, and keep his shirt sleeve rolled up while, Redneck, the tattoo artist, went about his work.

He looked at Dee when Redneck turned the buzzing pen off, and said, "That's a Dee bird."

Hubble was putting away Dee's bird watching binoculars from one of their weekend camping trips when he remembered seeing a large white Molocan cockatoo in the pet store next to the deli where he often ate lunch. The next afternoon he rolled a large black iron cage into the living room, filled with small plastic brightly colored toys with bells and mirrors tied to the end of them. He assembled the toys for the bird on perches that lined the cage, then filled small metal bowls with water and bird seed.

He went outside, and Dee came into the living room from down the hall when she heard the door of Hubble's truck slam shut. When he returned, the small white cardboard box rustled under his arm and Dee replied with, "What's in the box?" He carefully pulled open the flaps, and the large bird poked its black beak into the air, then turned its head to get a better look at Hubble and Dee standing over them.

"C'mon, Rambo," Hubble said, taking the bird into his hands, walking it over to the cage.

"Wait a minute. Let me see him," Dee said, reaching into the cage. Rambo perched on Dee's small hand, and she brought him out of the cage, and they studied each other, trying to figure out if one was just excited about the other.

During the fall after Hubble brought home Rambo, Hubble came home almost every week with a new bird tattooed on his body. He would only go out on nights Dee would accompany him. Most nights she'd start the night out slowly, then after a couple hours start to feel ill, and drove home, insisting that he stayed at the party.

One morning Dee found him on the couch. He'd been out a little later than usual that night. She walked over to Rambo's cage, pulled the blanket from over it, and Rambo stood, a silver engagement ring tied to his talon. Dee jumped back, then carefully reached in to retrieve Rambo and the ring. She sat on the edge of the sofa, letting Rambo walk along the back of it, shaking Hubble gently.

Cory Wallace, Age 17
South Carolina Governor's School for the Arts and Humanities
Greenville, SC
Teachers: Scott Gould, George Singleton

ENGLISH BREAKFAST

You forgot your summer dress when you left, and
I cut it into little shining squares of ivory.
I used them to steep my tea, so they have
slowly stained brown, but I didn't think you'd mind.

I remember how I used to have to train myself
not to point out the similarities between you
and your father, the way you fold your napkin
in your lap, the way he looks up at the ceiling
when he drinks his tea.

It is Christmas 1982 and our heater coughs and dies.
We chew sandwiches of dark chocolate and graham crackers,
and you're cranky because you don't like the cold.
You murmur, "I just want hot tea, Jesus,
is that so much to ask?" I hold you closer.

Kayla Krut, Age 15
The Bishop's School
La Jolla, CA
Teacher: Chad Bishop

THE FUNERAL

The lights were down
as I watched
the room full of people.
People all saying,
they remember holding me as a baby.
All saying that we should get together again some time,
sometime,
not at a funeral.
Yet all of us knew we never would,
not until another funeral.
Most of the people in the room
were sisters of the deceased.
Most of them looked old enough
to be my grandmother's grandparents.
They spoke to me in shaking voices,
in languages I didn't understand.
Sometimes Spanish, sometimes Italian, sometimes I picked out
a word of English.
Just as we left,
one lady took me aside.
She said something to me, but
the words had no meaning.
Her eyes looked into mine,
looked down into my soul and told me
in the end everything would be all right.
Saying goodbye to her was harder
than losing someone to begin with.

Cora Johnson-Grau, Age 13
Los Angeles Center for Enriched Studies
Los Angeles, CA
Teacher: Velicia Chartier

SONG EVER CHANGING

She stands at the base of the main road leading out of the camp, watching dust settle back into the gravel. The faces pressed up against the back window of the bus grow smaller and smaller, and eventually disappear as the bus rounds the corner out of the camp. So that's that. Most of the campers are gone, only a few linger until their parents will arrive on the 2:30 connecting flight from Bangor to Augusta, the biggest town anywhere near Stearns Pond.

She hadn't wanted this at first. "We're sending you to camp," her parents had told her. "It's in northern Maine, and it's musically oriented."

"Band camp?" she remembers saying. "You want to send me to band camp?" She could imagine the jokes and taunts she'd suffer if anyone found out. But her parents ignored her, told her it would be good for her violin skills and might help her get into regional orchestra next year. July rolled around and they shipped her off on a bus to Camp Encore-Coda, ten hours away in what was essentially Nowheresville, Maine.

But now she watches the buses pull away one after the other and she wants more than anything else to stay here, grounded, feet firmly planted on the sandy soil. Her bags are packed, her bunk stripped of sheets and the cabin floor swept clean, but she's not ready. It will not be easy to leave the soaring pine trees and the sunny waterfront and campfires every evening. But hardest of all will be to leave the tall boy with his cello and his green eyes and lopsided smile.

The morning air is cool and damp and slides into the folds of her sweatshirt, making her shiver even in the sunlight, which shines through the trees, turning the edges of the leaves glowing green and dappling the ground with gold. She hears him coming before she sees him. She's learned, like the Indians with their ears pressed to the ground, to tell when he is coming from the cadence of his footfalls. Here in the forest, where there is no cacophony of sounds from the highway, every sound is clearer. Her senses have sharpened as the outside distractions have fallen away. Even his scent stands out among the crispness of the pine trees.

He comes and stands beside her, but she cannot bear to look at him. He radiates warmth in the cool air and so she steps closer to him, still averting her eyes. After a moment, he speaks.

"I won't say I don't want you to go," he says, "because I know you have to."

"It won't make things any easier," she admits.

"I'll come back next year," he says. An offering.

A year is the longest time, she decides. "It won't make things easier," she repeats, and he is quiet. She looks up at the sky with her eyes open wide, trying to dry her tears before they spill.

"Lily," he says, and the weight of his breath on her neck is enough to make her swallow a sob. She puts her arm around him and presses her face against his shoulder. When she closes her eyes in the middle of winter, trying to find some warmth inside herself, this is what she will think of. This is how she wants to know summer in her mind.

"We could visit sometimes," he says, trying anything to stop her from crying.

She sighs and pulls away. "No, we couldn't. I can't afford a plane ticket, even if my parents would let me go. California may as well be another planet."

"We could write, then."

She wants to say yes. She wants to pen him love letters and spray them with her perfume like she's seen in movies and sign her name followed by a trail of Xs and Os. But she knows that soon enough, feelings will dissipate into memory. Love will become obligation, and that's the last thing she wants. She wants to preserve the perfection of this moment and never let it sour.

"No," she says. She takes his hand and presses her palm to his, memorizing the shape of his calluses. "I don't want to talk about goodbye anymore."

He clings to her hand. They're both out of ideas, and they know it has to be like this. Nobody finds their soulmate at fourteen. She wishes, in the part of her that still believes in magic, that they'd met when they were much older. Nobody marries the person they meet at summer camp. The grown-up part of her knows this is silly, that she'll probably forget all about him by the first week of school. That was the part of her that was controlling her brain when she gave in and let the cute boy in the cello section buy her a soda during rehearsal break. That part of her didn't think about how it would be, four weeks later, to have to say goodbye.

She thinks about how you spend your life building walls around yourself. Little by little you build, until you think you're finally safe. And then along comes someone who can knock down the walls with the softest touch of his hand. She knows she was never safe, not really. And for a while she welcomed the intrusion. But now she wishes her heart was made of stone so it wouldn't be so easily crushed by one little word.

"I hate summer camp," she says suddenly. "How do they expect us to do this? How are we supposed to go to the middle of nowhere for a month and meet all these people and then leave them? Who came up with that idea?"

He doesn't say anything cheesy, or try to offer trite advice about how it's better to have loved and lost, and all that nonsense that means nothing to a person actually saying goodbye. He just leans forward and whispers in her ear.

"This is real," he says. "Just because it's short doesn't mean it's not real."

And for the moment, that is all she needs to hear. Confirmation that the Maine air hasn't made her crazy. Love can take the shape of years upon years, but sometimes it's only given a few weeks. That doesn't mean it's any less all-consuming or life-altering.

She steps back from him, still clutching his hands, and closes her eyes. She wants to take it all in, every memory of every moment of the past four weeks. She might only be fourteen, but she knows some things. Violin will come and go. She might make regional orchestra, or she might decide in September that horseback riding is her new thing and give up violin entirely. It doesn't really matter either way. She won't remember the high second finger in the third measure of her solo piece, or how many hours she spent toiling through private lessons in un-air-conditioned practice rooms.

This is what she will remember. The way a viola sounds murmuring through trees heavy with rain. Waking to a new trumpet player stumbling through Reveille. The sound of mournful saxophones singing her to sleep. Playing cards in the cafeteria on a rainy afternoon. Holding hands under the table at dinner. Kissing under the eaves on a night so warm the air feels like a second skin. How hello feels like a symphony and goodbye feels like a lone violin, playing on a darkened stage. And this, above all: The music is beautiful and it will play on, song ever changing but never really gone.

Jenna Devine, Age 16
The Pingry School
Martinsville, NJ
Teacher: Thomas Keating

A TWISTED STOMACH

I glanced down at the speedometer as I flew down the hill leaving Landisburg. Wow, I thought to myself, after this I'm going to have to talk to him about speeding. I did the best I could to keep up with my father without going over the speed limit too much, as he led the way to Ralph Albright's farm. Whenever we arrived, the smell of the barn enveloped me. The odor was not as pungent as other barns, I thought, as I slipped off my sneakers and grabbed my boots on the passenger side of the car. Fitting my white-socked feet into the steel-toed boots, I noticed Dad hustling along, grabbing a bucket, crate, and other various items from his truck and hurrying into the barn. When I laced up my boots, I recognized an all-too-familiar sound. Glancing upward, I saw a cow less than one hundred feet from me, doing its "business." Here we go, I thought, as I grabbed my clipboard and made my way to the barn.

Today I would be observing a surgery called an LDA, which stands for "left displaced abomasum," also known as a twisted stomach. An LDA occurs when the cow's fourth stomach has gotten out of proper position and makes a cow stop eating. Left displaced abomasums most commonly occur in dairy cows one to four weeks after calving. The exact cause is unknown; however, it is associated with high grain and low forage diets or with other health problems.

When I entered the barn at 10:38 A.M., no one was in sight except for my father. One of my first observations was the paucity of repulsive odors inside the barn. Apparently, the huge new ventilation fans greatly reduce the usual odors found in barns. Although no other human life was present, two long rows of cattle shuffled about in their stanchions. The chains rattled on the cows' necks as they swayed back and forth. Every once in a while a cow would raise her tail and relieve herself and the waste would slop into the gutter behind her. Bedding mixed with manure was lightly scattered across the walkway between the two rows of cows. The Holstein my father would be operating on was at the end of the closest row, less than ten feet from the barn entrance.

The black and white cow was about four years old. My father started by tying her head to one of the rust-covered nails with a slipknot. He then injected her tail vein with a tranquilizer. Using a wire-toothed currycomb, my dad scraped the crusty manure and dirt off the side he would be operating on. Taking some power clippers, he proceeded to trim a 30-by-30 square inch area into the coarse hair behind her ribs. What was once black and white was now a pink area of flesh with veins scattered throughout. Then Ralph Albright entered with his golden lab, Mel. The dog growled at us for a few seconds, then ignored us. A young woman named Kelsey came into the barn, along with an older man.

The surgery incision would be through the para-lumbar fossa, the depression behind the cow's ribs. My father grabbed some gauze sponges, soaked them with iodine soap, and started to scrub the surgical area. The iodine turned the clipped square a sickly yellow color and made several bubbles appear on the area. Soon after, the cow began grinding her teeth, possibly due to the pain of her ailment. After he was finished disinfecting, my father took a bucket of warm water and rinsed off the soap. Steam rose off the warm flesh as it came in contact with the cool air. He then sprayed the surgical site with rubbing alcohol. I was given the job of pushing up on the Holstein's tail as my dad disinfected the area with Lidocaine.

Forcefully holding the tail had two purposes. First, the bovine could not swing her tail and contaminate the sterile area. Second, pushing up on a cow's tail would immobilize her, preventing her from kicking my father as he injected the local anesthetic. Nervous about standing behind the cow, my father warned me that the cow would kick if I did not forcefully elevate the tail. As I applied upward pressure to the tail, I received several gaseous surprises in my face. Ralph and his coworkers let out a few chuckles at the face I made upon the rank smell hitting my nose.

After the injection was completed, we tied the cow's tail to her left rear leg. Little swelling appeared where my dad had given the injections, in the shape of the number "7." He slipped on a thin, sterile, orange plastic glove that ran up to his shoulder, and washed both arms in a bucket full of hot, soapy water. My heart quickened as the surgery was about to commence.

My father picked up a scalpel and started to slice through the quarter-inch thick hide. Blood oozed out of the fresh wound and dribbled down the side of the cow, collecting in the uncut hair, then slowly dripping onto the hay like a leaky faucet. After he struggled to make an eight-inch vertical incision through the thick hide, he cut through three muscle layers and into the abdomen. The muscle layers appeared to peel away like an orange's skin, as blood quickly filled the incision. As soon as he cut into the abdomen, air rushed in, creating a flatulent sound.

At this point, Ralph removed a long sterile tube from a plastic bag. The six-foot tube with an attached two-inch, 14-gauge needle was pulled from the bag by my father. The end opposite the needle was attached to a Shop-Vac. The vacuum would be used to suck all the air out of the displaced stomach, to make moving it much easier. My father took the tube and reached inside the cow, over the top of the first stomach and across to the left side of the cow. There he found the gas-filled abomasum and he inserted the needle. My father's orange-sleeved arm disappeared from sight as the cow's side engulfed it. Ralph turned on the Shop-Vac, and the vacuum deflated the fourth stomach. Ralph and his coworkers had been watching with interest, but now they left the barn to complete other jobs.

After emptying the stomach of air and removing the tube and needle, my father stuck his arm down the inside of the cow's right side and pulled out her omentum, which is connected to the stomach. The omentum is a surgical landmark during an LDA operation. A flap on the omentum called the "pig's ear" told us we were getting closer to the stomach. The flap actually looked like a pig's ear, which fascinated me. Locating the stomach, Dad pulled it up and into the incision to show me. The stomach was the color of cottage cheese and looked extremely slippery. Veins were spread across the stomach like an intricate spider web. I wanted to touch it, but I could not since my hands were not washed.

My father grabbed a towel clamp to hold the omentum into the incision opening. He was going to suture the omentum into the first muscle layer. As he began, I squatted and looked inside the incision. An expansive cavity loomed above all the internal organs. Whenever the cow breathed, I watched as the organs slowly rose toward the spinal cord. Dad placed five sutures to tack the omentum. While suturing the abdominal lining, the cow breathed deeply, causing some intestines to spill out of the opening. Many times I imagined intestines as round and tubelike, but this cow's intestines were flat and pale because of the lack of food in her diet. My father quickly caught them in his clean hands, and skillfully placed them back inside the Holstein.

Suddenly, the cow decided she was going to lie down. If she had lain down, she could have gotten dirt and manure in the wound, contaminating the surgical site. I stood by helplessly as my father yelled and kicked her back legs to keep her up. I let out a sigh of relief when the cow decided it was better to stand than to take the abuse from my father. I could only imagine what damage would have been caused if she had lain down. My dad prepared to start suturing up the muscle layers.

A mild annoyance developed as he found a knot in the middle of the suture line. Unable to untie it, he mumbled under his breath and decided to bear with it. Every time he yanked it through the muscle layer, a popping sound was audible. My father put four throws on all the suture knots so they would not untie. He continued to close the opening with a simple interrupted suture pattern. When the stitching was completed, he closed the hide with an interlocking stitch. An interlocking stitch allowed him to close her much faster. I could see the frustration on his face as he struggled to push the needle through the thick hide without poking himself. The completed stitching looked like a zipper. My father finished the surgery at 11:34 A.M.

Ralph returned and asked how the surgery went. My father stated it went well. I then sprayed the incision with a silver coating called an aerosol bandage. The bandage glistened as sunlight from a dusty window hit it at just the right angle.

My dad shed the bloody sleeve, washed his hands and arms, picked up his equipment, and walked out to the truck. When he re-entered, Ralph had him check three other Holsteins. Two of them also had twisted stomachs. I'm sure glad I do not have to stick around to do them, I thought to myself. My father decided he would come back later that afternoon and attend to them. I thanked my father for allowing me to come and made my way out to the car. I took off my manure-covered boots and put on my comfortable sneakers. As I placed the key into the ignition, I thought about how busy my father was going to be for the rest of the day.

Joshua P. McMillen, Age 17
West Perry High School
Elliottsburg, PA
Teacher: Carol Weishaar

ON BEING EXPERIENCED

"Experience is the name everyone gives to their mistakes."

—Oscar Wilde

1.   My mother always wore a purple-knit sweater. From my youngest years, that's all I see: her long straight hair framing a blank face and then the violet, harsh and expansive. The same color they taught us about in photo class. It's sensitive to light, taken straight, extracted from mollusks. Early, it was mollusks I wished I could crack open on her plate, but I didn't have the technique, the fingernails, or the strength. Instead, my father split each open, and her lips pursed a perfect downwards bow when he spliced a shell unevenly; but she ate them anyway.

2.   Once my brother Adam cracked his head open on a rotisserie grill. The spokes were perfect cylinders, but mechanical, robotically violent. He walked over and pressed his fat toddler hand to the machine, setting the wheels in motion, shapes like block work from a simple toy. We were in the meat section of a supermarket. He spun obliviously near one spare grill, which lay in pieces on the linoleum, disassembled hastily for cleaning. The crunch of bone is something instantly recognizable, but nearly impossible to remember afterward. Blood is different; it has a common taste, connotative of platelets, transfusions, canker sores and scraped knees. Bones are animalistic, cracking, splintering, making fillets of themselves, bent like piano keys that went down with the *Titanic*.

3.   Owen had huge hands. His lifeline stretched farther than the entire span of my own palm, a sure sign he'd live forever. He was a god that way, Aries or Apollo, or maybe just the real thing, G-O-D all the way through. Some boys are all golden inside, and he was it: spilling out of his eyes, and then even smaller, from the tips of his sockets. We were best friends for years but I only swam with him once. We were still tiny then, and our bodies looked the same in our bathing suits. The pool was viscous, dirty, with last year's leaves at the bottom. We didn't dare to retrieve them, but we swam anyway.

He held my head underwater for a long time. His wide fingers deep in my hair, holding the strands tighter then the actual head itself. I was pounding with the lack of something essential. It may have lain at the gritty bottom, always a little ahead, out of reach. When he let me up for air I didn't say much. "You're so hurt-able," he muttered, with his hands on my shoulders.

4. Bill has always been skinny as hell. His body always a straight line, with no curvature at all; sometimes he was so slight it was hard to look at him. He never had calluses of any kind. Even his feet were plush and soft, like the hairless stomachs of puppies; his hands were the same too, long joints with perfect fingertips. His eyelashes were elegant and black: Maybelline lashes. Most girls would have killed for them. In the summer, we'd all go sunbathe on the basketball courts, each of us glowing golden except for him. His long green veins matched his neon swim trunks; we could see each bone, every vertebra. Our long-nosed vanity was caused by our precocious, coddled nature, and we looked down at his jutting form. A simple prejudice: we were beautiful, and he was less than, not equal to, our fine fat deposits and long femurs. Later, he ended up in the hospital, all hooked up under his blue, blue skin; and we went to visit him.

5. After dental surgery, John's mother wouldn't let him drive anywhere. She claimed he was too hopped up on codeine, the orange bottle with the childproof cap, and a label warning about a loss of depth perception. He seemed fine to me, but we stayed in that night anyway, watching an old movie on the VCR. The next weekend when his mom was out of town, John drove himself to Seekonk—drunk, racing down the highway, for no particular reason other than wanting to drive fast and watch the colors blur. Funny, what parents think they can prevent, what they think they know.

6. No one else in the city lived like this. We were home alone: James's parents out until tomorrow, and we kissed for hours on the couch in the front living room. We spent the rest of the day walking around in socks; I did my stepping jig to no music while he watched. His house always reminded me of my grandmother's back in New Jersey: all glass and steel, with crystal figurines and potpourri in a basket. The smell was the same: of clean civilized human beings and wealth, not extravagant, but immediately apparent. His backyard looked over a ravine that stretched down for a quarter mile until it suddenly dropped off into the bay. He took me out there with two cans of Coca-Cola and showed me how to hit a golf ball. I would just close my eyes and swing, not bothering with the form he taught me. It struck me as strange that we were still in Providence, but I forgot the minute, showing off, he hit a ball into the water.

On the ferry back from Nantucket we read the paper. We split the Life Beat section, me with the comics, and he attempting the Jumble. I got bored with Family Circle and started reciting the scripture my father chanted in his yoga classes. The other passengers would look over occasionally, but I kept on going, and James never took his eyes off the page. I stopped speaking when the ribbon of my memory coiled itself from my reach, writhing away like a little Egyptian snake, diamond pattern shaking. I looked over his shoulder. He was puzzling out "uippl"; he had written it out several times incorrectly. "Pupil," I said aloud suddenly, and he looked up at me and rolled his eyes.

We lasted until June. Later, sitting in the back of his car, he would tell me little things, into my skin, pressing hard. He left small marks all over me. Then he'd drive me home, and my mother would ask where I had gone. "A few of us were just driving around," I always told her, and I could almost see the scene in my head: an alternate reality, without me in it. My mother and I watched his headlights disappear down our street, two perfect yellow circles spit out onto the concrete.

7.   Carolyn took another draw from her cigarette, flicking ash on the kitchen table, her eyes trained on the TV, on the pageant girls all lined up in a row. "You know what my mom told me, when I told her I wanted to be Miss America?" I watch the runner-up cross the stage in her deep blue gown, eyes sparkling with tears, manicured hand at her throat. "I was twelve, I told her I wanted to be as pretty as Miss New Jersey." She gestured towards the screen, her cigarette run down almost to the filter. "You know what she said?" I barely moved as I watched the program, the winner reaching for her crown. I'd known Carolyn for a long time, long enough for it to be all right not to respond. "She told me it was only about who you know," she paused for a moment. Her cigarette finally out, she reached for another, "But I know what she meant about girls who mess around." Carolyn held out the lighter to me, and I took it between my thumb and forefinger, and thought maybe she only understands now because she is one.

Rosetta Young, Age 16
The Wheeler School
Providence, RI
Teacher: Kristine Palmero

TANTAMOUNT

Twenty young men and women, the very best of the best in science, sat around a long rectangular steel table. It was a cold looking room, with a single glass window to the outside, fogged by frost. Above them was the building's rooftop, where neon letters spelled out: Pulcher Laboratories: Human Perfection Studies.

A clean man in an unwrinkled suit sat at the head of the table: the Director. His words started out terse and staccato, but toward the end they became loud and loose. He asked his colleagues why the newest generation, at the age of three years old, still couldn't speak. Yes, they were only the fifth generation so far created since the Great Integration, but still...shouldn't three-year-olds be talking? His words were matter-of-fact, but his rising anger boiled over. He started to yell, a map of blue veins becoming prominent on his forehead.

"What's wrong?" His jaw tightened. "We've created a stable community. We've created the perfect human: a blend of all races. The Grays replace the Caucasians, the Asians, the Africans, the Semites, and any other race that ever existed. Everyone is now Gray with ash-colored skin, gray eyes, and dull brown hair. Everyone feels equal. Everyone feels spectacular. But now what? Now the children can't speak?" The scientists sat still, a deep ruby flushing their cheeks. Failure was a new feeling for them.

Two floors below was a sterile room. To say it was clean would be an understatement. The walls were white to a degree of purity. The indirect fluorescent lighting left no shadows. Nothing was unseen.

Twenty-five three-year-olds. Gray children clothed in white, gurgling drool in and out of their small mouths. Seventy-two wooden blocks, painted white, lay on the floor. From two speakers anchored to the walls, sentences were uttered. "The man washed his car. I opened my refrigerator. I like the color blue. All colors mix to gray." Their purpose? To teach the children to speak.

The children played in silence, picking up the blocks or throwing them or stacking them into tiny towers. "I am lying down." Little bodies, fresh and sweet, bumped into the towers and knocked them over. No dreams fell. No voices raised. No flood of salty tears. The children were learning how to build; they were learning to create a world with their little blocks so that when they grew up, that's just what they would do: Build a world.

And if they'd been tall enough, they might have pressed their little fingers against the glass window in the door to their room. They could have peered out of the window and down the narrow hallway. They might have caught sight of a slender figure, a middle-aged woman, dressed in a long white laboratory coat. They would have seen her leaning against a wall, holding something in her hands. And, had they been able to understand language, they would have heard her cursing in tightly-knit sentences. They would have heard her remind herself of her opposition to the Great Integration, and her personal alignment with the Great Segregation. How wondrous society would be again if only there was diversity and segregation when it came to the races of children . . . Latinos and Africans and Caucasians all functioning together but still individually enjoying their rich, unique cultures. She mouthed the horrors. Oh, but extermination! If she were caught? Well, there would be no trial. She would be directly exterminated.

However, she could make a difference. She could show twenty-five fresh minds a Different child—twenty-five minds not yet hardened, not yet corrupted. Even if she didn't have enough time to teach them how to accept, she could make them see. She could provide their impressionable minds with information they'd never be able to unlearn. And that she knew she had to do, no matter the risks for herself.

Back in the room, the door slowly opened. "The man shovels dirt." A woman in her late 40s entered the room. Her shoes softly clicked against the spotless, tiled floor, snapping the children's attention away from the blocks and to the center of the room. She bent down, placed something on the ground, then quickly straightened and left the room. Fifty gray eyes widened.

The balance in the room suddenly shifted. "I have a pet dog." On the floor before them was a child of their age, a boy. His face looked distorted; his skin was olive brown and his hair was a color they had not seen before: jet black. His eyes were small and his nose hooked. The pupils, a charcoal hue, appeared as if someone had bottled up nighttime and poured it into them. The children stared.

The Different child stepped forward, unaware of the sudden electricity running through the air. "She opens my refrigerator." The children's fingers twitched as the boy clutched a single white block, turning it over in his small hand. They wanted to snatch the block away, but walking toward him would be like treading on foreign soil. So they started to cry.

But there was one; one child whose eyes weren't wet, but curious. This child crawled forward, reaching out with his fingers and touching the Different child's face. The Different child dropped the block, looking at the gray-skinned child touching him. A smile broke across his olive skin face and he started to giggle, feeling tickled by the touch. The Gray child pulled his hand back, startled because that sound was new to his ears. "The girl and the boy dance happily."

Then, the most miraculous thing happened. The Gray child burst out in happy shrieks. He cackled away and fell over, completely surprised by his laughter. The Different child smiled and giggled more. The rest of the children looked in shock at one of their own, on the floor, making that noise. But the laughter was contagious, and soon they were all chortling, too.

"I love to build. Building is fun."

Soon, an alarm sounded. Hearing the noise, a group of laboratory workers burst into the room. They caught eye of the Different child and stared at him with confusion. After the initial shock, a member of the group pulled on latex gloves and picked up the Different child, quickly carrying him out of the room.

The laughter ceased and the happy tears in the children's eyes turned hot and angry. Then one screamed in an upset tone, "Boy! Boy!" The rest picked up the idea and they all started to scream any word they remembered to vocalize their disapproval. "Dog!" "Dirt!" "Buiwd, buiwd, BUIWDING!"

The adults swayed, falling to their knees in joyful appreciation. The children had spoken their first words! As suddenly as they had entered, they dispersed, running to the stairway to go up two floors.

After a chorus of explanation to the Director, who was seated at the head of the steel table, they all broke into smiles, pleased that they had witnessed the children's first words. Then they proudly ushered him down two floors below and opened the door to the sterile room. Inside, it was silent.

The Director was perplexed, and their smiles disappeared. He turned in anger, "Do you think this is some sort of joke?" He looked at each of them directly in the eye, deflating their high spirits. Just a minute or so ago, they assured him, the children had been speaking.

Finally, after a prolonged awkward silence, the Director turned and smiled, feeling suddenly connected to the chubby-faced children. He reached his hand out, ruffling one girl's hair. She looked upward and pouted; he noticed her gray eyes were sad. Then he turned again, straightened his face, and cleared his throat to address the workers: "Go get me the Different child. Come back promptly."

"Flowers are very pretty."

The electricity returned to the room, but this time, it was from the adults. They felt uncomfortable, looking at such a Different thing. At first, the three-year-olds didn't notice because they all had their heads down, staring at the floor. One by one, they looked up and saw the Different child. The speaking began again: "Car?" "Open?" "DOWN!" Again, the children shrieked with joy. They jumbled forward, smiles spreading across their faces. "Place the Different child down," commanded the Director. The workers obeyed.

Promptly 25 pairs of hands reached out to touch the Different child. Hands brushed against his cheeks, his arms…all with the same intent: to make sure he was really there. For the third time that day the children cried, but this time their tears weren't caused from laughter or anger, but from happiness.

The workers stared, their faces furrowed with new confusion, even with disgust. They turned to the Director, silent questions streaming from their faces. He regarded the children, his eyebrows narrowing, feeling like he had just heard a joke he did not understand. But then he smiled with sudden realization and shook his head.

"They need…Different."

"How?" a worker inquired.

"Invite Different in."

"The song was strange."

Sindha Agha, Age 13
University Laboratory High School
Urbana, IL
Teacher: Elizabeth Majerus

THE SWEET FORGOTTEN LIFE

The thump, thump, thump of my heart
    echoes through the worn Appalachians
    and the rolling plains of blackberry bushes.
The pad, pad, pad of my bare feet running
    along the red dirt road,
    over forgotten coal mines,
    warns the majestic pine trees and
    the fierce mocking birds
    to watch for me.
I steal through the Magic City,
    racing along the rusty train tracks
    shadowed by the black-blue star-splattered sky.
The raccoons rob the doves of their sunflower seeds
    in the dead of a hot, humid night.
The cicadas gossip
    and the books in the library rustle
    while it rains and lightens outside.
The cars pollute the city in the valley
    and the stores there struggle.
I question my surroundings
    and those who try to control me.
I sit on Vulcan's torch,
    observing it all.
I live in a place of the
    sweet forgotten life.
I wait for opportunity to come,
    and when it does, I'll labor 'til I'm free.

Antoinette Forstall, Age 13
Alabama School of Fine Arts
Birmingham, AL
Teacher: Iris Rinke Hammer

A SMALL ADJUSTMENT

The notice announces in bold letters that the government's new public improvement program is putting our tax dollars at work: they are going to build a sidewalk on our street, and they will need half a meter of our land along the front of our property. "A Small Adjustment for Our Services" they ask from us. My hands freeze in the middle of knotting my graying black hair at the nape of my neck. My bangles stop in mid-jangle.

"They are going to what!" I exclaim. My husband takes off his rectangular glasses and shakes his white head. "I suppose it is for the best of the neighborhood. We must just bear it. Anyhow, it is only half a meter. Let us go tend to it one last time." I slowly pull my sari over my head and follow him outside.

I have always liked to think of us as two shadows, or ghosts maybe, that float out in the dawn dew, neither visible nor invisible. He in his white veshti and I in my cotton sleeping sari (dating back to my great-grandmother's time) tucked securely around my waist. After over fifty years, our early morning routine is nearly the same: wake up, heat water for bath, say our prayers, then tend to our garden. By now, the small bulbs and seeds we had lovingly sown into the earth have grown strong and big, but we still remember them young, just as we remember our own children. To imagine half of this piece of our lives together wiped away wrenches my heart. My husband goes to the back to get our gardening tools and I stand in the rectangle of pavement in front of the garden, seeing the antics of our grandchildren over the years, the three brick stumps they used for cricket, hearing the shouts from the Deevalis from long before as the fireworks burst like fountains through the air, reaching up toward the heavens and falling back. Children screaming and running away in delight. All witnessed by the silent, leafy aunties and uncles growing around our house.

I should tell our tenant upstairs to move his auto rickshaw. I still remember the fateful day when we decided to rent out the upstairs floors. One week after my husband, in the middle of his meeting, had gotten the fateful notice that our child had been critically injured in a motorcycle accident. After our son was gone, the house just seemed too big. For hours, my husband would stare blankly from his desk or calculate endless stock prices as I weeded the garden even after it was completely purged of weeds. And I began sleeping on the floor of the living room to hear the crickets chirping rhythmically outside and the poor people bustling on the streets. Always busy, light the stove, clean the floor, pump the water. The hands must keep moving. There were other chores to do.

My husband comes with the tools. He walks, plant by plant, checking for infestations, weeds, rotten things thrown in by passersby. Pruning here, there. And I inspect the smaller pots lining our doorway, transplanting the medium-sized flowers, testing their supple stems for strength before lugging out the bigger pots, the next level before connection straight into the earth. I sometimes wish there was someone who had done the same for me, guiding me by the hand to the next best place, always knowingly traveling toward the end goal. But there never was. Gardening is time-consuming. It is easier to throw the seeds and hope for beauty, rather than to cultivate it. Women as a group will always be a lost people, wandering around, searching for the bigger pot, the fertile soil for our seed that we will never find, that no one wants us to find.

I glance over at my husband beginning to water my favorite little plant, the tulasi, which I had planted myself years before for good luck, a prayer to Lord Krishna. The water flows out in a thin stream with the virility and conscientious accuracy characteristic of my husband. He leans effortlessly against the low wooden frame above our garden, still exuding the ease of life at the age of seventy-three that he had shown since our wedding day. Everything was simple for him. No hard choices, no difficult decisions. Everything would work out in the end. I smile to myself at how different we are. My nervousness aptly accounts for the high blood pressure for which I take five gray tablets a day.

I move to my jasmine, the flower of the common woman. Lining any street near shopping areas are poor women of all ages, stringing jasmine flowers together into garlands for privileged women like me to wear in our hair. I don't know if they know that the jasmine fades. It becomes sticky and brown and lodges in our privileged hair like burrs that we must pry off. I sometimes have the urge to tell them that all the pretty white flowers decay. But seeing their eyes, lined with wrinkles of pain, I don't. I inhale the sweet smell of the jasmine as I pluck some flowers for my puja later. Sweet and sickly all at once. Always a duet. The poor and the rich, the sick and the healthy. Jasmine is the flower of India. My granddaughters do not understand why I ask them to wear the jasmine flowers in their hair even though the scent is so overpowering and different. When I tell them that I do so because the smell is different, they shake their heads and walk away.

The Spinach Lady's calls reach my ears faintly. She is turning down the street now, balancing on her rusty blue bicycle with one arm holding in place the expansive basket of spinach leaves on her head. When I was growing up, I had once hugged the Spinach Lady's mother because she had told me I was pretty. That evening, my older brother told my parents what I had done, and they gave me the worst chastising I had ever heard. She was not like us, she was dirty. We are Brahmins and we don't touch them and they don't touch us. There are certain rules we have to follow. Other things I didn't understand through my tears and bewilderment. Spinach Lady the Younger bikes by and looks at me, and I nod. We are friends, but in the distant way, where we both know each other well but acknowledge our bond through a nod or a small lift of the corner of our lips. I don't know why I never ask her how her family is, whether she is getting by all right without her husband. I heard her son is doing well in the government school. Most people like her have children who drop out and become drunk or homeless.

My husband is pruning the bushes with his long pair of scissors. Last year, my son brought a big machine from America to cut the bushes. I screamed and began to cry when he turned it on. The teeth on the monstrous thing looked like it would bite off anyone's hand in a second. He took it back, needless to say.

The daisies are beginning to fade early this year. I look closely and see broken glass in the middle of the flowers. People in my village used to call me pretty, like a daisy. Always smiling. I feel silly now, knowing that I was smiling like a little fool when there were people who begged daily for my father—a lawyer—to loan them money. Daisies are silly flowers. I don't blame the drunk man who threw the bottle into the heart of the daisies. I pick up the broken shards and hold them up to the orange sunlight. Fragments of light reflect off each piece, onto the pavement in a kaleidoscope of shapes.

My childhood cuts through my thoughts. Images of my brothers playing, of me washing dishes in the back, the residue of food running in rivulets down the street. Answering only "Yes" always. I grew up knowing that my opinions were a useless waste of time. Why does it matter what you think when whatever unfolds is what will be and thinking will not lead to solutions or change? That was the school of thought of my parents. We live, we exist, we survive, we die. For some reason God only knows, we are invariably here, on this giant spinning planet soaking in the sun. Somehow we must persist, reach the final goal written in the Vedas of Moksha, union with God. When will the Spinach Lady attain Moksha? I wonder.

Then, in a jagged piece broken off of my childhood came adulthood, in a rush of change and uncertainty. I can still remember my wedding day: the nervousness, the folds of my rich silk sari, the glittering gold and diamonds that covered my face. I had never seen my husband-to-be before; I had merely been informed two weeks before that I was to be married. I laugh softly to myself, thinking of all the questions my grandchildren from America ask me. Did you love him? Did you want an arranged marriage? I feel a blush spread over my cheeks and I bend closer toward the mint leaves so my husband does not see it. There was no question of love or want. Only of necessity, duty to my parents, duty to my progeny. Love? Only mutual acknowledgement of each's services to the other through a nod, a small smile. No, there was none of that flashy lust with hands on bellybuttons like they show in the cinema. My American grandchildren could not understand, naturally.

It's funny how as I age, I seem to remember more from the early years of my life. Life goes in a full circle, like a vine, intertwining with others yet returning to its origin. I hobble over to the rose plant—my ankle is paining me—and begin gently to pull up the drooping stems covered in buds, fastening them to the protective surrounding cage. I had never liked that there had to be a cage. My mother-in-law was the one who had suggested it long ago, when the plant was merely a fledgling—a few weeks after my marriage, when I was rushing, sweat dripping off my forehead, to grind dosa batter for nine mouths.

"How in the world are you going to get anything to grow like this! Stupid girl," she had exclaimed in her authoritative way. Everyone else had a cage for the roses. Yours would be the only droopy ones, hanging low like an old woman's breasts, and none the prettier. The cage would make the vines of the rose stronger, as they would never be strong enough to stand on their own.

She didn't say that every single rosebud would also be trapped in its cage.

My mother-in-law was a very blunt woman, caustic and arrogant. Her death two years ago from all kinds of cancer came more as a relief to her children than a sorrow. I wonder who will grieve for dead flowers but the gardener. Are the people passing my garden gaining any delight from seeing the blossoms? Some people do great things in life: Mahatma Gandhi, Jawaharlal Nehru, Indira Gandhi. People grieve for the deaths of great souls, mahatmas who make deep imprints on society and give their life's breath to the bettering of their country. Destiny puts them in such situations so they can bring change. Who will grieve for the Spinach Lady's death? I wonder. Where will be the throngs of people who remember her daily call and her daily good mornings after she breathes her last?

Roses are unpredictable. Sometimes, even in the right season, the plant will deign to give two or three blossoms, and then will haughtily stop. Or is it haughty? Is it merely a product of its incarceration, a protest to the cage that constrains its body and beauty? Memories of an old poem drift through my mind—yes, the poem that my first daughter had memorized for a contest. Did she win? Perhaps. "Gather ye rosebuds while ye may." What was next? As a schoolgirl, my teachers had always told me that I have an elephant's memory. I chuckle, remembering the time I told my granddaughter the same phrase—the granddaughter from America. The granddaughter burst into tears and screamed, "I'm not an elephant!" It was one of my first experiences of culture shock. Then the consoling, the explaining, the laughing.

"Gather ye rosebuds while ye may." Why the buds, why not the roses themselves? I suppose, in the bustle of life, in the dearth of time, we have only a moment to gather the rosebuds before we rush off to the next arena of life—the next birth, the next visit, the next meal. And wait to see if the rosebuds will bloom in our hands.

When I was younger—maybe in my early twenties—I would ask my mother what was the purpose of all of this. The cleaning, the cooking, the subservience. The purpose of this cage around the rose. A thorn from the rose pricks my finger, drawing some blood. My reward for carelessness. My mother knew I had wanted to be a lawyer, like my father. She would secretly buy me books with the little spending money she had, though he had already pronounced that I would never amount to anything, going to college. "There is no place for a woman in our world except in the home!" he had shouted upon discovering my little library, eyes furious at my mother for encouraging my dreams. His turban had come unwound in his rage, and I remember having the unseemly urge to laugh amidst all the emotion in the room. And that was all. End of discussion.

Pansies. I remember my grandson from America as I stoop to pluck some pansies for offerings. He calls spineless people pansies. I feel like a pansy when I half-acknowledge the Paper Boy, the Spinach Lady, the Ironing Man. When I look at the caged rose. Each traveling through a miserable life in the shadow of the past, following the withered footsteps of their ancestors. The same. Even if the rose could stand on its own, we would never know. It will always be in its cage, with the pansies growing upright, beside it.

A boy across the streets runs around without pants. He squats and begins to do his business. I avert my eyes and tend to the flowers. I wonder if his mother, as a little girl, envisioned her children squatting outside houses without clothes. You sometimes wonder if God hears the little people. Perhaps the famous, important people have a hotline in their air-conditioned offices to God. To request personal favors. But the little boy across the street doing his business prays only to faraway gods in faraway temples behind wrought oak doors. And there is some refuge in knowing that God isn't listening. Here, in this night, we are all on the same street with garbage lining the side.

With a heavy heart, I wipe my hands on the edge of my sari. My day's gardening is done. Half of our garden will be destroyed within hours. Each year, each day, each step has been leading to this moment, when I sit on the concrete slab in front of the three make-believe cricket stumps, watching my husband water a rose in a cage. So much of life is unexpected. I would never have dreamed of having a television in my living room and a car parked outside. I would never have dreamed, as a little girl growing up in Pudukottai, that I would have daughters with Masters degrees living in houses with central air-conditioning in America, the golden land. Looking outside, from this worn sack that shrouds me, the world around seems to have aged while I remain the tiny figure in a bright skirt, running through the village streets. This little garden, which started out as a disfigured collection of weeds and shrubbery, is now our—mine and my husband's—little diary.

The gentle tendrils of the rose wrap around the cage, up and up. They do not break. I'm sure they will never break. My husband gathers his tools and walks over to me as I stand beside the metal grill. You have leaves in your hair, he tells me. He sifts through my hair and removes two leaves, a twig. We stand side by side, with deliberate space between us, deliberate silence between us, watching our garden. And as we watch, side by side, the vines seem to grow together, the fragments of the sunrise seem to collate into one beam, and, together, we walk inside our house.

Shalini Ramachandran, Age 17
Parkview High School
Lilburn, GA
Teacher: Marylynn Huie

FALLUJAH
(EXCERPT)

(Lights come up on Jack, leaning up against the headboard of a bed and reading. He is wearing a rumpled gray t-shirt, covered by blankets from the waist down. A wheelchair sits next to the bed. There is a knock on the door.)

JACK: *(not looking up)* Yeah!

(Annie enters.)

JACK: *(surprised at first, then grinning)* Annie Calhoun.

ANNIE: Hi, Jack.

JACK: Look at you. You're all grown up.

ANNIE: *(looking around the room)* I'd say the same of you but your posters prove otherwise.

JACK: *(defensively)* They're memorabilia.

ANNIE: *(scoffing)* Of what?

JACK: *(looks around and shrugs)* Hair metal.

ANNIE: I'm sure history will appreciate your careful preservation of White Snake.

(Pause. Annie steps further into the room, picking up a picture and studying it.)

JACK: You cut your hair.

ANNIE: So did you.

JACK: Army wasn't too fond of it.

(ANNIE puts the picture down.)

JACK: What're you doing here?

ANNIE: I was in the neighborhood.

(She sighs and sits down at his feet on the bed, leaning against the wall.)

JACK: Who told you I was back?

ANNIE: Norma Potter. Remember her?

JACK: Yeah, she works at the flower shop now.

ANNIE: *(nodding)* She sent me a Christmas card. Some picture of her and her husband and their dog. You know, *(mimicking Norma)* Hope you're doing well! Jack McGuire's home from Iraq! See you at the 10th reunion!

JACK: There's no chance you decided to shoot the messenger is there?

ANNIE: *(shaking her head)* She's a born-again Christian now. If I shot her I'd be damning myself to an eternity in purgatory and I'm determined not to do that until I'm at least thirty.

JACK: Wise.

ANNIE: I know. My morals are flawless.

JACK: Close enough.

ANNIE: *(smiling)* Your mom really didn't want me to see you.

JACK: *(sighing)* She gets protective. What with my, you know, *(gestures to the wheelchair)* state of affairs.

ANNIE: You seem all right.

(Jack's face darkens.)

JACK: *(laughs sarcastically)* Yeah, I'm fantastic.

(Annie looks at him, alarmed at his mood swing. He sighs.)

JACK: Sorry. *(obviously changing the subject)* So are you going to the 10th reunion?

ANNIE: *(shakes her head)* Are you?

JACK: Well, I've always wanted to be the token cripple.

ANNIE: Point taken.

(Awkward silence. Annie wanders over to his bookshelf, kind of pokes around. Looks at his CD player, hits the play button. It starts playing "Jeremy". Annie looks skeptical.)

ANNIE: *(incredulous)* Pearl Jam?

(Jack laughs.)

ANNIE: *(smiling)* Don't laugh. I'm trying to be disgusted with you.

JACK: What's wrong with Pearl Jam?

ANNIE: No one has been in this room since 1994.

JACK: *(shrugging.)* I moved out. So sue me. What've you done over the last decade?

ANNIE: I moved to New York for a couple years.

JACK: How was that?

(Annie sits at the foot of the bed, below his feet, leans back against the wall.)

ANNIE: *(shrugging)* My laundry got stolen.

JACK: What?

ANNIE: My laundry got stolen. Out of my car. I was going to the Laundromat and I stopped to get breakfast at this deli and someone smashed the window on the Oldsmobile and took my laundry.

JACK: You still have that Oldsmobile?

ANNIE: No, this was a while ago.

JACK: And that was the highlight of your time in New York?

ANNIE: *(smiling)* Pretty much.

JACK: Maybe we should make some sort of rule. You know. Stick to major life events or some—

ANNIE: I quit smoking.

JACK: *(shaking his head, amused)* Sure. Why not. *(To Annie)* Congratulations. Did you chew gum or get one of those patches?

ANNIE: Neither. Started chewing pens.

JACK: I guess that's an improvement.

ANNIE: Hard to say.

(Silence.)

ANNIE: I got married.

JACK: I know.

ANNIE: What'd you mean you know? How do you know?

JACK: *(gesturing to her left hand)* Well you've got quite the rock.

ANNIE: Oh. Right.

(Pause.)

JACK: Someone told me.

ANNIE: Who?

JACK: Norma Potter.

ANNIE: You're kidding.

JACK: I wish.

ANNIE: Oh god.

JACK: Uh huh. I didn't even get a card. I was getting milk at the supermarket and when I turned into the dairy aisle she was just standing there with this look like she was about to tell me my dog died.

ANNIE: Must've been fun.

JACK: Tons.

ANNIE: She creeps me out.

JACK: *(nodding)* Made me drop my milk. *(pause)* So you married whatshisface.

ANNIE: David.

JACK: Never liked him.

ANNIE: You never met him.

JACK: It's a matter of principle.

ANNIE: You never liked anyone I dated.

JACK: That's generalizing.

ANNIE: Name one.

(Pause.)

JACK: Seventh grade. Marcus Lieberman.

ANNIE: He was gay! He had a crush on *you*.

JACK: Semantics.

(Annie gives him a pointed look.)

JACK: *(sighs)* Fine.

(Pause. Annie continues to fiddle nervously with the blanket.)

JACK: How was the wedding?

ANNIE: Marcus didn't even get to second, Jack. There was no wedding.

JACK: I meant with this David guy.

ANNIE: *(smiles)* Oh, right, that. *(shrugs)* It was okay. It was in July—that summer there was a drought? *(Jack nods.)* Right, well my mom got heatstroke and fainted halfway through, which kind of put a damper on things. But other than that it was nice. Quiet.

JACK: *(smirking)* Not like ours.

ANNIE: *(smiling)* This groom didn't throw up on my shoes.

JACK: Hey. My motor skills weren't exactly at their best that night. It's not like I meant to.

ANNIE: Not helping your case.

JACK: Like you could've come up with a better way to celebrate graduation.

ANNIE: Several.

JACK: Oh c'mon, it was fun. All the cool kids are doing it. Look at Britney Spears.

ANNIE: The priest was wearing a T-shirt that said "Don't Mess with Texas."

JACK: *(grins)* Oh yeah. I liked him.

ANNIE: *(smiling)* You would.

(Pause.)

JACK: So, what're you doing now?

ANNIE: Nothing, really. We just moved out to San Francisco. I'm looking for a job.

JACK: How's married life treating you?

ANNIE: *(smiles)* It's good. Nice. You know.

Rebecca McCarthy, Age 17
Greens Farms Academy
Greens Farms, CT
Teacher: Elizabeth Cleary

THE LUMP OF INSPIRATION

We emerged from the dank garage, its corners saturated with fermenting urine and my own with fermenting frustration. The sun was at its zenith, so you held my hand only in spirit; as we moseyed across the hospital lawns, it was my own puppeteer, maintaining my posture and purpose with its golden beams. You scanned my eyes for the tears they hid, told me this was an opportunity. Most unfortunate, yes, but some people never experienced a thing like this in all their lives. If one was positive, a thing like this would only make one stronger, and could inspire one one's whole life through. Your words stung with basic truth, and my future lurched before me, its essential composition denatured. I would one day write with a sincerity I had never before wielded.

It was a Wednesday, and I could only think beyond the doctor's appointment. I sat in the waiting room, confined my hands to my lap so as to gratify my mysophobia and desperately hoped that Room #1 would not deflate my feeble courage with booster shots. My adamant suspicion? That my first pediatrician had cultivated in me this fear of shots. Dr. D., who bought only razors and always sought to collect my blood sample himself, had always been determined to puncture my finger with a single, forceful jab. My fear had since swelled beyond recognition as fear of pain, and I would bawl and scream incoherently at the sight of any needle. To an acquaintance who claimed to fear everything else, I circuitously explained the foundation of my fear: "You see, I don't mind pain. I bear pain pretty well, like when I get a rather vicious facial and I prevent myself from physically harming anyone. But with a shot, you don't have any control over the insertion of the needle, and you're not supposed to look. I like to know when something's going to happen, like if I'm on my bike and I'm riding into a tree, at least I know what's coming, I can predict exactly when the pain's going to hit." In other words: Hi. My name is Nicole and I'm a control freak.

In the lobby, I had been soothed by the predictable romance of "Lady and the Tramp," and was swathed in a hazy, tranquil gauze as I entered Room #1. My calmness was protracted by a normal checkup routine. Dr. D. had failed to send my files; I was spared any booster shots just yet. My blood pressure, and my blood and urine samples were fine; I was confident the physical examination would progress as it always did, without mishap. Dr. O. scrutinized my body from kidneys to neck, where her hands kneaded my flesh for a suspiciously long time. She left the room—to call for another doctor, she said. Her absence was yeast on my fears; they rose to fill the room. The reassurance my mother administered could not shrink them. "I'm sure it's nothing," she said, reading the newspaper. "They just like to double check."

The lump that Dr. O. found would be double checked, triple checked, quadruple checked in the week that followed. It would be rubbed, pinched, fondled by a multitude of curious hands—but the night after the checkup, I formally introduced myself with my own hands. I approached the mirror with hesitation, but was warmly received with a familiar reflection: keen hazel eyes, a helping of freckles, and a blaze of auburn hair. I lowered my eyes to the invasive lump, that trespasser smugly settled above my collar bone, and with my fingers diligently compared the cavity on one side of my neck to convexity on the other. I wondered how the lump had so sneakily arisen without my knowledge, or, more importantly, my consent. But its past was irrelevant; it only spoke to me of molted auburn locks on the bathroom floor, dimmed eyes, and chemicals coursing through my body, absorbing my freckles and strength. I shivered violently.

I shivered more violently when I went to get the sonogram that Dr. O. had recommended. The lump objected to the cold, wet goo the nurse slathered on my chest, and the pressure she applied. She asked me if it hurt. It had been molested the week long, and the lump was justifiably incensed. The moron disappeared, and I pulsed in anxious unison with the sonogram machine. It was a hefty, impressive machine, and as I idly swung my feet, it assumed a pompous air. Your fate is my data, it beeped, and I couldn't possibly stand for that, so with my mother in tow, I went to the waiting room.

There I was relatively content, among your average sort of people and the most beautiful fish. I determined the pageant winner: a fish the color of the Bahamian waters that my grandparents annually sailed. The fish cheerfully swam about the tank, munching on the drifting particles he found with his snout and nestling in coral when it pleased him to do so. The lump should have left me to emulate that happy fish, but the nurse rematerialized, and the lump only reaffirmed its presence. Stubborn lump: the doctor thought it was an enlarged lymph node, but he could not be certain.

For days, I determinedly dismissed the lump from my consciousness. Then, on the night preceding Orientation, you made an announcement: "Tomorrow, you have an appointment with a specialist at 11:00." The lump was instantly reinstated in my mind.

"No. No, I won't go. I have to meet my Little Sibs, and then I have my orientation. It's just not possible. I can't leave early; there are important things I have to do." A big, nasty bite of bitter escarole, and my face bloated with impending tears.

"We're very lucky he made time for us; he's a very busy man, and you have to go," you admonished firmly, but your words were coated in concern.

"No. No! NO!" Tears intermingled with the no's as they convened on my lips. As the dinner table blurred, the lump came into focus. I no'ed for fifteen consecutive minutes, banishing that irritable lump with my demanding word. I no'ed about the house, up and down the stairs, in the bathroom, on the couch, in my bedroom, in search of preferable acoustics. I chanted my no's, screamed them, sang them—anything to empower them. My parents remained stationed at the dinner table, and when I collapsed in my seat at the end of 15 consecutive minutes, we argued the logistics of the coming day.

Stocky, short, and balding, the specialist I met the day of my orientation was a catalyst in the evolution of my relationship with the lump. He was very knowledgeable about his field. As his faults lay, he lacked a versatile command of the English language, and he was utterly incompetent. He had a very oblique way of explaining my situation, and as he bore his fingers into my armpits and my neck, investigating the state of each and every lymph node, he spoke with a curious accent and pouting lips. He sat back down confidently in his puffy chair and spoke of something being where it should not be. He tried to incite my nonexistent anger. When he spoke directly to me, he blinked continuously. His eyes were dry from recycled hospital air. He was a liar. He told me to ask questions; I had none. What would happen? How could it happen? I bit my lip and peered at the tiled floor, and then at my watch, my annoyance receding with the minutes. He'd finish quickly, and I'd make it to my orientation. He addressed my parents' questions about cancerous growths and details that metastasized in my imagination, and he then rotated his chair towards me, patent leather shoes squeaking across the tiled floor. But I had no questions, no aggression. Shiny head, shiny shoes—and my shiny makeup dissolved by the welling tears. I'd never make it now. My nose leaked a steady drip of diluted mucus, staining my lips with a salty gloss, and I reached for tissue after tissue. My toes curled, and my eyes squeezed shut as Dr. K. explained the biopsy; though my tears were restrained by unyielding eyelids, my whimpers were released by slippery lips. They assembled on my chest: it collapsed, and once on the floor, I lay sobbing into a heap of crinkled tissues and nasal excretions.

This was junior year, and didn't the lump know that? SATs and PSATs, and extracurriculars galore. There was simply no time for this lump and certainly no space in my mind to accommodate it. My father said that it was much worse when a lump visited a person who had to work to support himself, who would spend his days at the hospital and come home to an empty refrigerator. Dr. K. said that it was much worse when a lump visited a person and he didn't know it for many months until one day his busy mind came home to a diseased corpse. We'd so fortunately caught my lump early; we would familiarize ourselves with its nature, and if it had a disagreeable disposition, of which there was a 90% chance, we'd flush it out with chemicals in a standard six-month procedure. With blinking eyes, he said we would most definitely cure me. No future repercussions. I was sixteen and too young to care about birthing healthy children.

Conscious that life would stall for the next six months, I lived the week fully. I embraced the positive attitude you had recommended. I shed my bitter outlook, my anxiety, and came to school social, productive, and merry. Louis described his odd, but usual summer experiences—I smiled knowingly. Zack vented his frustration at the scheduling programmer—I laughed in concurrence. People shared with me their stories, and, soon enough, I was able to reciprocate. Why wasn't I going to gym tomorrow? I could say it very collectedly by the end—I'm having surgery. And Casey said, "You're very brave, I wouldn't let them cut me open, I'll let the lung cancer that runs in my family take me alive." But there was never a possibility of stopping them. I could only stay calm and rational, and laugh as much as possible; I laughed heartily at her obstinacy.

On the day of the surgery, I remained composed, smiling at the children building starships with Legos and inaudibly chuckling when one boy chucked them at his father. It was a hollow laugh, sustained awkwardly, but I consciously projected it. Anyone who heard it would know I was prepared to enter the O.R., lie passively, and wake up to find a mediport inserted in my skin. They were to take a frozen sample during the course of the surgery; if they found the lump to be cancerous, they were to take immediate action. As I followed a resident to the O.R., my loose scrubs sailing behind me, I accepted the possibility that I could wake up a different person without having had any input in the transformation.

In a medical show, the climax always occurs in the operating room. Stimulated by drama, the patient's wound cries profusely, his heart seizes with empathy, and surgeons pass utensils with unparalleled efficiency until the wound is bound in reassurance and the overarching drone recedes to a dim, pulsing beep. A shrewd director films the scene in bird's eye view to compel one to watch just a little longer and wish just a little more devoutly—to willfully mellow the drama, and resuscitate one's bleeding hope. From the opposite end, the operating table, it seems like only someone else's fervent wishing could make a difference, and one might as well let the anesthesiologist insert the IV without retracting in fear. Chilled by the metal needle, rattled by the beeping of unfamiliar technology, it is easy to panic, but it makes no sense to hyperventilate. One shivers with an oncoming flood of anesthesia, and suddenly, the doctor is only distantly requesting another deep breath of oxygen.

Three hours later I awoke with a throbbing above my collarbone. Someone had been wishing hard, had been merciful and hadn't changed the channel because the surgeon happily came to my bedside: the lump was benign.

Or someone had gotten bored and changed the channel. The surgeon trudged to my side, telling me dutifully that chemotherapy would begin in two days.

Either way, as the scar and the pain fade, I don't want to lose my inspiration, sincerity, composure. You see, I'm letting the pen do its own thing.

Nicole Levy, Age 16
Hunter College High School
New York, NY
Teacher: Christopher Zegers

NATURE AT OUR DOORSTEP:
FOUR SEASONS ON AN OHIO FARM

SPRING

I was cutting brush along the pasture fence line this spring when I saw a redwing blackbird nest built into the weeds. As I carefully cut around it, I noticed that besides three blue eggs with black splotches there was one white egg with brown spots—evidence of a cowbird's visit. As many people know, the cowbird female lays a single egg in another bird's nest, leaving the foster parents to raise a cowbird chick along with their own young.

Although birds sometimes are not fooled by this trick, it seemed to be working with the redwing, since I saw her happily sitting on the full clutch of eggs later in the week. That might have been in part because the cowbird egg is similar in size to a blackbird egg. And, coincidentally, the nestlings would also be similar, since redwings and cowbirds are both in the Icteridae family of American birds.

The blackbird nest was an unusual choice on the cowbird's part; they usually target smaller species so that the cowbird nestling over-competes with the other birds in the nest. The other chicks often starve, while the mother bird is kept busy feeding a young cowbird already bigger than her.

Cowbirds' lazy habits have not endeared them to us, and neither has their grating, hoarse call. In describing the cowbird, a 19th century naturalist said, "This bird forms a striking contrast to other feathered neighbors, and indeed is almost an anomaly in the animal kingdom," and went on to give the opinion that the cowbird's character "is thoroughly bad." The redwinged nesters on our farm probably agree.

I was ten years old when I first saw a crayfish, and I had to travel several hundred miles to see it—from southeastern Ohio where we used to live, all the way to the Black Fork River in Ashland County for a canoe trip. I saw the small, lobster-like crustacean as it swam in the shallow water alongside a sandbar. It was about four inches long and greenish-white, with a meaty tail and large claws on either side of its head. A few minutes later I saw another one, burrowing into the mud.

They were the only crayfish we noticed while on the river, and I was surprised even to see them. Many years ago, crayfish could be found in almost any body of water, from ditches to rivers, and were in fact considered a nuisance by fishermen whose bait they stole. There is a larger species that digs burrows in low-lying fields to get into the groundwater, and when it was more common it actually did damage to crops by biting off the stems. But even this larger species has been nearly exterminated, probably from pesticides sprayed on the fields.

Pesticides and fertilizers end up in creeks and streams and now crayfish in Ohio are rare; a fisherman would probably be thrilled to see one. It would mean the waters he was fishing in weren't badly polluted.

My father has told me about the time he returned to the woods he had played in as a boy. The forest was ripped up with dirt bike trails, causing massive erosion. Natural gas wells had been drilled, and brine and pollutants had spilled into the streams he had played in. The whole woods had been used up. The creek was deserted now of water bugs and minnows.

And there were no crayfish.

Dad got into the creek and began to turn over rocks, looking for crayfish that weren't there. People haven't been able to drink creek water safely for a long time in our part of the country, and evidently nothing else can, either.

SUMMER

While digging fingerling potatoes on a hot and sunny day this summer I happened on two unusual things. First, as I pulled back the hay mulch from a plant, I saw a group of small potatoes sitting with all their "fingers" pointing upward. Then I spotted about a dozen bumblebees rising off the "potatoes" to buzz in my direction. The next thing I knew, I was running.

I had sprinted 30 feet before the bumblebees gave up the chase. But I got up the courage to go back and get my produce crate, as well as to take a look at the bumblebee nest I had bumbled into.

What I had mistaken for potatoes were actually wax nectar pots. Slightly more than an inch long, they tapered at both ends. I could see that at least one of the half-dozen wax pots was partly full of nectar. With the exception of the queen, the colony does not live through the winter, and does not need a lasting supply of honey, but the workers do save nectar for rainy days when the bees can't eat nectar off of flowers.

It is hard to tell how many bumblebees lived in the nest I found; there were only a few bees in among the nectar pots, but on a sunny day most of the workers were probably out gathering nectar. Besides the queen and her workers there would be several young queens and drones, or male bees, hatched into the nest by early autumn. When winter comes and the temperature drops below freezing, the old queen bumblebee, drones, and workers die, but the new queens have already begun to hibernate in the ground. They will start their own nests the next year.

I re-covered the nest with hay and left it alone, along with the nearby potato plants. People kill many bumblebee nests each year by spraying pesticides, but bumblebees are the sole pollinators of red clover, and I don't want to lose a single colony on our small farm.

In a fringe of second-growth black cherry, maple and ash bordering the hayfield on our farm, an apple tree is growing. The trees around it are taller, but the apple tree is on the edge of the fringe, and gets plenty of sunlight. The apple tree seems out of place now, but I'm almost certain it was planted intentionally.

The seed an apple tree grows from does not necessarily determine its variety. To get a golden delicious or northern spy, you have to graft branches or plant slips from an existing tree. Wild apples (or "unintentional" apples, as they ought to be called, since all apples came here from Europe) are almost always sour, but the apples from our tree have a good flavor.

Our apples are hard to get at, since the tree has grown to over thirty feet tall. At its base, you can see the remnants of an old applewood stump, proof that in the past the tree rotted or was blown down, and a new sprout grew from the old tree. I wouldn't want to guess how ancient this tree is, but it must be at least as old as the nearby rock barn foundation and hand-dug, rock-lined well.

It could be much older, though. Sitting on the table-sized boulder that lies against the old tree, I can just see State Route 95, which was once the Cuyahoga War Trail. John Chapman—better known as Johnny Appleseed—often traveled this path in the 30 years he wandered over north central Ohio, going from his camps along the Mohican river to "Mohican John's Town," now Mohicanville.

Our apples, as near as I can identify them, are Johnny's favorite variety, "Rambo," which is green on one side, red on the other. But if Johnny Appleseed planted the tree, it would have to be nearly 200 years old, and only one such tree has been confirmed to still be living.

Sometimes I wish our gnarled old tree could talk.

AUTUMN

As the temperature drops lower in autumn, the deer mice in the woods and fields of our farm look for a warm place to spend the winter. Most of them hole up in hollow stumps and trees, but a few find something more convenient: one of our half-dozen bluebird nesting boxes. So, every year around the end of October, I make the rounds of the boxes to clear out rodents.

The necessary equipment is simple, just a stick and a five-gallon bucket. I have to transport the mice away from the bird box in the bucket. If I scooped them out onto the ground, along with their nests, the mice would simply transfer the whole clump of dry grass, shredded paper, and animal fur back into the bird box, piece by piece. So instead, I use the stick to push mouse and nest into the bucket, and then release the mouse in the woods.

Deer mice and the similar white-footed mouse are American natives, unlike their cousin the house mouse, an immigrant from Asia. Deer mice have long whiskers, flat, gray fur, white paws, and tails that are often longer than their bodies. They heap their shredded bedding into cavities and do not weave a freestanding grass nest like house mice do.

I've always liked these drab little animals, but they ruin bluebird boxes with their gnawing and urine. They also drive the bluebirds away if they happen to stay in the boxes through the spring. With few skunks, foxes and coyotes around—their natural predators—deer mice overpopulate our farm. And so I evict them, because unlike the bluebirds, deer mice don't need nesting boxes to survive.

❧

Now that most of the plants of summer have died back in the wooded and brushy areas on our farm, the trails left by woodchucks, deer and rabbits can be plainly seen. These animals are plant eaters and over the summer they have worn paths from their homes to their food sources. Woodchucks seem to leave the shortest, most worn paths, because they situate their holes as near as possible to alfalfa and clover. The woodchucks are hibernating now, but their packed-down little paths reveal dozens of trips from hole to hayfield each day.

The rabbits are still using their trails, which are harder to find. Cottontail paths are more like tunnels, running through brambles and brush. Sometimes when I startle a rabbit, I can only hear—rather than see—it race away beneath the bushes.

The deer have left the most plentiful and obvious trails. And now that the plants are dead, the paths are accessible and easier to walk. They are surprisingly narrow—often only a few inches wide at the ground. There are dozens of paths around our farm that lead from browsed areas, crabapple trees, and nearby cornfields to the crowded thickets where these overpopulating animals sleep.

The bare ground of these paths is covered with the small prints of fawns, larger prints of does, and even larger, heart-shaped buck tracks. I've left my own tracks on a few of them this autumn as well, but in general I stay away from the woodland trails during hunting season...there's always the chance of being mistaken for a deer.

WINTER

As the last leaves fell into the frost of early winter, I eventually noticed that a hornet nest was hanging in a pignut tree at the edge of our woods. The nest is empty now, since hornets only use their nests for one season. Although it held a colony of hornets that built it through the summer, I never saw it then because the tree's leaves hid it.

The nest stands out now: cone-shaped and about a foot long by a foot wide at the top, tapering to a few inches wide at the bottom. Hornet colonies add onto their nests throughout the one season they live in them, and I have seen nests twice this big.

Young queens that were born and fertilized in autumn hibernate in the ground or in hollow trees over the winter, but all of the workers die in the first freeze. The nest in the pignut tree is already beginning to show signs of weathering. Hornets make their grey nests out of a paper they produce by chewing wood and plant fibers. The paper is somewhat waterproof, but once the hornets aren't repairing and adding on to the nest, it soon decays.

American hornets are really a species of yellow jackets, and have a painful sting. Many people dislike them and destroy their colonies with poison, or fire. Hornets are a danger when they build a nest near people, because they are quick to defend their home from both real and imagined intruders. And, unlike honeybees, hornets don't die after stinging.

Some counter that hornets are beneficial and should be left alone because they eat crop-damaging insects, but then again, taking that stand could stir up "a hornet's nest" of controversy.

⟶◦⟍⟍⟍⟍⟍◦⟵

 This afternoon I saw nearly two dozen sparrow-sized gray and white birds searching for seeds on the lane. They were juncos, the first ones I've seen this year. Juncos often are the most common birds at a feeder, and are known as winter rather than summer birds, but they are here year 'round. They spend their summers deep in the woods, and are seldom observed. At the beginning of winter they move to yards and fields, and are then a common sight. It seems several dozen have moved into the fir trees along our lane.

 Although juncos are one of the best known "feeder birds," birdseed wasn't what brought them to our farm this winter. We haven't filled our feeder because of problems with mice. I tried to stalk the juncos with binoculars, but ended up chasing them into the trees along the lane. Juncos aren't very wary, though, so I got to within twenty feet of them. At that moment I also noticed a downy woodpecker looking for insects in the pasture fence posts. The downy is another bird that is rarely seen during the summer, but migrates close to people during the winter.

 The birds I chased were dark-eyed juncos, but occasionally Oregon juncos and white-winged juncos are seen as well. These different juncos were believed to be separate species, but in reality they interbreed and their differences are very minimal.

 I am glad to know a flock of juncos is wintering on the farm. Life on our farm is lived by the season, and in a season when so many birds leave for the south, it's nice to have a few new ones show up to take their places.

John Savage, Age 13
Savage Home School
Loudonville, OH
Teacher: Scott Savage

FINDING HOPE

I'm not even sure what day it is anymore. My little brother Sam and I are living in a daze, practically sleepwalking through our lives. Dad has not gone to work, or indeed, even strayed from his room. His once handsome face is shadowed by thick stubble and his eyes are vividly red, gray tear runnels making paths down his sunken cheeks. Our answering machine's message button is permanently flashing red. We haven't answered the phone since *it* happened. All I know is saltwater—it seems my world is being flooded with tears. Yet I cannot cry. Sam can't grasp *it*, forever asking where she is, when she's coming back. He doesn't understand. She will never come back.

Our mother died four days ago.

She sips at her thermos, filled with her morning black coffee. Dixie, her Great Dane mix, wearing the doggy grin that he always displays on his walks, the grin that says "What a great day to be running," trots by her side as she jogs along the towpath, early morning sunshine dappling the ground. She passes others who smile at her, but don't waste their breath on words. She does the same and keeps jogging.

Dad comes out his shell on the fifth day. While Sam and I eat the last of the breakfast cereal around our plastic picnic table in the middle of the kitchen (the family table had become so encrusted with molding food, we had to abandon it), he shuffles downstairs. His face is haggard. "She needs a proper funeral."

We don't have to ask who she is. We know.

He continues, "I have called your grandmother. She's coming down with the rest of them."

"Oh." I rack my brain to remember my grandmother. I come up with an overly-high voice and the wrinkled brown skin of a cheek. "The rest of them?"

"The rest of the vultures on her side of the family, yes. The ones who detest me." He replies. Noticing the shocked look on my face, he adds dryly, "Why did you think you hadn't seen them for all these years?"

> *She keeps jogging, feeling adrenaline pound through her bloodstream as she speeds into a sprint. She savors the feeling of her arms pumping effortlessly, the feeling that she might fly if she jumped, the feelings that always flood her when she runs. Dixie lopes beside her, his long, pink tongue flapping. She stops abruptly, almost tumbling to the ground as a laughing group turns the corner, nearly twenty people striding in a pack, grandmothers, uncles, children...She wonders why her family can never be that way, never laugh with ancestors, never cry with cousins...She sighs, and resumes her run with Dixie as the cluster passes, not even sparing a glance, caught up in their perfect world.*

The family spills through the door, laughing, joking, shouting greetings, and yet dampened as a whole by the house's atmosphere. I feel envious of their closeness. I am an outsider. Sam hovers uncertainly on the fringe until a loving aunt swoops him up ("Look! How cute! What's your name, honey?") But I'm too old to be cute, too young to talk to my teenage cousins. Only Granny skirts my father—he too is enclosed in sympathetic hugs, all past conflicts forgotten. He smiles for the first time since the accident.

Later, around the newly-scrubbed table (my various female relatives had exclaimed over the state of the kitchen, and gotten down to work) we gobble lumpy mashed potatoes and fried chicken from huge buckets. Only my name makes me look up from my meal.

"So...Henrietta!" A big-jawed man with watery brown eyes and a weedy mustache, who I think is known as Ralph, says amiably. "You've not met Hope."

I raise an eyebrow. *Is my uncle a religious fanatic, one of the people that ask you quite seriously if you have seen happiness?* I wonder.

Seeing my silent query even behind the mane of unbrushed bangs, he adds, "Yer cousin Hope. She's about yer age, y'know."

"No." I reply sullenly. I know I am being stubborn, but I don't care. Why would I want to meet this Hope? The only person I want to see right now is Mom. "I don't know." *And don't care*, I add under my breath.

"You'll love Hope. Everyone loves Hope." One of my thirteen aunts pipes up (Don't ask what her name was—I wouldn't be able to tell you…). The rest of them join in. I hate this Hope already.

She sees the bridge ahead. The few cars on it move sluggishly. Dixie pants as they slow to a jog. The morning is getting hotter as the sun moves higher in the cerulean blue of the sky. She and Dixie trot up the ramp to the road from the towpath. While leaning on a wooden post to catch her breath, she sips at her still-warm coffee thermos. The street is still. She yawns and stretches, then walks to the edge of the long strip of asphalt.

Two days later, I hide out on our sagging back porch. It's only a matter of time until the uncle task force gets around to it, but I'm dreading it. I've always loved it back here. But you have to hide these days, if you don't want to get suckered into smiling weakly at your wacky cousin's new tattoo, or snatched away from your e-mail to put everyone's underwear in the washing machine. So I've taken to veiling myself with self-pity, sewing my soul into a shroud of solitude, and concealing my emotions with the same winding sheet. It's much easier than actually feeling anything. Right now, I'm just numb.

All I know is that having thirty-odd relatives in the house is not exactly enjoyable after a few weeks of utter grief (*why* they couldn't have forked out for a nice hotel, I honestly have no idea…it must be better than this place). I am suddenly required to give an effort, to smile, to buy countless family bags of chips at the grocery store. I was trapped yesterday by no less than five aunts, who first insisted on me calling them "Auntie, dear," and then shoving a vacuum cleaner's handle into my unwilling hands and plugging it in. The house is so crowded, I practically have to wade through assorted relations.

You can virtually guarantee that a few are on the stairs tying shoelaces and running up and down the steps as part of their new exercise regime. While this is going on, the younger cousins are putting on a puppet show in the garage, in which a kind great uncle serves as both audience and cameraman, using our ancient camcorder. Today, a few of the jock and jockette cousins are in the den watching some sports final with my grandfather, while Granny and at least half of the aunts are nattering and cooking up a storm in our kitchen. Various uncles, sullen teenagers and quite a number of people of unknown relation to me are scattered around, and even our unfinished basement is littered with pillows and duffel bags.

Dad is hiding, like me, but he claims that he's "working" in his study and only comes out for meals. This doesn't feel like a funeral gathering. This feels like one enormous, never-ending party, of which I am not a part.

The rusty blue pick-up (Great-Uncle Waldo's, I'm told) sputters to a halt in the driveway. He climbs out muttering to someone in the back. My mouth goes dry, and I am frozen to my wooden rocking chair. Long legs, clothed with dusty blue jeans extend from the door. I suddenly realize what I am waiting for. I had been waiting for Hope till now. The rest of her swings out. My jaw drops. I had been expecting a girl with perfectly neat, straight blonde hair, an ample figure, and incredible poise. I had been wrong. So wrong.

She wears loose jeans and a T-shirt that proclaims, "I went to Camp AlpenKidd and survived!" Her mouse-brown hair is tangled, and she is gawky, her legs too long for her torso. Her voice is soft and shy, as she murmurs something to Great-Uncle Waldo. He laughs and hugs her tight, like Mom used to do. I am nauseated, and run inside. I skulk in my room, an occasional tear dripping, hoping she won't notice me, wanting the world to leave me alone.

Looking along both sides of the street, she steps off the curb. Halfway across, Dixie yelps, and sits down. She attempts to drag him off his firm seat, but, being part Great Dane, this is not possible. She notices he holds his left paw slightly off of the road. Ah ha! she thinks triumphantly, and grabs for his dangling limb. His yelp echoes around the street, as she locates the sharp piece of broken glass firmly embedded in his paw. She tugs and he cries out. She strokes his head for reassurance. Through his sorrowful howling, she doesn't hear the car coming until it is too late. A dented silver BMW barrels up the narrow lane. She screams, flies through the air—she collides with solid concrete, and everything goes black.

Hope knocks softly on my door. "Henrietta? Are you in there?"

I remain silent, hoping she'll go away. I still my breathing, willing her to leave. She stands there for a minute, and then I hear her walk away, obviously bare feet padding back down the stairs. I heave a sigh of relief. I kick at the duvet on the floor, suddenly frustrated. *This is my house!* I scream silently. *Why do I have to hide?* I look down, catch a glimpse of a picture on the floor, a captured moment previously covered by crumpled blanket. Dixie sits with a doggy grin on his face, sandwiched by Mom and a younger, happier me. I pull the duvet back over the photo, but it is too late. The memories are flooding back.

I try desperately to staunch the repopulation in my brain, but my pitiful attempts at thinking of something else are unsuccessful. This is exactly what the numb feeling was supposed to hide. I grasp at the slipping numbness, but it tumbles away and I am swept into the past.

I remember the months of walking neighbor's dogs, the Barbie sneakers that eventually gave way to Converse high-tops, thudding on dark asphalt. Dragging the dachshund from next door until finally giving up and carrying it the rest of the way home. Being dragged by the German Shepard who lived on the next block. Almost two years of memories, a myriad of reminiscences, are overpowering my ability to control my thoughts. Because with the dog memories, there is also the memory of going to the Humane society with Mom countless times, me pacing up and down in front of the tiny enclosures, Mom waiting patiently at the door for news of my latest object of desire.

There are more, of Dixie and Mom making friends, her requests to walk him, after all the walks she made me go through for that privilege. The tornado begins to slow, and I am able to make my eyelid screen go blank.

The pain, the grief, the longing for mom's soft embrace and Dixie's warm licks are all renewed. *I loved them both and they're both gone!* I cry silently. *If there is a God, why did he let this happen?* I flop on my bed, spent, and try to fall asleep. I never dream, not since it happened anyway. Asleep, I don't have to deal with memories.

My eyes fly open with a jolt at a tap at my door. "Henrietta?" It's Hope. "Can I—come in?"

I shut my eyes again. *Get out of my life!* I desperately wish she would just admit defeat—I don't care about her or anyone else's stupid condolences.

Without waiting for an answer, she enters my grief-mussed room. I look around, and realize what a mess it has become. All the shredded pictures of Mom are spread around the room, a destroyed Mom collage partially covered by the duvet that lies limp on the floor. Mom's old T-shirts are clumped on my unmade bed, and my attempt to paint my room black with watercolors is all too apparent on about half of the west wall. She simply picks her way neatly through the maze of dirty laundry and crushed breakfast cereal, and flops on my bed. We both wait for each other to say something.

I burst out rudely, "Lemme guess. You've lost a family member, too, and you're gonna tell me how hard it was, and how you got over it with a combination of classical music and lots of chocolate donuts."

She giggles a bit, and sighs. "Well…I've never had that happen to me, but people tell me I have an active imagination. I'm sure I could come up with something—though I'm not partial to chocolate donuts…"

I can't believe how passive she is. Most people would have anxiously attempted to soothe my nerves after this explosion, becoming flustered. She hasn't even turned a hair. "Look. What do you want?" *I know what I want! How about you leave now?*

"I want you to tell me what it's like."

Oh, no! Another child shrink! I think. "And why do you want to know, huh?" *Why would you* want *to know what this feels like?*

"If someone dies in my immediate family, I'll know what to do."

I ponder this. I have never gotten an answer with "dies" in it before. *Oh, no, Henrietta is far too delicate at the moment to hear the word "dies."* I think sarcastically.

"God," I grumble.

Her triumphant smile makes me want to smack her even more, but I tell her how my mother had gone running on the towpath with Dixie, had come to the road, had been hit. I tell her we had gone to the scene, called by the ambulance, my mother lying on the ground, her inert body crumpled, EMTs swarming around her. I tell her of Dixie's three broken legs, his badly fractured tail. And finally, I tell her of Dad's fury that Dixie had survived, and not his beloved wife, sending him away to the pound in his grief…

I still cannot cry. The pain fills me until I can't breathe, can't see, can't hear, and Hope vanishes behind a whirling cyclone of sorrow. I miss them so much at this moment I can hardly stand living. I want to throw myself off a cliff. At least then I'd be with her. And then it subsides, as Hope shifts on the bed. Instead of patting my shoulder (which, in my opinion, is the most idiotic thing to do when someone is dying inside—and yet that doesn't stop ninety-nine percent of this new population in my house from doing it) she sits, and waits. Just waits for me to stop, to calm down.

When I am as composed as possible, she leans back and regards me. "Hmmm…That was interesting." *I don't care about you either.* I turn my back on her, now regretting ever telling her about my mother. She doesn't deserve to know. She didn't even say "sorry for your loss" like most of the less weepy acquaintances do.

I want to throw her off the cliff as I go down. For the few seconds before impact, I think the cliff method would be fun. I've always wanted to know the feeling of flying, as our old lumpy sofa knows well enough.

She clears her throat, trying to break the awkward silence after her stupid trying-to-be-unique comment. *All you need to do now is rub your foot uncomfortably on the floor and you'll be a regular Charlie Brown at a school dance.* I want to say it, but rein in my sarcasm.

Hope stands, clears her throat again. "I—I'm gonna go get a snack. Uh…do you want to come w—"

"'Kay. Bye." I interrupt hastily, trying to keep the invitation at bay. I guess I'm successful, because she shrugs and walks to the door.

Lunchtime, three miserable days later, Hope drags me from my bagel to the front yard.

"Whadoyouwant?" I ask groggily, still tired from a bad night of sleeping in stops and starts.

"You'll see, Henri." She leads me around the garage, heading for the backyard.

"Since when have you called me Henri?" I ask through gritted teeth, seething. "Henri" is my mom's name for me, no one else's.

"Since now!" She laughs, practically skipping with glee at her cleverness.

I grind my teeth even further. Her irrepressible cheerfulness makes me want to strangle her. "No, Hope. Not Henri."

"'Kay—Henri. Shut those baby blues."

"Baby blues?"

She sighs, exasperated. "Your *eyes*."

Right. I shut them and I am led blindly through the yard, dead leaves crunching underfoot. When we stop I feel things falling around me, brushing my arms, my hair, my shoulders ever so lightly. I can tell we are under the maple tree. *It's autumn,* I realize suddenly. *The leaves are falling.* I can't remember the last time I looked out the window since it happened.

Hope interrupts my revelation. "Hold out your hand."

"This had better not be worms..." I warn her.

"Here h-it is!" I feel warm, wiry hair under my fingers. I open my eyes.

"Dixie!" I start bawling and hug him, letting the warmth of his solid body soak into me as my tears seep into the gray fur. I cry out the pain, the anguish the way I hadn't been able to before, and it washes away in floods. This, if anything, was the proof that Mom was up there somewhere, still loving me. She and I loved Dixie almost as much as we loved each other. My cousin made a miracle happen. I turn to a blurry Hope and hug her tightly.

She whispers in my ear, "I convinced your dad that you needed him." I see a twinkle in her blue eyes, the baby blues that mirror mine.

"I—I think..." I am blubbing really hard now, so that she can probably hardly make sense of my words. I say it anyway. "I think my mom would have really loved you," I sob.

And Hope just smiles and hugs me tighter, just like Mom would have done.

Clare Grieve, Age 14
Martha Brown Middle School
Fairport, NY
Teacher: David Dunn

GRATEFULNESS RUNS IN THE FAMILY

As the puck hits the ice, the players are off and skating and Natasha Meunier sprints to receive the pass. A teammate with the same last name shouts to her in Russian.

When Suzanne Meunier found out that she was not able to have any children, she and her husband Rick decided to look into adoption. As soon as they saw pictures of Russian twins, Olya and Jhenya, it was love at first sight. They didn't plan on adopting any more children, but after flying all the way to Siberia, they met the twins' friends, Natasha and Masha, and decided they had to adopt them, too.

"I was so excited to meet them," said Jhenya Meunier. "I remember seeing all the other kids getting their parents but no one ever came for us until they showed up."

When Olya and Jhenya's parents abandoned them, they were placed in a Russian orphanage. They were nine years old when they were adopted by the Meunier family. Sisters Masha and Natasha were brought to the United States after two years of what seemed like "endless paperwork."

"We didn't speak any English when we came here, so our mom had to teach us everything. She also home schooled us," said Natasha Meunier.

Their new life did not come without adjustment, as the girls had to grow accustomed to new kinds of food, a remote language, and life with a loving and caring family.

"We now have our own room which is so cool," said Natasha Meunier. "I think most of all, though, we are so thankful to have parents that care for us and are there for us when we need them the most. We never had that back at the orphanage and we would have been thrown out to fend for ourselves at age 16."

When the girls first arrived in Alaska they began playing recreational hockey, until this year, when all four sisters decided to join the South hockey team.

"The minute I saw them it was like a breath of fresh air," said South girl's hockey head coach Donna McCarrey. "They are the epitome of gratefulness and they shake the coaches' hands and thank them for such a great practice every day."

As the hockey team prepares for the season ahead and the culminating region tournament, the players are optimistic about their chances of winning the regional title.

"If we connect as a team and work hard then we can do it," said Nina Sutherland. "The key is believing that we can win [the regionals]."

South features the leading scoring line in girl's hockey with juniors Rachael McEahern and Lynsey Clowers and sophomore Brie Forrest leading the way for the district.

"South hockey is not long a 'learn to skate' program, Everyone on my team is working so hard at practices and I keep telling them that no matter what happens on the season, we're a success if we work harder than any other team," McCarrey said.

While the team's biggest challenge has been integrating the less-experienced players with the players who have played for a long time, the Meunier sisters appear to be fitting in without any mishaps.

"Their work ethic is incredible and they are always listening to instructions and nodding their heads. They even echo the coach's statements with enthusiasm on the bench. They are just so excited to be out there," McCarrey said.

Sutherland said that the sisters are the perfect teammates who always show up early for every practice or game.

"They are just good people and caring is obviously something that matters a lot to them. They always want to make sure that everyone is happy, but on the ice, they are just as aggressive as everyone else," said junior Lynsey Clowers.

It appears that others outside the hockey arena are also taking note of the sisters' enthusiasm and gratefulness for life.

"Every morning without fail, Masha says good morning to me with a huge smile on her face, and she always says thank you when she leaves class or when I hand her a test or a paper," says social studies teacher Jessica Williams. "I'm thinking to myself, why is she thanking me for a test? It really speaks volumes about her. She honestly cares about her education, and as a teacher I love to see that."

As three of the sisters start thinking about college and graduation, the opportunities seem limitless compared to what they had back in Russia.

Jhenya plans on studying a subject involving animals. After seeing stray dogs and cats running the streets of Russia without a home, she feels for them.

"We would always take the stray animals into the orphanage and make a home for them, but the owners would get mad at us," Jhenya Meunier said.

Natasha, on the other hand, hopes to become a nurse after getting her degree from the University of Alaska at Anchorage. After having a lot of surgeries when she was little for reasons that are still unknown to her, Natasha feels appreciative to the people who took care of her. Because of this experience, Natasha wants to help people.

But hockey seems to be what the sisters do best together. During South's 9-0 win over Mat-Su a few weeks ago, Jhenya scored a goal in the second period, Natasha scored in the third period, and Masha assisted. Olya was unable to play due to sickness.

"These girls are truly part of the team. They represent the Americanism that you don't leave the people you love behind, and they remind us all of how blessed we are to be Americans," McCarrey said. "These girls are the best thing that ever happened to me."

Brenna O'Tierney, Age 18
South Anchorage High School
Anchorage, AK
Teacher: Rebecca Gerik

TIP TAP

OPEN! The neon light casts an orange glow that drapes across my nose.

It's not like I had big plans or anything. After high school I figured I'd take a break, pack up my Mustang, and drown my sorrows with the engine's purr. For the main course, I'd go to art school and get a nice job. But life has a way of smacking you in the jaw, doesn't it?

Now I'm here. Mike's Mini-Mart. The midnight shift, with fluorescent lights attacking me from every angle. I'm starting to feel insecure about how my complexion is reacting. I look up at the mirrored ceiling, ignoring the disorderly aisles of junk, and examine my crumbling mascara. My appearance proves I've given up. As my boredom climbs, I strum my jagged fingernails along the plastic counter. The tiny black radio churns out "Songs of the Seventies" behind me. My head slumps down; I can feel my exhausted eyelids coming to a close. As I start to get fuzzy, I pray for a pleasant dream. Maybe a credit card, new car, or true love. Cling-clang-ring-ring! My momentary lapse from reality is interrupted by a cluster of bells. An ancient man with crinkled skin waddles in, his patent leather shoes slowly tapping against the linoleum floor. It's unusual to see the elderly at run-down convenience stores this late at night, especially men who can barely walk. I wonder what he wants.

That's the one perk of my job—it's interesting to see what people buy at midnight. Something desperately needed or desperately desired.

Regardless of my curiosity, I refuse to make eye contact. Exhaustion is pumping through my veins; I look like a train just hit me, and I'm a failure. Eye contact will surely bring this to his attention. The man slowly weaves in and out of the rows, making his way to the canned foods. I try to ignore him, but he's a label reader. With each massive ravioli or spinach can he reads, he clunks it down on the metal shelf, making me jump. His feet continue to tip-tap toward the refrigerators, stopping in front of the energy-drink section. I would hate watching him read the labels of every energy-drink, especially because the list of chemicals is endless, so I grab a magazine and turn my face to the cigarette wall. The glossy pages crinkle between my fingers as I read about the successful, rich, and happy. I almost vomit. Behind me I hear the suction lining of the fridge-door seal, and the taps get progressively closer. I wish this guy would hurry up, so I can be left alone. Our usual midnight customers make it quick—grabbing their beer, condoms, or Tylenol with Olympic speed. I swear the fluorescent light-bath scares them away.

Finally, I hear a soft thud against the plastic counter. A quick turn of my neck reveals the final purchasing decision. A pack of spearmint gum. A sting of annoyance hits me, but I decide to let it go.

"A dollar-nineteen please," my voice croaks out.

One-Two-Three-Four-Five-Six coins clink on the counter, followed by a crisp dollar bill. I appreciate the exact change. Section 6 of the Employee Contract requires me to always ask if they'd like a receipt, and always ask if they'd like a bag.

But tonight I'm feeling dangerous.

The man starts to tear open the pack of gum, and then places it in his palm. I turn my back, and listen to his slow tapping toward the door. As I let his image slip my mind, zoning back into a pathetic trance, I notice a sudden silence. His walking pattern abruptly stops. When I turn back around, the man is standing there facing me, looking at me as if I were a science specimen. After his peculiar head-to-toe examination, his bug-blue eyes zero in on my pupils.

"You may think it's rather late," he says, glancing at a gold wristwatch, "But we all deserve something more." Then he pops a piece of spearmint gum in his mouth and tip-taps out, the doorbells clanging behind him.

Ryan Beiermeister, Age 16
The Kinkaid School
Houston, TX
Teacher: Carolyn McCarthy

WRITER'S STATEMENT

I can't get away from my family. I can't get away from being Ethiopian. As a kid I'd go to great lengths to hide the fact that my parents were from a country that people had either never heard of, or only seen on infomercials featuring children with waists small enough to thread through Cheerios. I have a list of American names I use to place take-out orders (I normally go by "Allie") tucked in my wallet, and sometimes I refer to it before leaving for a party, because I get a kick out of stepping inside as Lydia and waving goodbye as Briana.

I've spent the last fifteen years of my life in a state where people think pierogis are Italian cars. My writing instructors always remind me that uncomfortable situations are prime real estate for an essay, and I find this fact to be uncomfortable enough. My parents always remind me that writing silly papers about my upbringing won't get me an MD, but the fact that their frantic attempts to shape me into Ivy League material (by age five I was more familiar with Mozart's concertos than Raffi), are sillier.

The writing in these pages could be described as terminally caustic, sardonic, buffoonish, ironic, sarcastic, irreverent, shrewd, derisive, et cetera, but I prefer to think of it as the wanderings of a mind exposed to the spell of the South—not just the American region, but the Ethiopian one, too. It's sort of like water: You don't usually get enough of it but occasionally you do, and when that happens, it's got to get out somewhere. My out just happens to be onto paper.

BROWN OR BUST

I spent the bulk of my childhood watching television, particularly nature documentaries. They offered a more intriguing body of information about the world than school did, so I idled weekdays away, meditating on the bathing habits of Japanese macaques while the rest of the St. Anne 5B class copied transparencies about Manifest Destiny. This greatly troubled my Ethiopian parents. Despite holding PhD's in quantum mechanics and microbiology, my mother and father constantly grappled with why I couldn't solve a linear equation with the same, single-minded purpose I applied to constructing a peanut-butter and banana sandwich. They dreamed of the day when *Where's the remote?* turned into *What's a parabola?*—a distant, sunny afternoon when their wealthy post-grad daughter would enter a bistro and say, "I'll have the sea bass and a Pellegrino." For eleven years they'd lived with one terrifying realization: that their expectations were buttressed on someone with an encyclopedic knowledge of every episode of *Walking With Dinosaurs*. An intervention was required—I needed an example, a paragon of success. That summer, instead of the perfunctory family trip to Myrtle Beach, we drove to Baltimore, Maryland to stay with my cousin Meheret.

"Call me Mimi," she said, kissing the air beside my cheeks. Mimi ushered us to the couch, an Ethiopian–flag afghan draped over her shoulders, and poured coffee for my parents while chatting in fluent Amharic. After she produced Cokes for my brother and me and excused herself upstairs to get her parents. My mother set her cup down and looked at me meaningfully.

"Mimi's going to South Africa in a few weeks. Her school is sponsoring a trip for potential pre-meds, you know, to see what it's like to work in an AIDS prevention clinic."

"Cool," I said, examining my pitted Coke can. I recalled a segment of the local news about deadly intestinal parasites breeding in dented cans. Somewhere in the depths of the house I heard a stereo blaring an Ethiopian folk song "Salaam Adenan Nen"—"I Found My Love at the Market Stall."

"She did well this year," my mother continued. "All A's."

"Uh-huh." I said.

My parents made the decision to have children the same way people select a new car or compatible breed of dog. Words like "honor roll" and "mathlete" seemed like appropriate tradeoffs for the down payment of food, shelter, and cable television. At the age of three, I began to read. At four I was finishing short chapter books and tying my own shoes. By six I was able to tread water for more than thirty seconds, and as far as my parents are concerned, this is where all significant achievements stop.

I watched Mimi ascend the stairs and wondered what could have occurred during *my* development: an erroneous gene splice, head trauma, adoption. Whatever the case was, my mother had a right to be crestfallen. The den was a veritable shrine to Mimi's accomplishments: equestrian medals, Youth in Government awards, perfect attendance plaques. Over our mantelpiece was a hazy photograph of me in second grade, standing beside a failed science project with an aluminum foil cone on my head (to harness the power of the sun). Mimi's parents sent out holiday e-cards fashioned like newspapers, in which an entire section would be devoted to her: *Mimi Wins District Geography Bee!* or *Mimi Interns at UNICEF!* In popular dinner conversation at my house, I ranked somewhere between my father's stock portfolio and an attractive set of coasters.

My mother blew on her coffee. "Mimi is taking violin lessons, you know. She hopes to continue them at Cornell, but the medicine major should occupy most of her time."

Dad chimed in. "You really should be thinking about what you want to do." He was referring to the requisite career survey fifth-graders took before middle school. I circled the most interesting occupation I could find, *mortician*, and wrote in the margins of the Goals section that I wanted to host a landscaping show called *Horticultural Hijinks*, attributing the decision to my newfound taste for the Home and Garden network.

The second night of our stay Mimi and I were dispatched to Bi-Lo for barbeque sauce. Her parents were having a cookout and were inviting their extended family. Upon hearing the news my mother whispered, "Good! Lots of kids your age!" a phrase I'd come to learn meant I'd spend the evening watching Power Rangers.

I examined myself in the vanity mirror as Mimi guided the Honda into two parking spots. What would I say to these people? My cousins regarded me with the amused curiosity reserved for photographs of six-legged calves or late night talk shows featuring children nibbling cheese slices into the shapes of Canadian provinces. Mimi did things differently, attempting, in vain, to correct my behavior. She'd interject benignly, saying things like "*My* parents don't let me cut eyeholes in *Zoobooks* covers," or "The remote control isn't a Geiger counter." We took the back route around the store, hugging the meats section so she could read the aisle signs more clearly.

"I'm trying to avoid eye strain," she explained. "Stronger prescriptions totally kill your reading speed." I shivered and pulled my arms into my Pokemon T-shirt, listening to the thrumming freezer behind the Bonuscard beef brisket.

"So how do you do it?"

"Read so fast?"

"No, be so *Ethiopian*. My parents love you. They think you're perfect." Mimi squinted and moved her lips silently. For a moment I thought I'd gone deaf, but she was reading the nutrition facts on a package of fudge rounds.

"So, how?" I repeated.

"The thing you need to do is prioritize." Mimi continued as we rounded into aisle five: *condiments*. "You freak out over the stupidest things, like, remember when they cancelled *Wild Discovery* last night? Remember how I was like, it's not a big deal, think about those Agent Orange kids in Cambodia?"

I listened to the sharp cadence of Mimi's voice, trying to replace the rows of mustard behind her with steaming Sumatran jungles, the bleak expanse of the Sahara. I couldn't picture her saving the world. She sounded more likely to open a package of press-on nails than hold free clinics for Haitian children.

She sounded like someone named Tiffany.

"I guess it's about putting things in perspective, you know, making super-huge decisions." Mimi hovered anxiously over two bottles. "Hickory-smoked or chipotle?"

As we drove back, I watched Mimi signal a left turn and apply lip gloss simultaneously. I'd hoped that she would impart some kind of special wisdom, steer me onto the path to enlightenment. I began to formulate a plan to respond to my parents' impossible demands. I couldn't beat them or join them, so I met their criticisms with a realistic standard to hold them to: sitcom parents. True, I would rather floss with barbed wire than study algebra, but when was the last time my mother set a steaming casserole on the table? Why couldn't *my* dad wear a hat and carry a tin lunchbox? My family never went shopping in coordinated outfits, let alone traveled the country in a psychedelic bus. Family shopping trips were a more crowded affair and usually ended with my uncles and aunts gathered around a display model at Sears, waving their arms at salespeople and asking things like "does it julienne?"

At the cookout, whenever one of my relatives asked to hear my future plans I shrugged and changed the subject. This behavior was met with tutting and shaking heads. It was bothersome at first—like living in a house of bobbleheads—but after a while, not only did I adjust to these lower expectations, I embraced them. Now I had a role to play: the charismatic underachiever. Ask me what colleges I'm considering and I'll be stuck for a response. Ask me if I caught the PBS special on the love lives of single-celled organisms and I'll let you borrow the tape.

During a lull in conversation my mother pulled me aside to relay the latest filial tidbits from relatives: Jarred placed second in a cross country meet, Kidest will represent Ethiopia in model UN, Samson was accepted at Yale. She gave me a look as if to say, "Surely, you must feel eclipsed! Doesn't this make you want to *do* something?" I reminded her that June Cleaver would never tell her children such things.

"Well, Mimi is grilling outside, go help her," she said. "I just wish *you'd* do something constructive around the house."

I hesitated, watching my family gather around the grill, idly chatting about scholarship opportunities. Mimi's hands moved smoothly above the meat, as if she were directing a choir. I imagined her leading the beef patties in song, a rousing battle hymn. As one manicured hand maneuvered the spatula,

I watched as the other, as if guided by some perverse force, rise slowly and lodge a finger in her nostril.

"Mom," I said, "Mimi's picking her nose."

My mother fiddled with the straps of her purse. "That's unsanitary. Mimi knows better."

I pointed outside, but Mimi lowered her hand, absentmindedly wiping it on her jeans.

"Are you sure you want to let her serve food?" I asked. "Shouldn't she wash her hands?"

"She knows what she's doing. She's helped *her* mother before." My mother pulled back the sliding door and I opened my mouth to protest, but stopped to watch my family form a line. Mimi flipped the patties onto the waiting plates with the precise execution of a conveyor belt, and I smiled for the first time since we'd arrived in Maryland.

EVERYTHING I NEED TO KNOW IN LIFE I LEARNED FROM GENGHIS KHAN

I entered a Hallmark store for the first time at the age of seven. My family had stopped at a strip mall just outside Myrtle Beach so my mother could use the bathroom after polishing off a 64-ounce iced tea—a setback that, according to my father, could have been avoided if we'd had a funnel and jar on hand in the minivan. While he was sitting outside the store on a plastic bench folding over a page of his favorite issue of *Scientific American*, he instructed me to find an item on the personalized gifts rack with my name on it. What he'd failed to tell me was that the Hallmark corporation had yet to produce a line of Ethiopian-specific gifts, and cards written in his native Tigrinia were a longer way off. Therefore what had started as a misguided attempt to teach me that my name was unique ended in tears and a reaffirmed sense of isolation.

"Try the keychains. If you find it there I'll give you a dollar," he said, running his finger down a gossip column about the Hubble telescope. Here was a man that wondered frequently and aloud why things like experiments concerning the effect of zero gravity on cellular respiration did not crop up more often in dinner conversation. It made sense that someone with a worldview so absurd assumed my name would appear in the row just below "Tiffany" embossed on what looked like a purple brontosaurus driving a tractor. As I tearfully returned to work, a small crowd of people began to migrate from the seasonal cheeses kiosk to watch what they thought was a bizarre form of time out.

"I can't find it," I called. "Why couldn't you name me something easy, like Samantha?" He examined the magazine's cover and through the window I read "Why the Ground Is Brown," p.74.

"Your mother and I named you after your great-great grandmother. She was a midwife in her village. Be proud of that. Be proud of your culture." I wasn't unaccustomed to advice like this: my father seized any moment of free time to dispense what he thought were nuggets of wisdom about cultural identity——as he pumped gas at Citgo, in line at Starbucks, at the zoo while we watched the elephants eat. He always ended with the same line: *If people can't appreciate your uniqueness, then they aren't worth your time*. He said this with a clinical air, as if the statement revealed the logic behind his decision to raise children in a state where people accessorized with fishing lures.

"What's a midwife?"

"Someone who helps women have children."

I flinched. Although I was unsure of the more intricate details of the process, the very idea of childbirth made my stomach churn. I'd heard that when the infamous womanhood tape was screened for the sixth-graders Mallory Smith's loss of consciousness had coincided with the arrival of the placenta.

"If that's not good enough for you," he said, turning a page, "then you can wear a blonde wig so you can fit in with all your little friends." He chuckled at his own joke.

I didn't know what to say. I was expecting a heartfelt apology, for him to grovel at the tips of my flip-flops, begging forgiveness for the crime that was committed the moment the ink on my birth certificate dried. Abstract concepts like nonconformity didn't apply to the discomfort my name and culture created in the classroom. So much for my "little friends": Caitlin Weldin laughed when I said my ancestors were goat-herders, during show-and-tell Ashley Ledford told the entire class my family hunted with spears, and Caroline Bolt followed me around during recess making clicking noises with her tongue. ("Can you understand me? Doesn't everyone in Africa talk like this?") It was times like these that made me question the necessity of school. I considered how far I'd go to avoid alienation caused by my name and resigned myself to a dead-end job and an exclusive diet of Ramen Noodles. It seemed like elementary school was a rite of passage—Indian braves fought bears, I had to endure roll call.

Grade 4-B's scheduled activity for morning period was creating an Easter motif for the classroom door. Our substitute, Miss Leslie, was a leggy, tan brunette with a heavy southern drawl. She picked up the roster from the podium and The Name Game began. As I waited for the inexorable pause between "Scott, Samantha" and my name, I wondered how many assisted and unassisted attempts it would take her to get it right. Her mouth opened and closed, then shut and pursed. Her brow furrowed. She seemed to be gathering resolve.

"Tameek?"

Strike one.

I corrected her hopefully, crossing my legs. I only allowed one freebie.

"Tuhmeet?"

Strike two.

"What an interesting name. What language does it comes from?" She couldn't have made her stalling more obvious.

"It's Ethiopian." I guided my pinking shears around the edge of my egg.

"It's what?"

"I mean, African." A small wave of laughter crested and fell across the front of the room. I stared at the hairs on Miss Leslie's upper lip and imagined her husband taking her out to dinner, her mouth moving like a goldfish's as she worked her way around tricky words like "masala," "guacamole," or "dim sum." The girl behind me tapped my shoulder with a crayon. "Do they have Easter in Africa?"

"Yeah," I said, reluctant to delve into further detail. While my American classmates stuffed their faces with Cadbury eggs and jelly beans, my brother and I waited in line at the Halal market while a balding Pakistani man in a sportcoat weighed bags of cubed goat. We would spend the remainder of our afternoon at Orthodox church where gnarled old women with henna crosses on their foreheads would try to feed me curried bean paste, urging that it would make me more fertile.

At 12:30 Miss Leslie dismissed us for lunch. I often dreamed of a day when some corporate bigwig would conceive ethnic Lunchables and the youth of America would grow up seasoning their own kimchi or scooping falafel into miniature pitas, but until then my Tupperware box of stewed lamb would continue to be received with comments like "That looks like dog food!," or from the more ironic, "Ethiopian food? Isn't that an oxymoron?" I saved as much face as possible by scraping the lamb into the trash and accepting a stale peanut-butter sandwich from the cafeteria staff, fare reserved for unfortunate kids that forgot their lunchboxes on the bus.

At recess I began a chalk rendition of the jetline being overrun by the undead and purple robots. I was adding the laser beams jettisoning from the robots' eyes when a Velcro Cinderella sneaker appeared in the corner of my drawing. I looked up. Above me, Amy Clinton ran a glittery pocket brush through her stringy hair. A dour girl with the build of a car antenna and the complexion of a saltine cracker, Amy took it upon herself to feed Jerry Garcia, the classroom guinea pig, at such opportune times as the middle of a spelling test.

"I have a question." She scratched at her flat nose. It was said that it retained its shape from a Marsha Brady-esque encounter with a polo mallet at the Rock Hill Country Club.

"Okay, what?"

"It's Ashley's question, too—HEY ASHLEY! Do you still want me to do the thing?" She pointed at me and brayed at the swing set, where Ashley Richardson flashed her a thumbs-up. "Okay. So, are you an African butt kisser?"

I must have looked like I'd been jabbed with an electric cattle prod, because she pointed back at the swings where Ashley Richardson tried to look nonchalant. "Jeez, it was just a joke, go ask Ashley." Ashley had asked me for an answer during our last history test, and I'd managed to convince her that the Aztecs were native to the Blue Ridge Mountains. She was also the student that would later have the unfortunate distinction of lauding "F-Stop Fitzgerald" as one of the greatest photographers of our time in an eighth grade term paper.

"How do you spell your name?" I asked.

"Why?" Her mouth was puckered; since I'd seen her open the package in math, I knew she was working on an enormous wad of Sour Apple Dubble Bubble.

"Is it C-L-E-M-E-N-S?"

"Yeah. What's it to you?"

I answered with a phrase I'd picked up from the copies of *Consumer Reports* my dad left around the house, because it sounded official and concise:

"Thank you for your input." As her sneakers gradually left my field of vision, I added the finishing touches to a green pile of smoldering humanoid labeled "AMY CLINTON."

A week into Christmas break, I situate myself in the Laz-E-Boy with a large bowl of Frosted Flakes and the digital cable remote, a thick, matte black instrument that looks more suited to use on the Death Star. *The Little House on the Prairie* marathon ends at 3:00 A.M., culminating with the episode in which Laura and Mary learn the value of sharing when winter hardship leaves them nothing to play with but an inflated pig's bladder. I flip up to the Discovery Channel and catch a documentary on the life of Genghis Khan. I am immediately hooked. The narrator announces against reverberating tympani that the young Khan did a myriad of amazing things before the age of 30: directing the effort to establish a writing system for the Mongolian language; leading a successful campaign against the Persian Empire; and uniting the Central Asian confederations underneath one sword. He was a judicious ruler: to quell intertribal squabbles he advocated tried-and-true methods of conflict resolution, such as torching villages and the ritualistic disembowelment of enemy cattle.

The detail that really captures me is that "Genghis Khan" was a moniker given to him by his people. His birthname was Temujin Borjigin, something neither Miss Leslie nor the entire administrative staff of St. Anne Catholic School could pronounce, even with the assistance of UN interpreters. War crimes notwithstanding, I admire Temujin. In a country full of weird names, a boy with one of the weirdest rose to the top through bloodshed and pillaging and had it changed to something slightly less weird. It dawns on me that I could find acceptance, maybe even greatness and admiration in a place like the Gobi Desert. I briefly entertain the idea of relocating to Mongolia. The documentary's actors portrayed what seemed to be a pretty good life: I would get up at the crack of dawn and put on tea for the family, enjoy a refreshing gourd of mare's milk, then brave the sub-zero winter weather to feed the livestock while making small talk with the neighbors.

Your yurt is looking a little crooked, Jamuka!

I was planning on taking the old thing down anyway. Haven't you heard? We're moving to Ulaan Bator!

Present-day Mongolia was quite progressive by today's standards. Public execution was deemed unnecessary and done away with in the mid-1970s and the nation's newest president campaigned successfully with the help of an all-female beat-boxing group. These two facts alone say quite a bit about the national character. I try to fight down resurging waves of sticker shock when I look up the price of a one-way ticket—surely, taking lungfuls of fresh Mongolian air, admiring the periwinkle expanse of the sky, finding the place one truly belonged, all of these meant more than a college education.

I return to school with buoyant morale. Nicholas Childers wouldn't have asked me where my spear was in P.E. if we were in Mongolia. I am unfazed when Caroline Bolt asks if there is electricity in Africa. Katherine Swindon fails to provoke a reaction with her Sally Struthers impersonation. It isn't their fault I'm in the wrong country. When the bell rings I am the first to exit the room, frog-shaped backpack swinging from my wrist. I lean on the side of the administrative building under the enormous crucifix and await my mother's Honda, brimming with the confidence of a Mongol.

Temnete Sebhatu, Age 18
South Carolina Governor's School for the Arts and Humanities
Greenville, SC
Teachers: Scott Gould, George Singleton

MY FATHER SAYS HE HATES POETRY

My father says he hates poetry,
but I do not believe him.
He has given himself away before he begins,
for I see the poems within him,
wordless and complete.

There is one.
I am five,
unnatural on skis as a baby doe
on spindly birth-legs.
We stand at the top of the world,
point ourselves into white and white and blue,
and he shows me how to find my way down,
this man who tells me he has no poems.

I am thinking of another—
seven years old,
he and I are walking to the bus stop.
Too much sunrise
makes my shoes gleam black
as the glossy coats of the pigeons
who live on our roof,
and our clasped hands are like Escher's,
one beginning from the other
in perfect symmetry.

At eleven,
I am taught to capture these poems,
to lay out my trap
with words and lines and a single sheet of paper,
and then to wait
for the snap of metal jaws,
something to paint with formaldehyde
and pin into cases,
rigid and still.

He, the one who taught me about words,
does not know the hunt
and tells me only that there is
another good novel
he thinks I should read.

Today, I am sixteen.
I am sixteen and still waiting
for poems to spread before me
as perfectly as they did
when I was five and seven
and too young
to cover them in language.

This morning,
my father told me
of how once,
so many years ago,
he told his father he loved the ballet
and how he laughed,
my grandfather
(that heavy laugh
that I would someday inherit).

He didn't understand, my father said,
the way limbs stretched over music,
and caught flight between notes,
the way they hesitated in perfection
and how only he could see it.

Ryan Brown, Age 17
Denver School of the Arts
Denver, CO
Teacher: Jana Clark

ABOUT THE AUTHORS

Laura Ball will start high school this fall in Milwaukee, WI. In her fantasy world, she would spend one year of her life after college on Broadway and then proceed to pursue a more academic career. She also hopes to write novels as a way to keep in touch with her creative side.

Zara Kessler makes her home in New York City, and says its frenzied pitch—from Broadway to a ride on the subway—assures her that she can write about anything and everything. She aspires to become a professional dancer, and cannot imagine dancing without writing about it.

Amanda Picardi comes from Southborough, MA, a small town outside Boston. She hopes in ten years to be living in Paris, writing by the Seine, and reciting old French poetry to anyone who will listen. She plans to dedicate her first book of poetry to her brilliant creative writing teacher, Daniel Bosch.

Grant Hailer lives near Boston, MA, which he defines as a melting pot of different cultures that has certainly influenced his writing. Though he enjoys writing poetry that focuses on his individual emotions, he also loves to play football and values the camaraderie and teamwork that is found on the field.

Erin Weeks attends high school in Greenville, SC. A South Carolina native, she enjoys going to the beach, shopping at flea markets and knitting. Her teachers have been her greatest source of inspiration—they are living proof that a career in the arts can be rewarding.

Anna Isaacs lives a metro ride away from the heart of American history and politics, Washington, D.C. Having that sort of proximity has greatly influenced her writing—she plans to one day become a journalist in New York City. Aside from writing, she has played the piano for nine years and is an alto in two choirs.

Phoebe Rusch has spent her high school years at the Interlochen Arts Academy in Interlochen, MI. She plans to double-major in international relations and anthropology next year at Princeton, and hopes to study somewhere in West Africa during her junior year.

Andrew Halterman comes from Norman, OK and will be a freshman at Amherst this fall. Besides writing and debating, he roasts his own coffee, sings in two choirs, and plays ultimate Frisbee. He hopes to work in the Peace Corps and teach Political Science at the college level. His writing skills, he hopes, will enable him to write a dissertation without long, dry, passive sentences and weak verbs.

Jasmine Hu lives in San Jose, CA. When she was younger, her dream was to become an explorer of the khaki-wearing, binocular-toting variety; in a less literal sense, she still holds on to this dream. She wants to explore the world through language and writing; bridge gaps between people and places; and make unusual connections; with or without the khaki.

Leila Dashevsky will spend the next two years far from her Springfield, MA, roots, working in Israel with recently-arrived immigrants from Ethiopia. She hopes to earn a degree or two from an Israeli university, and live there working hard until she becomes a famous writer, after which she will write all day long.

Suzannah Isgett lives near beautiful Charleston, SC. Contrary to what outsiders may think of the South, she is proud to be a product of her genteel city and all its influences. If she decides to go the "starving writer route" after high school, she plans to temporarily teach piano lessons to make some extra cash.

Michael Lambert hails from Helena, AL. Most of his inspiration to write derives from what he calls the wild accidents of his life and from the people who showed the greatest depth and personality he's ever seen. He would like to become a screenwriter. In the meantime, fate keeps sending him material, and he keeps taking notes.

Maya De Vitry grew up in Columbia, PA, and keeps writing because there are stories to tell. She also plays classical violin and traditional fiddling styles, and is inspired by ordinary people with extraordinary wit, curiosity, and courage.

Michael Yashinsky comes from West Bloomfield, MI and believes that written words are not mere inkstains on a page but represent ideas and sentiments that can build bridges between people, cultures and nations. He aspires to a career in international relations and diplomacy, and will attend Harvard University as a freshman this fall.

Denise Rickman has lived in the same house her entire life in Apex, NC, but hopes to one day travel around the world. In ten years, she hopes to become either a fiction writer or a journalist. This fall she will be a freshman at the University of North Carolina at Chapel Hill, where she plans to study creative writing.

Margaret Hayertz is from West Linn, OR, but spends much of her time in Portland, where she gets inspired to write. Walt Whitman's work has also had great influence on her writing. She likes to sing and hike and hopes to one day own a publishing house.

Monica Klein will be a freshman this fall at Oberlin College and hopes to study Political Science and Journalism. She has been involved in two nonprofit organizations, which work to raise awareness about the HIV/AIDS epidemic. She would eventually like to become an investigatory journalist for either a newspaper or magazine.

David Pederson is from Edina, MN, but says that placing himself in another culture has proved the most fruitful in generating ideas. It was Seamus Heaney, the Irish poet, who initially awakened the muse within him and impelled him to put pen to paper. He enjoys snowboarding, baseball, and British comedy. However, his favorite hobby is thinking.

Kathryn Llewellyn has lived in her hometown, Westport, CT, all her life. But the bright lights and smog of New York City are only an hour's drive away. As a Chinese-Welsh-German-American, Kathryn finds Chinatown particularly inspiring and tries to capture the complexity of its ambiance in her writing.

Erin Guty is from Dillsburg, PA, a suburban area which she says comes through in most of her writing. Her hobbies include reading, running, and photography, but she hopes to eventually become involved in medicine as her life progresses.

Eugene Stockton-Juarez lives in Carlisle, PA. In addition to writing prose, he also writes, plays and improvises music with many of the local players in his hometown. He hopes to study anthropology, sociology and economics, and to have opportunities to write in whatever profession he chooses.

Lisa Pang is from Herndon, VA. Though many think the Virginia suburbs don't possess any inspiration or creativity, Lisa has learned to develop an eye for details. She also likes to draw in her sketchbook—she tries to capture the mood and vitality of the people she loves. She hopes writing will play an integral part in her future.

Katharine Eisenberg calls Bedford, NY, home, and hopes to become an actress, playwright and performer. She thanks everyone for inspiring her to write: the toddler who grabbed her leg and thought it was his mother's, the people in a crowded elevator who stare at the numbers like their lives depended on it when she enters, and every child whose lemonade stand she has stopped at over the years.

Elizabeth Motich was home schooled throughout high school in Dillsburg, PA, a town best known for dropping a giant papier mache pickle from a ladder every New Year's Eve. She enjoys studying mythology, world religions and crazy historical facts. She will be a freshman at Dickinson College this year, majoring in Humanities.

Kaitlin Sanders lives in Newton, MA, a town that is consistently ranked "the safest city in America." She writes for her high school's newspaper and literary magazine, and hopes to prolong these hobbies for as long as she can. When she is not writing, she volunteers at homeless shelters and plays catcher for her school's softball team.

Anne Reece is from St. Paul, MN, but attended boarding school in Michigan. In ten years, she hopes to be teaching at some place quiet in the woods. She is taking a year off after high school to focus on her writing, and then it's off to college.

Jack Anderson lives in Provo, UT. He toured Germany last summer, which inspired him to write several works of fiction. He is also interested in the technical aspects of computer science and hopes this will factor into his career in the future. Currently, he is writing a novel and a screenplay.

Alyssa Fowers developed her interest in the strange and subversive from her hometown of Miami, FL, a city bursting with diversity. She enjoys folklore, costuming, figure skating, and guitar. In the next ten years, she hopes to own a personal library complete with floor-to-ceiling bookcases and sliding ladders.

Naomi Funabashi is from Phoenix, AZ, but attends high school in New Hampshire. When she is not writing, she enjoys figure skating, stargazing, and playing the violin as sources for her inspiration.

Margot Miller hails from Wilmington, DE, where she attends an all-female high school that she says has greatly influenced both her style of writing and her subject matter. She hopes to teach writing for a living.

Eric Roper lives in Greenville, SC, and thanks Mrs. Dowling—his sixth-grade guide to the writing path—for inspiring him to express himself. He enjoys skateboarding, swimming, biking, visual arts, creating practical things out of recycled or unusual materials, and over-analyzing ridiculous hypothetical situations.

Jillian Kinsey lives in Middletown, PA. She says much of her inspiration comes from her family's Italian and Czechoslovakian background as well as her friend Alicia Appleman-Jurman, a Holocaust survivor. She has been involved in many art areas, but believes that all life experiences can be used in writing.

Katherine Sedivy-Haley comes from Providence, RI, and plans to earn a Ph.D. in biochemistry, have at least one novel published—perhaps three or four—and a number of short stories as well. Writer Isaac Asimov taught her to love fiction. The story here was a birthday gift for her mother.

Thomas Renjilian is from Clarks Summit in northeastern PA, named by the *Washington Post* as a contender for the coveted distinction: "Armpit of America." Though this may not seem like a pleasant title, he can't imagine any other bodily crevice of our nation providing more inspiration to a writer.

Cory Wallace attended boarding school in Greenville, SC, although he has lived in many different corners of the American South. The landscape and people he has encountered have greatly influenced his writing. He will attend at the University of South Carolina and hopes to become a teacher.

Kayla Krut lives within walking distance of the Pacific Ocean in Del Mar, CA. She enjoys playing volleyball and tennis, and plans to study educational psychology. In ten years, she hopes to be sitting on a mountain somewhere writing poems.

Cora Johnson-Grau is from sunny Los Angeles, CA. She says heading to the beach inspires her—the waves lull her into writing about distant lands and magical powers. She also plays the violin and participates in many sports.

Jenna Devine lives in Lebanon, NJ, and has wanted to be a writer since kindergarten, when she published her first book with Crayola markers. She hopes to go to Princeton to study with writers like Paul Muldoon, and Toni Morrison, and to become a creative writing teacher.

Joshua McMillen comes from Loysville, PA, a small town in a rural area just west of Harrisburg. Besides writing, he likes to read, be part of his high school's marching and symphonic band, go hunting, and play paintball. He plans to become an orthodontist and set up a practice in his hometown.

Rosetta Young hails from Providence, RI. She says the over-Americanized, simplistic cultural blandness of her environment motivates her to reach for something grittier and imaginative in her writing. She is also interested in photography, but plans to choose a career path with some sort of writing involved.

Sindha Agha is from Champaign, IL, a town, he says, that is filled with many different personalities. The interaction between these types of people has been a great inspiration for his writing. He is also a budding photographer and hopes to combine his talents and pursue both writing and photography in the future.

Antoinette Forstall lives in Birmingham, AL. Besides writing, she also likes to paint, draw, and play volleyball. She hopes to one day write about the history of New Orleans, where her family is originally from. In the future, she can see herself as a journalist, editor, screenwriter, or teacher.

Shalini Ramachandran comes from Lilburn, GA. In ten years, she sees herself not as a starving author in a New York apartment trying to create a masterpiece, but as an author—perhaps still starving—who has the betterment of humanity as the goal in sight; a writer who seeks to sing out those voices that are not readily heard.

Rebecca McCarthy calls Monroe, CT, home. A book about a changeling child that Rebecca read in first grade launched her on a creative path. She plans to be a writer, and since there is no specific career path for that goal she is sure that she'll end up waitressing to support her art.

Nicole Levy lives in Flushing, NY, which is near New York City. She is inspired by the city's diversity, pace, and stimulation. Aside from writing, she is interested in biology and opera, which she hopes to continue with in college. This past summer, she volunteered at an opera festival in France.

John Savage is from the Mohican River area of Ohio, a valley once home to one of his favorite authors, Louis Bromfield. When John is not writing, he enjoys working on his family's small farm, bird watching, and observing nature. He writes a weekly nature column for a local newspaper.

Clare Grieve lives in Fairport, NY, and credits authors Markus Zusak and Chris Crutcher, as well as her most-excellent English teachers, for inspiring her to write. She likes to read, play soccer and field hockey, ski, dance, sing, play the violin and piano; but she loves to write. She hopes to be a journalist or a novelist.

Brenna O'Tierney is from Anchorage, AK. Though she says living in Alaska is unique in many ways, it was studying abroad in Ireland for a year that really sparked her interest in writing. She is also an active volunteer with the Special Olympics organization. She will attend at Northwestern University this fall, where she study broadcast journalism.

Ryan Beiermeister lives in the Houston, TX area, and spends many weekends traveling and discussing everything from nuclear war to space robots with her high school debate team. She's considering a career in journalism; traveling around the country and world; investigating social issues; and refusing to sit at a desk to work are all on her agenda.

Temnete Sebhatu is from Rock Hill, SC. In ten years, she imagines herself in the same place: in her chair, in front of the computer, trying to think of a first line. She also enjoys knitting scarves and beekeeping. This fall, she will be a freshman at Wesleyan University where she hopes to study English and creative writing.

Ryan Brown will attend Duke University in Durham, NC this fall but is originally from Denver. She is also interested in filmmaking and political science. In ten years, she hopes to be working as a lawyer, diplomat, documentary filmmaker, or for a political nonprofit organization. She knows writing will always be an important part of her life.

NATIONAL WRITING JURORS

American Voices
Aracelis Girmay
Martin Walls
Jim Savio
Carolyn Meyer

Dramatic Script
Bronwen Bitetti
Michael Ramirez
Heidi Schreck

General Writing Portfolio
Billy Collins
Roger Mummert
Ellen Hagan

Humor
Jeff Kinney
Chris Bannon
Kate Klise

Journalism
Ianthe Jeanne Dugan
Jim Sheeler
Glenn Thrush

Nonfiction Writing Portfolio
Andrew Solomon
Jennifer Lyons
Ken Foskett

Personal Essay/Memoir
Millie Davis
Julie Bowe
David McMahon

Poetry
Lee Bennett Hopkins
Margo Figgins
Sherry Robbins

Science Fiction/Fantasy
David Clement-Davies
Christopher Golden
Todd Mitchell

Short Story
Laura Bowers
Lara Anderson

Short Short Story
Candie Moonshower
Emmett Shkeme Garcia
Malachy McCourt

Want to know more about the national jurors?
Go to **www.artandwriting.org** to read juror interviews.

SPONSORS OF REGIONAL PROGRAMS

Central Pennsylvania Region
Regional Affiliate: The Patriot-News Co.
Additional local support provided by: The Times-Tribune and Marywood University

Colorado Region
Regional Affiliate: Colorado Art Education Association
Additional local support provided by: Colorado Data Mail, Colorado Language Arts Society, Colorado Writing Project, Denver—The Mile High City, ExxonMobil Foundation, Hewlett-Packard Foundation, Jerry and Marty Berglund, Kent Denver School, Newman Family Foundation, The Rotary Club of Denver, The Auraria Higher Education Center: Community College of Denver, Metropolitan State College of Denver and University of Colorado at Denver, and Health and Sciences Center

Delaware Region
Regional Affiliate: The Arts Center/Gallery at Delaware State University
Additional local support provided by: The Art Educators of Delaware, Colonial Rotary of Dover, and Dr. Donald A. Parks

Harris County, Texas Region
Regional Affiliate: Harris County Department of Education

Lancaster County, Pennsylvania Region
Regional Affiliate: Lancaster Public Library

Metro Area Richmond, Virginia Region
Regional Affiliate: The Visual Arts Center of Richmond

Miami-Dade County, Florida Region
Regional Affiliate: Miami-Dade County Public Schools
Additional local support provided by: Miami Art Museum, and The Miami-Dade County Fair & Exposition

Mid-Carolina Region
Regional Affiliate: The Arts Education Department of the Charlotte-Mecklenburg Schools, and ArtsTeach

New York City Region
Regional Affiliate: Alliance for Young Artists & Writers, Inc.
Additional local support provided by: Scholastic, Inc., The New York Times Company, Accenture, Command Web Offset, CDW-G, and Brooklyn Museum. Additional support provided by: The Maurice R. Robinson Fund, Jack Kent Cooke Foundation, The Jacques and Natasha Gelman Trust, The Jean and Louis Dreyfus Foundation, Inc., The Richard and Mica Hadar Foundation, and Three Bridge Trust

Northeast Indiana Region
Regional Affiliate: Fort Wayne Museum of Art
Additional local support provided by: The News-Sentinel, Macy's, a Division of The Federated Department Stores, and Chase Manhattan Bank

Northern Kentucky Region
Regional Affiliate: Northern Kentucky University, Department of Literature and Language
Additional local support provided by: First Security Trust Bank, Northern Kentucky University, Department of Literature and Language, Thomas More College, Staples, Inc., Kentucky Council of Teachers and English/Language Arts, The Greater Cincinnati Foundation, and Robert and Judith Frey

Pinellas County, Florida Region
Regional Affiliate: Pinellas County Schools
Additional local support provided by: St. Petersburg Festival of States, General Dynamics, Raymond James Financial, Inc., Verizon, and the Salvador Dali Museum

Southern Nevada Region
Regional Affiliate: Nevada Foundation for the Arts
Additional local support provided by: CCSD Partnership Office, CCSN Photography Club, The Art Institute of Las Vegas, Henderson Art Association, UNLV, and Blanche & Phil Meisel

Southwestern Pennsylvania Region
Regional Affiliate: Waynesburg College
Additional local support provided by: CONSOL Energy, Community Foundation of Greene County, The Observer Reporter, and Pennsylvania Rural Arts Alliance (PRAA)

About the Alliance for Young Artists & Writers

As we celebrate the 85th anniversary of The Scholastic Art & Writing Awards, the Alliance for Young Artists & Writers continues to bring outstanding visual arts and writing created by teenagers to a national audience by showcasing their remarkable work and encouraging their creative journey and career development. The Alliance, a nonprofit organization, was formed in 1994 to support aspiring young artists and writers through The Scholastic Art & Writing Awards program. The Alliance not only seeks to identify emerging artists for college scholarship consideration, but also invests in the critical role of creative development for students by offering six years of eligibility beginning in seventh grade. The Alliance also collaborates with colleges across the country to leverage an additional $1.5 million in financial aid for award recipients who demonstrate exceptional promise.

Special projects of the Alliance include:
Providing Showcase Opportunities
The Alliance brings remarkable art and writing to a national audience, presenting showcase opportunities for creative expression in the visual and literary arts including:

The Scholastic Art & Writing Awards Showcase, an annual publication and virtual gallery that showcase nationally-recognized work;

The Best Teen Writing, an annual anthology and virtual gallery of teen writing exemplars from The Scholastic Writing Awards;

Spark: Young Voices and Visions of 2007, a curated publication and virtual gallery that showcases the creative excellence of 7th and 8th grade emerging artists and writers across the country;

Kids Reconstruct with Creativity, a curated project of authentic voices and expressions of students, grades K–12, responding to the Gulf Coast hurricanes of 2005;

P.S. Art, outstanding artwork, grades K–12, from New York City Public Schools;

ARTifacts: Kids Respond to a World in Crisis, a curated project in response to the events of 9/11.

PUSH Anthologies: The Best Young Writers and Artists in America (published by Scholastic Inc.)
> You Are Here, This Is Now
> Where We Are, What We See
> We Are Quiet, We Are Loud

Visit www.artandwriting.org for more information about the Alliance, including participation information for the 85th Anniversary of The Scholastic Art & Writing Awards of 2008, and to view the Virtual Gallery of nationally-recognized work.

Support the Alliance for Young Artists & Writers

The Alliance gratefully acknowledges the generous leadership support provided by Scholastic Inc. and The Maurice R. Robinson Fund. The Alliance is a nonprofit organization supported by charitable contributions and offers opportunities to individuals, foundations and corporations to underwrite national and NYC-based program activities that impact the development of creativity in our nation's youth. For more information, contact Venas Matthews, Senior Manager, External Relations, by phone at: (212) 343-7717, or by email at: vmatthews@scholastic.com.

To make a contribution, go to: www.artandwriting.org and click on DONATE NOW to review giving opportunities and be a part of our 85th anniversary. Select the appropriate option and make your secure contribution via credit card. Contact: SupportTheAlliance@scholastic.com with questions.

If you would like to make your contribution by mail, send your check to:
Alliance for Young Artists & Writers
557 Broadway
New York, NY 10012

CALL FOR SUBMISSIONS
The Scholastic Art & Writing Awards

The Scholastic Art & Writing Awards offer early recognition of creative teenagers and scholarship opportunities for graduating high school seniors. Supported by their visual arts and writing teachers and other community mentors, participants create and submit their best works in any of the following categories:

Visual Arts
Art Portfolio, Animation, Ceramics & Glass, Computer Art, Design, Digital Imagery, Drawing, Mixed Media, Painting, Photography, Photography Portfolio, Printmaking, Sculpture, Video & Film

Writing
Dramatic Script, General Writing Portfolio, Humor, Journalism, Nonfiction Portfolio, Novel, Personal Essay/Memoir, Poetry, Science Fiction/Fantasy, Short Story, Short Short Story

Each October, program materials are made available to students in grades 7–12. Award recipients are recognized through awards ceremonies, exhibition and publication opportunities, as well as scholarships on both the local and national levels.

High school seniors who submit portfolios compete for more than $1.5 million in tuition scholarships at colleges across the nation. Twelve $10,000 scholarships are presented to Portfolio Gold Award recipients in art, photography, and writing.

Visit our Web site at www.artandwriting.org to learn more about The Awards, for deadlines and entry information and to view galleries of previous national award-winning art and writing.

Alliance for Young Artists & Writers
557 Broadway, New York, NY 10012
(212) 343-6493
www.artandwriting.org